Reminiscences

of

Rear Admiral Robert Halley Wertheim
U. S. Navy (Retired)

U. S. Naval Institute
Annapolis, Maryland.

REAR ADMIRAL ROBERT H. WERTHEIM
DIRECTOR, STRATEGIC SYSTEMS PROJECTS

Rear Admiral Robert Halley WERTHEIM assumed his present duties as Director, Strategic Systems Projects, Department of the Navy on 14 November 1977.

As Director, Strategic Systems Projects, Admiral WERTHEIM is responsible for the research, development, and operational support production POLARIS, POSEIDON and TRIDENT missiles. Admiral WERTHEIM exercises overall management control of the civilian-military Strategic Systems Projects contractual team which brought the FMB system to operational readiness.

Admiral WERTHEIM has additional responsibilities related to the British Polaris Force. He is U.S. Project Officer for the program resulting from the Nassau Pact and later the U.S./U.K. Sales Agreement under which the U.S. provided the Polaris missile system (less warheads) to the United Kingdom and continues to support the system in the four British FMB submarines. In addition to missiles, the subsystems which make up the weapon system are also provided for installation in British-built nuclear-powered submarines.

Admiral WERTHEIM was born in Carlsbad, New Mexico, to Joseph (now deceased) and Emma Vorenberg Wertheim on 9 November 1922. He attended New Mexico Military Institute at Roswell, N.M., for two years prior to entering the U.S. Naval Academy at Annapolis, Maryland, in June 1942. Upon completion of an accelerated three year wartime program, he was graduated and commissioned an Ensign in June 1945. Through subsequent advancements he attained the rank of Rear Admiral, to rank from November 1972.

His initial assignment in August 1945 was as an engineering and communications officer in the destroyer USS HYMAN (DD 732) and involved duties with the American occupation forces in Japan following World War II. On USS BORDELON (DD 881), he participated in operations with Task Force 77 of the U.S. Seventh Fleet in the Far East. During this tour, Admiral WERTHEIM served as an engineering, communications and Combat Information Center (CIC) officer.

After attending the Navy's Electronics Material School at Treasure Island, San Francisco, California, he was assigned to the destroyer escort USS MALOY (DE 791) as communications and electronics officer.

From January 1948 until December 1949, Admiral WERTHEIM served with the Navy's first special (nuclear) weapons assembly team at Sandia Base, N.M., and in January 1950 he reported to the experimental guided missile test ship, NORTON SOUND (AVM 1) as Instrumentation Officer.

Following this early involvement in the military applications of atomic energy and guided missiles, he pursued advanced studies in ordnance engineering at the Navy's Postgraduate School and Massachusetts Institute of Technology. He received a master of science (M.S.) degree in physics and was elected a member of Society of the Sigma Xi in July 1954.

Admiral WERTHEIM was then assigned to the heavy cruiser USS LOS ANGELES (CA 135) which was the first U.S. surface ship to be armed with the REGULUS surface-to-surface missile system. During this tour, he was designated an Ordnance Engineering Duty Officer.

In June 1956 Admiral WERTHEIM was one of a select group of naval officers and civil servants assigned to the Special Projects Office of the Bureau of Ordnance in Washington, D. C. This group, working in close cooperation with their teammates in government and industry, developed the world's first submarine-launched ballistic missile, POLARIS. His prime responsibility during this period was organizing and managing the joint efforts of the Atomic Energy Commission and the Navy to develop the re-entry system for POLARIS. For his contributions as Head of the Re-entry Body Section from June 1956 to June 1961, Admiral WERTHEIM was awarded the Navy Commendation Medal.

From 1961 to 1962 he was assigned to the Naval Ordnance Test Station, China Lake, California, as Assistant to the Head of the Weapons Development Department. It was at China Lake that he conceived and aided in the development of the CHAPARRAL, a tactical surface-to-air missile system later adopted by both the U.S. Marine Corps and Army.

Admiral WERTHEIM reported to the Office of the Secretary of Defense in September 1962 for duty with the Director of Defense in September 1962 for duty with the Director of Defense Research and Engineering. He served as Military Assistant for Strategic Weapons until August 1965 and was awarded the Joint Service Commendation Medal for his contributions to Air Force and Navy strategic programs.

In 1965 he returned to the Special Projects Office (renamed Strategic Systems Project Office), successively serving as Head of the Missile Branch and Deputy Technical Director. He attended the Harvard Business School Advanced Management Program during 1968-1969. In August 1968 Admiral WERTHEIM assumed the position as Technical Director, Strategic Systems Project Office. In this assignment he was the senior technical manager for the development, production and operational support of the Navy's strategic weapons systems POLARIS, POSEIDON and TRIDENT.

Following initial deployment of the POSEIDON system in 1971, Admiral WERTHEIM was awarded the Legion of Merit for exceptionally meritorious service in coordinating diverse governmental, scientific and industrial resources and facilities to support Navy strategic weapon system programs vital to the national defense.

Upon completion of the development phase of the TRIDENT-I (C-4) submarine-launched ballistic missile, Admiral WERTHEIM was awarded, on 15 October 1979, the Distinguished Service Medal for exceptionally meritorious service to the Government of the United States as Technical Director and Director, Strategic Systems Projects from September 1971 to October 1979.

In addition to his military decorations, he has been honored by the Navy League of the United States with their Rear Admiral William S. Parsons Award for outstanding contributions to scientific and technical progress in the Navy, and by the American Society of Naval Engineers with their 1972 Gold Medal Award for significant contribution to Naval Engineering. In 1977 he was elected to membership in the National Academy of Engineering.

Married to the former Barbara Louise Selig of Los Angeles in December 1946, Admiral WERTHEIM has two sons -- Joseph H., and David A. Admiral and Mrs. WERTHEIM currently reside in the Virginia suburbs of Washington, D.C., but maintain their official residence in Carlsbad, N.M.

DECEMBER 1979

Preface

This volume contains a transcript of five interviews with Rear Admiral Robert Halley Wertheim, USN (Ret.). They were taped in his home at Annandale, Virginia, during January and February, 1981. It was an ideal time in that the Admiral had just retired from the Navy (Nov. 1980) where he served as Director of the Strategic Systems Projects. Shortly after completing his interviews he departed for Burbank, California, and his new duties as Senior Vice President, Science and Engineering, the Lockheed Corporation.

Researchers who use this manuscript will find in it an excellent account of the development of the Navy's strategic weapons systems--POLARIS, POSEIDON, and TRIDENT. Admiral Wertheim first became involved in the program in 1956 under Admiral Raborn. He remained there until his retirement except for two tours of duty elsewhere; at China Lake in 1961-62 and in the Department of Defense (1962-65) where he had duty with the Director of Defense Research and Engineering.

The Admiral has corrected the initial transcript. A subject index has been added for convenience. An appendix is also added: a copy of an address delivered in April, 1980 heralding the success of the TRIDENT I program; a copy of the retirement ceremonies of October 30, 1980; a copy of orders to Ensign Wertheim on Dec. 2, 1947 - orders which launched him on his career with the Navy's atomic energy program.

It has been a great pleasure to record the recollections of this brilliant navy scientist and to make them a part of the Oral History collection of the U. S. Naval Institute.

John T. Mason, Jr.
Director of Oral History

December, 1981.

DECLARATION OF TRUST

The undersigned does hereby appoint and designate as his (her) Trustee herein, the Secretary-Treasurer and Publisher of the United States Naval Institute to perform and discharge the following duties, powers, and privileges in connection with the possession and use of a certain taped interview between the undersigned and the Oral History Department of the United States Naval Institute.

1. Classification of Transcript.

(X)a. If classified OPEN, the transcript(s) may be read or the recording(s) audited by the qualified personnel upon presentation of proper credentials, as determined by the Secretary-Treasurer of the U.S. Naval Institute.

( )b. If classified PERMISSION REQUIRED TO CITE OR QUOTE, the user will be required to obtain permission in writing from the interviewee prior to quoting or citing from either the transcript(s) or the recording(s).

( )c. If classified PERMISSION REQUIRED, permission must be obtained in writing from the interviewee before the transcribed interview(s) can be examined or the tape recording(s) audited.

( )d. If classified CLOSED, the transcribed interview(s) and the tape recording(s) will be sealed until a time specified by the interviewee. This may be until the death of the interviewee or for any specified number of years.

2. It is expressly understood that in giving this authorization, I am in no way precluded from placing such restrictions as I may desire upon use of the interview at any time during my lifetime, nor does this authorization in any way affect my rights to the copyright of my literary expressions that may be contained in the interview.

Witness my hand and seal this _1_ day of _October_ 19_81_.

[signature]

I hereby accept and consent to the foregoing Declaration of Trust and the powers therein conferred upon me as Trustee:

[signature] R T E Bowker Jr
5 October 1981

Interview No. 1 with Rear-admiral Robert H. Wertheim

Place: His residence in Annandale, Virginia

Date: Tuesday, 6 January 1981

Subject: Biography

By: John T. Mason, Jr.

Q: I have been looking forward to this interview. You have had a very significant, indeed a remarkable career in a very important area of operations and I am looking forward to having your account of this career on tape. This is a talking biography so would you begin by telling me where you were born, when you were born, and a little something about your family.

Adm. W.: All right, I am happy to do that. I was born in Carlsbad, New Mexico, November 1922. My father was an immigrant to this country; he emigrated directly to New Mexico from Germany in 1906 at the age of 17 and as for so many immigrants he was brought over by a cousin. He worked in a general store in a small town in New Mexico until he had earned enough money to repay his passage.

Q: How did he happen to select New Mexico and not the coast?

Adm. W.: Well immigrants are supposed to be sponsored by someone and he had a cousin who resided in New Mexico and why the earlier relatives had chosen New Mexico is something I don't know how to answer but I do know that there was a fair number of immigrants at that particular stage of our country's history that were coming over from Western Europe.

Q: It required a sense of adventure to go that far west, didn't it?

Adm. W.: Oh yes, I should say so and that was where the opportunity was. He was brought up in a society that was pretty rigid; you were born into a class and that is where you were going to be. He would have been apprenticed into some trade or other and he would have been a tradesman in Germany just as his father was and he would have served his time in the army and all that sort of thing, whereas in the New World there were opportunities limited only by one's industry and ability. That was very attractive to him and to many others in Germany. At any rate he came over to this country and after he repaid his passage and was on his own he became a travelling salesman for a period of time, and among others, for the Peters Shoe Company. It was while he was in that capacity he met and married my mother who was from an even tinier town in New Mexico called Wagonmound.

It was named after a prominent landmark on the Santa Fe Trail. They were married in 1913 and settled in Carlsbad. My mother's background is interesting if you would like to hear it?

Q: Yes I would, does it have a direct bearing on you?

Adm. W.: Yes, it did. She was born in a very tiny town called Cleveland, New Mexico, which no one I am sure has ever heard of. The town itself was given its name and was founded by her father who was himself an immigrant from Germany at an earlier time. He was running a general store up there and in order to correspond with his finacee' back in Philadelphia it was necessary to have a postoffice which they did not have in that town so he founded the town, named it after the then President of the United States, Grover Cleveland, got a fourth class postoffice and was able then to successfully correspond with his fiancee'. The postoffice was located in his general store, and ultimately he was able to persuade this red-headed girl from Philadelphia to come out and share the wilderness with him. She did and she raised a family of eight children, each one delivered by a midwife and educated by governess. They were one of only two anglo-white families in the town, all the rest were Mexicans and Indians. They were the Vorenbergs and the other white family were the Cassidys so you had a family of Irish Catholics and a family of German Jews, all the rest were Indians and Mexicans. There were about 700 people in the town.

In any event my mother, as were all the other girls in that family, when they were ready for high school they were sent off to Philadelphia for a couple of years. She went to Friends Central in Philadelphia and the boys of the family were generally sent to the New Mexico Military Institute.

Q: Great emphasis on education was it not?

Adm. W.: Yes. The family was multi-lingual, German, English, Spanish and my mother also learned French. While she was raised on a ranch in a tiny town nevertheless when they reached an appropriate age that iron-willed grandmother of mine saw to it that they got their education. When my mother announced that she had found a man that she was interested in marrying my grandmother announced that no way was she going to marry a travelling salesman. So, as one of the conditions for approving the marriage my father was informed in no uncertain terms that he was to get something that would allow him to settle down. He did that, he found a small store in southern New Mexico and with that the two were married.

Q: That became his kind of dowry.

Adm. W.: It is an interesting tale but not one on which I want to dwell too long but nevertheless he became a successful businessman in a very small town, at first in Artesia, New Mexico and later in Carlsbad, the town in which I was born. He was a successful businessman, widely known, widely respected, never wealthy but solid middle class, a civic leader he was the one always called upon to take on the thankless chores, the head of the Chamber of Commerce, the Exalted Ruler of the Elks, the Master of his Masonic Lodge; he always was the Fourth of July speaker at the ceremonies on the Court House steps--that sort of thing. He was deeply patriotic and was very, very involved in community service. As so many who have adopted America as opposed to being born into it, he appreciated the country in a very undemonstrative but sincere way and he passed that on to his kids.

Q: How many children were there?

Adm. W.: Just two of us; I had an older brother who died as a child and my sister, who was older than I by four years, were the only children. We were brought up in a very warm and close-knit family. By the way we were the only Jewish family in the entire county so in order to retain any kind of sense of identity it was necessary to work pretty hard at it but we did in a religious and undemonstrative way and in a patriotic and sincere and meaningful way. My father always believed that every young man should serve his country in uniform and so, even before I was born, he made a commitment to the then superintendent of the New Mexico Military Institute, that if it is a son he is coming to the Institute. I was committed before I was born, and that was what I was going to do.

Q: Did he make a conscious effort to shape your thinking in this area??

Adm. W.: Not really, it was just sort of assumed that I would spend a couple of years in uniform, that every young man was supposed to do that by his standards.

Q: That was a carry-over from the German background.

Adm. W.: I think so, but that background was what he left, what he abandoned, in the one case it was required. There is a difference in being required to serve and in volunteering. That was his view, he felt that this was his adopted land and everyone should be prepared to defend this precious liberty that gave people the right to choose as opposed to being mandated.

Q: What a marvelous heritage?

Adm. W.: That's right; and there were other things that they passed along to me which I thought might be worth mentioning at the outset.

Q: Yes, because this all has bearing on you as you grew up and developed your career.

Adm. W.: Both my sister and I then went all the way through the Carlsbad public school system. Carlsbad at that time had about 2000-2500 people and it gradually grew over time but it was still quite a small community even by New Mexico standards.

Q: It has scenic attractions, doesn't it?

Adm. W.: Yes, the Carlsbad Caverns are about some 20 odd miles outside of town. It actually drew its name from mineral springs found nearby which reminded some people of the resort in Europe--Karlsbad--and they tried to exploit it without success and when the caverns were found they took the name of the town.

Anyhow both of us went all the way through the school system in Carlsbad from kindergarten right through high school. And, as you have gathered, it was a very secure, very stable environment, a loving close-knit family; many of our friends had the same experience, born and raised right there. I remember I felt so sorry for people who had to move because to me that seemed frightening the thought of ever living any place else. I knew only one home and my mother still lives in this old house where I was born. Obviously there are advantages and disadvantages of everyone in town knowing you, you couldn't get away with very much and those kind of strictures are not bad but it does have an influence on what you are willing to try to do--you can't be very anonymous even to just soaping windows on hollowe'en night. One of the things I remember particularly about growing up there was how I always was expected to have a job. After school jobs, summer jobs; I delivered the Saturday Evening Post, sold them, delivered the local newspaper. I worked at various stores at various times. My dad felt very strongly about the need for people to do something to get some feel for the value of money. The first job I held was in the depths of the depression as a pre-teenager, with a local grocery store and I earned a dollar a week. It was much later in life that I discovered that that dollar was in fact given to the store by my father. They didn't have any need for someone like me but they were willing to have me around as long as it didn't cost them anything. But it was that important to my father that I be working; I didn't learn this until I was grown.

Q: A very significant story.

Adm. W.: I did reasonably well academically in school as did my sister--she did better than I did. We had this family respect for education and a certain amount of pressure to study and do our homework. Standards were set reasonably high and things were expected of us and we did them. As time went on I found I enjoyed mathematics and the harder sciences perhaps more than other things but I don't believe I was unbalanced in that regard.

Q: Were you attracted to history at all?

Adm. W.: Yes, I was and I liked English, I wrote reasonably well although it came hard to me, I labored over it. I was in school plays and in high school I won an essay contest. I remember how hard I had to work to make the words come out right. I envied people who could write easily. I don't.

Thinking back on those days I remember that I wasn't a particularly attractive kid, I was slow to reach my full growth so I was a little undersized; I wore braces on my teeth as they hadn't come in straight and I wore glasses. I wasn't terribly athletic, I played tennis fairly but I wasn't big enough or strong enough to play football. I was in the band, built model airplanes; photography was a great hobby of mine.

Q: Did you take languages?

Adm. W.: Spanish was the only language offered in school in New Mexico. It was required as New Mexico is legally a bi-lingual state; many people don't know that but it was required that Spanish be taught and the laws are published in two languages, Spanish and English.

Q: That comes in quite handy today, doesn't it?

Adm. W.: Rather surprisingly it came in very handy in my naval career and fairly early. We always had a Mexican maid in our house, she spoke nothing but Spanish, so I was brought up speaking Spanish although I have lost most of it because I simply don't use it though I reckon it would come back quickly if I needed it. Later on when I went to the Naval Academy the only elective you were offered in the course was language so I said to myself, I obviously don't want to take Spanish having had it all through school so I volunteered for Japanese or Russian both of which seemed to be particularly challenging and I wanted to do something like that. I was turned down on the grounds that my background only qualified me for Spanish. I had never taken Latin or any of the other things that were necessary to study languages.

Q: Well Latin wouldn't have helped you with either Japanese or Russian.

Adm. W.: I never did understand that decision.

I left high school in 1940 and promptly went to the New Mexico Military Institute, which was the first time I was away from home. By that time I had grown up, the braces were off the teeth and I could smile again, I had been Robert all the time I was growing up and to everybody in that small town I was Robert and somehow that name identified with my former personality, so when I went away to college I could hardly wait to rename myself Bob, and I have been Bob all the rest of my life. My mother, by the way, knew I wanted to be called Bob but she refused to let me on the grounds that everyone she knew called Bob ended up being called Bobby, and even at 50 years old they were still Bobby. Maybe there is something to being called Jimmy too. She just didn't want that to happen to me; it didn't bother her at all that I became Bob once I left home.

Q: How did you take to the military?

Adm. W.: It was a cultural shock of course, a cultural shock to leave home at all to be snatched out of that one environment into a completely different one.

Q: How large a school is the New Mexico Military Institute?

Adm. W.: It was at that time several hundred, there must have been around 300 boys and at that time it was cavalry, every boy rode, it was horse cavalry the horses provided by the army and we had army paid instructors, it was an ROTC school, fully approved and graduates were given commissions depending on whether it was Junior ROTC or Senior, either as officers or non-commissioned officers, in the cavalry. It was a high school and first two years of college and many of its graduates went on to other colleges that offered cavalry ROTC on which they were commissioned directly into the army.

Q: Did some go on to West Point?

Adm. W.: Yes many did and of course that was where I got the idea that I wanted to do the same. I did reasonably well there in the military sciences as well as the mathematics and physics and history and English and so forth, but particularly I enjoyed the engineering subjects in mathematics. I found it was a real luxury because for the first time I was really getting something I could get my teeth into like calculus, analytical geometry and physics. I discovered physics there and to me that was really the thing I loved. My professor in physics wanted very badly for me to go to Cal Tech from there. He felt I could do that.

But by that time, it was early 1941, war clouds were gathering and it became increasingly clear that we were probably going to get involved, so I was trading off the options as to what I wanted to do. I really wanted to finish college so the notion of going to one of the service academies, West Point or Annapolis seemed particularly the best of all worlds because I knew they were technical schools, that one could get a good technical education and it was also a way in which I could finish.

Q: I suppose your father approved of this?

Adm. W.: Yes, he did, he was so proud he was busting his buttons that his son wanted to do that.

Q: What about your mother?

Adm. W.: Mother was very supportive. My dad, once he got the idea that that was what I wanted, in his characteristically energetic way, he set about trying to persuade the Senators and Congressmen from New Mexico--there weren't so many you know--

Q: At that point there was only one Congressman.

Adm. W.: That's right but we had two Senators. Nevertheless he started working on every one, which wasn't easy; New Mexico is a democratic state and he was one of the very few republicans in that whole area of the state. But he got a lot of support from his friends and associates and people who had known me--I think more of him than me.

Q: That's understandable he had been a civic leader in his community and that was a help.

Adm. W.: Of course I had done well in school so that helped and I had very strong support from the Institute. I had finished second in my class academically and militarily so that was helpful. In due course I got a telegram offering me an appointment. I had done nothing to earn this, it was sort of handed to me on a silver platter and I accepted it.

Q: Did you have to take a competitive exam then for standing?

Adm. W.: I had to do nothing because of the fact that I had done two years of college and had done reasonably well and had taken the right courses, all of those things were weighed and to me it was a piece of cake handed over on a silver platter. As my Dad said, "I can make it easy for you to get in with the help and influence but now its up to you" and indeed it was.

Q: What a marvelous Dad you had, his guiding influence in those formative years.

Adm. W.: My word yes, and my Mother too. She was very strong but my father was really the dominant influence. My mother was an old fashioned girl who believed she should stay pretty much in the background, with support and amplifying her husband's desires in all regards. Later on she had a rude shock when she had to take over. My father died at a relatively young age and the whole thing was thrust upon her, then she showed what she was made of. She picked up the reins and with my sister's help ran my father's business.

Q: She took over the business?

Adm. W.: She did and the two of them made it go and continued to make it work, she is a marvelous woman, now in her late 80s, no longer what she was obviously. She has suffered a series of strokes and is a shadow of herself but nevertheless is quite a remarkable woman. In any event, I entered the Naval Academy in June of 1942 with the Class of 1946. And that really should have quotation marks around it I think because it was a three-year course which was to graduate ultimately in three years in 1945. We were the first class to enter the Naval Academy after the start of the war and because of the accelerated course and because of the fact that they were trying to crowd as many people as they could into these classes we were the largest class up to that time and for many, many years afterward.

Q: How many were in your class?

Adm. W.: Something over 1200, a typical class before that had been running between 700 and 800.

Q: Living quarters must have been awfully crowded?

Adm. W.: That's right, we were three in rooms designed for two.

Wertheim #1 - 15

We worked right through the summer, we took thirty days off but didn't have the time to do the things during the summer that had been done in the past. Some courses were dropped, some that were considered luxuries I guess.

Q: What was the plebe's summer like? was that truncated also?

Adm. W.: It was kind of interesting, not truncated but it was another cultural shock because I had anticipated that having gone to a military college it had somehow better equipped me to go to the Naval Academy than some others. Maybe it did and maybe it didn't but it turned out that the criteria, the standards, the style was very different.

Q: It was navy rather than army.

Adm. W.: That's right but both the Naval Academy and the Military Academy had honor systems but they worked very differently. The New Mexico Military Institute was patterned on West Point and the Naval Academy system was different and took some getting used to. The academic course work was easy because in those days there was no way of giving credit for courses already taken so I found myself repeating work.

Q: You were in a minority were you not, in terms of having had college?

Adm. W.: I would have been in a minority I think, in a normal class; but in a wartime class the academy was attractive to a lot of people. I won't be so crude as to call them draft dodgers but there was a natural desire on the part of a lot of people to get into the military through that route if they could which otherwise they might not have been interested in the military. Our class average age I think was a little older and probably there was a larger percentage of my classmates who had had college than might have been normal.

Q: What about the instructors, what was the caliber of the instructors in wartime, the percentage of civilians?

Adm. W.: Of course everyone was in uniform it seems to me as I look back on it. That wouldn't mean that they were all military.

Q: The civilians wore uniform also?

Adm. W.: Yes, I believe so, most of them did, but the style of instruction in those days was such that a great deal was not required of an instructor. We were given the books, given the assignments that covered the entire year at the start of the year so we knew for each class, for each day, what sections of the book were to be covered; we knew that we were going to be given a quiz, that some kind of a grade was going to be taken in every class on every day and generally speaking the instructor was a referee between the book and the boy.

Q: He could be almost a dummy up there, couldn't he?

Adm. W.: Almost. Now some of them were quite a ways beyond that; any naval officer could be taken off any ship and sent to the Naval Academy to be an instructor without putting great demands on them.

Q: That was done was it not? If they needed a short tour on land?

Adm. W.: Yes, that is the way it was done. It was studiously done this way because, I think, in order to be fair since it was all competitive and large class standings on graduation as to where we stood in the fleet as to seniority for promotions and all the rest of it for the rest of our lives, it was studiously fair and in order to make it fair since everyone was going to take the same classes though not necessarily at the same time, they tried to make it such that it didn't really matter which instructor you had--your particular class, that day, so that particular section of the math book was going to be covered the same way by the instructor for every group.

Q: It depended on your ability to study and you had learned how to do that.

Adm. W.: Yes that gave me a big advantage. It might have been too easy for me at first because I then fell into some pretty sloppy habits. Things were so easy for the first year or so academically and later on when the work wasn't all that easy I had to pull myself up by the nape of my own neck.

Q: Did you have to help your roommates if they were in need of some tutoring?

Adm. W.: One of them in particular needed help. I had one roommate who was very bright and had no problem at all and he and I had to help one of our other roommates. He was a wonderful, warm Texan, a big hulk of a guy, the nicest person you could imagine but academically just barely squeaked through and we all had to support him, help him as best we could. There were some others too. Sure, you help your classmates, you did the best you could particularly your roommates. In any case we were all expected to do something with regard to athletics and it was there that I discovered fencing of all things. I had never heard of fencing in New Mexico but it was something that I found I could do and reasonably well; I was on the varsity squad.

Q: It calls for great agility and dexterity doesn't it?

Adm. W.: Yes it calls for agility, dexterity and some strategy and skill, and there is no premium placed on size or weight so I took to it like a duck to water and I really enjoyed it. I still played tennis and other intramural sports but that was my great love.

In due course graduation day came.

Q: Could you say something more about what you did in the summer

Adm. W.: Well they were telescoped. During the wartime years at the Naval Academy the summer cruises were cruises in name only; the first one on the USS ARKANSAS, which was an old battleship and still swung hammocks.

Q: Fortunately you didn't have to do any coaling.

Adm. W.: No we didn't but I remember the shock of discovering there was no place I could call my own on that ship. When we upped hammocks in the morning and they were stowed away, there was nothing, no spot on the ship to call your own. That was a shock. And we did cruises in the Chesapeake Bay, didn't venture out because of the submarines.

Q: How were you occupied, with gunnery and that sort of thing?

Adm. W.: Sure, we worked through the departments in the ship acted like junior division officers and were instructed by the petty officers and the officers on the ship. Of course we had our own officers from the Naval Academy, some of the faculty came along.

The second cruise, the other cruise that we did was on the USS NEW YORK. By this time the war was in its later stages--in 1944--and things were secure enough for us to venture out from the Chesapeake Bay and we got down into the Carribean.

Q: In general the submarine menace had been diminished?

Adm. W.: It had been beaten back a bit and while we were

Wertheim #1 - 20

of course still escorted it would have spoiled somebody's whole day to have lost a battleship full of midshipmen, it was still considered safe enough to let us out of the Chesapeake Bay. I enjoyed those cruises, they were the first real encounters I had had with the ocean.

Q: Were you a good sailor?

Adm. W.: Not really, particularly later on when I took my first sea duty as a junior officer I discovered that I wasn't a good sailor. That was on a destroyer, they put me up forward in chief's country which is right up near the bow the peak of the ship where you got the full benefit of the ship's motion and it was quite a while before I got over the tendency of being seasick. I thought I was going to die and I was sure I had picked the wrong career. But all things pass and I ultimately developed my sea legs and didn't have these problems but believe me there was a time when I hoped I would die.

Q: In more normal years the summer cruises proved to be I suppose, a culling process for some boys who decided at that point they didn't want to be sailors. But with the war on it was different. How was that reflected in the attitude at the academy, with the war waged in the Pacific particularly?

Adm. W.: I speak only for myself--I was very, very impatient to get through the course and to get to sea and to participate.

I felt that we were moving at a snail's pace and that we should be getting out much sooner. I looked at some of the other officer programs, like the V-12, V-5 and V-7, these were different officer programs of one kind or another with those men getting commissioned with a much shorter period of training than we were getting and I didn't think it was fair; I felt something ought to be done.

Q: Did you have visiting officers who lectured on the war, who came back from the battles and told you about them? That kind of thing?

Adm. W.: Yes, the officers who were attached to the academy who were concerned with discipline and military training and that sort of thing as opposed to the academic courses, the executive department was made up of officers who had had combat experience and we hung on their every word, we ate it up, their experiences and what they said about what we should be concentrating on and what we should need to pay attention to.

Q: Who was superintendent at that time?

Adm. W.: Beardall was the Commandant of Midshipmen. As I have indicated the curriculum was fixed, everyone took exactly the same courses. We still marched to classes. The honor system as practiced there was your word was accepted as long as you could prove it. Anything you could prove would be believed. I thought, coming from a military school of a different type, that where everything you said was accepted and you didn't have to prove anything but if you were ever found lying or cheating you were simply out instantly. The same was true of the Naval Academy except that you knew you would have to prove it, signing in and signing out and that sort of thing.

Q: Were there fewer infringements in wartime than there would have been otherwise?

Adm. W.: I think there was more concern about not wanting to be expelled. The threat of expulsion was more impressive then than it would have been in peacetime.

Q: Was there any introduction to aviation at all?

Adm. W.: Yes, we had some introduction to that, it was part of our classwork and in the summer upon graduation those of us who weren't going into aviation had to spend a month at Jacksonville taking flying and getting exposed to aviation in a practical way. It was considered to be a part of the proper education.

Q: Did you reject the idea of aviation out of hand?

Adm. W.: No, not really. I hadn't thought much about it. It turned out that we were all given aviation physicals, one of the last things before graduation and it was sort of assumed that anyone who could pass the aviation physical would in fact choose to be an aviator. There were many obvious reasons for that, they were paid more money, promotions seemed to go faster if you were a flyer. There were all kinds of reasons and the life of a flyer seemed to be much better.

Q: I suppose there was the more glamourous aspect.

Adm. W.: You were one of the first class citizens of the navy if you were a flyer; everyone knew that aircraft carriers and aviation was the wave of the future and all that. Well I passed the aviation physical.

Q: No impairment to your eyes?

Adm. W.: I never wore glasses after I got to the Naval Academy, I took them off. You see me wearing them now strictly for reading, I only put them on in later years.

Q: You said that as a boy you wore them.

Adm. W.: I wore them because I had a muscle imbalance that caused one eye to cross. This happened when I was quite young and the optometrist there prescribed the glasses to relax the muscles and to take eye exercises, which I did all the time I was growing up. They told me when I was a youngster that I was going to have to wear glasses for the rest of my life and I accepted that. It was only when I went to the Naval Academy that I took the glasses off. I passed the physical exam and reached for them to put them back on again and they said, "Oh no, you leave them off now", it was then I discovered I could get along without them.

Wertheim #1 - 24

Whatever the problem had been was corrected over time.

Q: Did you continue with your eye exercises?

Adm. W.: No. It just turned out that I had outgrown the problem without ever realizing it; I never wore glasses from the time I entered the Naval Academy until I was in my forties when I started to use them to read.

Q: You passed the physical for an aviator and that was proof positive that your eyes were all right.

Adm. W.: As far as eyes were concerned the physical exam for a submariner I think was even tougher the idea being you had to see well enough through a periscope. What I really wanted to do was be a submariner. It just appealed to me.

Q: Why? Was it the engineering aspect?

Adm. W.: Yes that was it and I sort of felt that that was the wave of the future, that aviation was great now but some day it was going to be submarines. I took the physical for aviation, passed it, got to the end of the line and the last thing we had in the examination was an interview with a flight surgeon and the first question he asked me was "Why do you want to be an aviator?" He made a presumption that I didn't think was fair and I reacted to it in a negative way and I said, "I am not really all that sure that I do". Without thinking about it I was sort of saying,

"Well if someone wants me to be an aviator why don't they convince me I should". His reaction to that was to write on the exam "Poor motivation". In fact he said, "He doesn't look like a very good bet." So I was not chosen to be an aviator. As far as submarines are concerned there were far more boys who wanted to go into submarines than could. I think about 300 of us out of that class of almost 1200 who graduated had spots and could go directly into submarines. I drew a preference number which was by lot, the process by which we could determine who would get what. It wasn't good enough, it wasn't a low enough number to have gotten me into submarines; if I had asked for submarines with that number I knew that I wouldn't get them and they would put me at the tail end of the line and I would have gotten a battleship, or a heavy cruiser which I didn't want. So in fact I put down my first choice--which was really my second choice-- which was destroyers and that's what I got.

Q: What percentage of the class went into the marines?

Adm. W.: Around 100 or 150, most of the ones who did were ones who had come in from the marines.

Q: So you did get your second choice actually, to the USS HYMAN.

Adm. W.: I joined HYMAN in 1945 after graduating from the Academy and by the time I joined her it was August 1945. I had in the meantime spent a month at Jacksonville with the aviation training for us non-aviators and then a month of leave.

Q: Actually you graduated with Distinction which is quite something in a speed-up course, isn't it?

Adm. W.: Yes, I think I was like number 23 out of that class of almost 1200 but even so I am sure Admiral Rickover would have said something unpleasant to me because I didn't feel I had done my best.

Q: He would disagree with the kind of education you had gotten anyway.

Adm. W.: I thought it was very well balanced. I did enjoy the military elements of it, I was never a four-striper or a five-striper but I was a striper and I enjoyed my association with people, with other men, then as I have ever since. I never had any big affairs of the heart because there wasn't really that much opportunity to especially in those days.

Q: Will you say something about the social life in wartime at the Academy. It must have been very limited.

Adm. W.: It was. Opportunities for dating, for social life, were not very great. As a plebe they were non-existent altogether, we would have the tea dances and the hops and that sort of thing, formalized affairs where the girls would be imported--Annapolis really didn't produce anything like enough girls for all the demand from the Naval Academy and the local schools for the young men that were still there in wartime. So we used to import them from Baltimore, Washington and Philadelphia and I am sure that still goes on. Some of the more ambitious ones came all the way from New York. The old Baltimore and Annapolis Railroad (the old W.B.& A.) ran from Baltimore and I well recall standing at the train station in Annapolis patiently waiting for it to arrive and see what it was going to deliver to me. It usually was going to be a blind date--a friend of the girl friend of one of my friends, it usually amounted to somebody who has a 'marvelous personality and a lot of fun'. But it was great fun and we, especially during our first class year, had opportunities to take a boat out during the summer, or go out picnicking or the like. There was plenty of opportunity to get serious about a girl if there was a girl who had mutual interests. I never found anyone during that period that I was serious about, nor did I until the summer vacation after graduation, the war was still on in the Pacific in 1945, and I was on my way to join the HYMAN. I was on leave in my hometown in New Mexico and my mother announced that my aunt who lived in the town, had two young ladies as house guests who had come to see the Carlsbad Caverns and I, as the only eligible male in the entire family had an obligation to go present myself to these two young ladies, as a matter of courtesy, and I said, "No way was I going to spoil my last leave before going off to die for my country and wasting my time that way." I had all on my dish that I could possibly handle with the other town girls and no way was I going to do this. Mother informed me that that was all right for me to say because I was going to be leaving but she, my mother, had to live with my aunt (her sister) after I was gone so for her sake would I please just present myself, say something nice and then disappear as I would have done my duty and her life would be easier.

Q: And you had to appear in uniform too, didn't you?

Adm. W.: Of course. So I did, I appeared in uniform and I remember I went there bright and early in the morning to get it over with and the young ladies were up for breakfast but still in their bathrobes--not the most auspicious time to be making an impression on anyone--but I took a long look at one of them and decided, well a little overweight and not terribly attractive and I discounted her quickly. The other was a little bit harder to discount. She, I felt if you put a little weight on her she just might pass. Also it turned out she was from Los Angeles and I was going to be on a west coast based ship so I condescended to put her name in my little black book. Suffice it to say that in due course she became my bride. When I went to the west coast to look for my ship (in those days the ship movements were held very, very close) and I didn't really know where my ship was going to be. I was ordered to a particular place and there I should present myself and my orders and they would consult the secret files and then they would decide what they would do with me next. Sure enough the first place I was to present myself was Long Beach and this girl was from Los Angeles so we made contact there. At that point she looked even better to me. As I was shuttled up and down the west coast from one point to another looking for the ship I passed through Los Angeles a couple of times and each time we would have another date. By the time I was finally sent to Pearl Harbor where I finally did catch the HUMAN, we were corresponding. I will jump ahead a little bit then come back--we corresponded for the entire seven months of that deployment and by the time the ship got back I already had orders to another ship and I knew that the turnaround would be extremely brief. During that very brief turnaround we managed to see enough of one another for us to get engaged. Then I went to sea on another destroyer this time for nine months and of course the correspondence by now was that of an engaged couple and the arrangements were to get married as soon as the ship returned. In fact when we married we were virtual strangers because almost all of our association had been by letter and there was a moment of panic when I really wondered whether this was the right thing to do, whether I really knew this person.

Q: She may have shared the same feeling.

Adm. W.: She was marrying a sailor and one that she only knew by the two-dimensional means of letters.

Q: During wartime, correspondence aboard the ship must have been difficult, wasn't it?

Adm. W.: Yes, because the mail would arrive very infrequently and that was a highlight.

Q: It was still censored and read, wasn't it?

Adm. W.: It really wasn't; the war only lasted a few more months after I joined the HYMAN.

Q: Would you say something about the difficulty of finding your ship. Wasn't this a little disconcerting?

Adm. W.: It was really. I remember being sent from Long Beach up to San Francisco and then back down to San Diego. I can't remember all of the trips I made. The ship had returned from Okinawa where it had suffered Kamikaze attacks, it had gone to the yards and had been repaired--I think the shipyard was Mare Island--then it was sent back again and all this time I was on my way to it. They sent me up to San Francisco to catch it and by the time I arrived it had departed so I was ultimately sent to Pearl Harbor where I caught it.

Q: By that time she was enroute to Japan?

Adm. W.: And Soeul. We were enroute to Japan and the invasion of Japan was in the grand scheme of things.

Q: OPERATION OLYMPIA?

Adm. W.: Exactly, and we were going to be part of the invasion force, or the covering force. We were enroute from Pearl Harbor to that part of the world when the war ended. We were diverted and assigned to the task of taking the surrender of the Japanese islands. These were islands which had been by-passed during the island hopping. During the island hopping campaign in the Pacific some islands were completely cut off.

Q: What about the Bonins?

Adm. W.: These particular islands we were involved with were the Marianas and the Gilbert group and the Carolines-- that far down. The first one was an island called Kusai and that was on the 8th of September. We went in to this little island of Kusai; this had been fortified--these were islands that no one visited during the period of the Japanese mandate. By no one I mean no foreigners.

Q: Attempts had been made but they had not succeeded.

Adm. W.: We went in with just the destroyer and hoping the Japanese had gotten the word that the war was over, that they had lost, because the one destroyer here in the midst of all that enemy force wouldn't have done too well. We went in wearing our white uniforms but it was general quarters so it was kind of ?? but they had gotten the word; the Emperor had spoken and we went in and ended holding a miniature version of the big formal ceremonies of surrender with which we are all so familiar on the MISSOURI, and we did this on our destroyer. The local Japanese commander and other officials met with the American military officers and this was duly recorded. We had an American correspondent aboard who wrote it all up and it was sent to hometown newspapers, all about this event.

Q: What was the attitude of the Japanese once they surrendered?

Adm. W.: They were very impassive, no tears running down their cheeks, there was no emotion shown, it was just a formal thing, they were very polite, they turned over their swords, with some complaint as they felt they should keep them for ceremonial purposes but this was turned down and they were required to turn them in. Then we were promptly sent to another island after Kusai, and this next island was Ponape.

Q: Ponape had figured in the war.

Adm. W.: Ponape was quite another matter. It was a very large island in fact it was the largest island of the former Japanese mandated group and it had some 20,000 Japanese on it and a number of natives that must have been much larger than that. About half the Japanese were military of the three services, the rest were civilians.

Q: Still a single destroyer?

Adm. W.: Still the single destroyer, we went through the same process, the surrender proceedings followed the same procedure. As a photographer (I still retained that skill) I was assigned the job of recording all this so I took the pictures, still and movies.

Q: That was a matter of faith too wasn't it? To record the surrender in the far off Pacific.

Adm. W.: And instead of moving on we were told to stay put, to stay there as station ship for that island until the Japanese could be repatriated and until their navy, many of whom were forced laborers who had been brought in from surrounding islands by the Japanese, could be returned to their islands. We stayed there for some three months.

Q: Who provided the transportation for this change?

Adm. W.: Japanese ships would come in, transports or warships, and pick up the Japanese and take them home.

Q: Were they manned by the Imperial Navy?

Adm. W.: Yes. This was a very interesting experience and coming as it did so soon after my joining the navy on active duty, I got an entirely erroneous impression of what life was going to be like in the navy as a naval officer. These were quite unusual experiences. It turned out that among the people on this island were some Europeans who had been interned by the Japanese at the start of the war, Belgian planters and their families. There was a group of Spanish nuns and priests there. I told you I would get around to where my Spanish came in handy; I was the only one on the ship who could speak Spanish and so I was pressed into service as an interpreter for these folks who spoke no English and that too was quite an interesting experience.

Q: How had they been handled, and taken care of?

Adm. W.: They had a pretty rough time of it, they were literally imprisoned--interned--by the Japanese. They were cut off from their parishoners and not allowed to have any contact with the natives many of whom had been converted to Catholicism and the natives were not allowed to practice their religion. They had absolutely nothing; obviously they were fed, the island was self-supporting fortunately for them because they had been cut off from the Japanese homeland but they were able to raise their food enough to survive.

Q: Did you have a chance to inspect the Japanese fortifications?

Adm. W.: Yes. If in this interview I could show you pictures you would see many photographs of those fortifications that I took.

Q: The standard ones, pillboxes and that sort of thing?

Adm. W.: Yes. This was a relatively fortified and well manned and pretty well supplied with arms area, but since it was cut off it was a convenient training target for flyers who had gotten out and were in the process of being staged to the forward areas but who needed a little bit of a taste of live action without too much resistance. They would come over and take a crack at bombing the island of Ponape to get anti-aircraft fire and there were a few Americans shot down; their graves were duly identified to us by the Japanese when we arrived. It was real, they had a capability, they would have put up pretty significant resistance had any one attempted to take the island but that had never happened.

Q: They were fortunate Japanese weren't they?

Adm. W.: They were, so many of the other islands were obliterated. There are some wonderful stories that I will not relate because they have nothing to do with anything that I would care to repeat. But, we had to keep those Japanese busy during the time we were waiting for their ships to come and repatriate them so we were looking for projects to assign them and one of the projects was building an Officers' Club, a clear essential, after all we had twenty officers on that ship. We set up a club on the beach and I, as the junior ensign on the ship was sent in due course on ship's business to the Island of Kwajalein, there to find out about how to get stocks and supplies of beer. They had the impression--things were pretty much in chaos at that time at the end of the war--that the district supply officer (or club officer, I don't exactly remember which he was) was a very distracted individual; when I identified who I was and where I had come from, he said, "Oh yes, I hear you have opened a small base so I guess you want the standard small base club allowance".

Q: What was your transportation to Kwajalein?

Adm. W.: Seaplane, the weekly mail plane. I have buried in my papers a copy of the ship's orders that I was sent to Kwajalein on a 'no cost to the government ship's business'. And that ship's business was arranging to get supplies for the Officers' Club.

Q: It must have been quite a task to keep them busy when they didn't know exactly when they were to be taken off? It was an open ended thing.

Adm. W.: That's right. They were assigned things to do; there was no resistance, no resentment, no surliness on their part that I recall. As a matter of fact they seemed to be in relatively good spirits, they were looking forward to going home. I was prepared to be quite severe and grim, the typical conqueror in the presence of the hated enemy, but it was hard to maintain that pose because they were just people and a lot of them were women and children, some just newborn, children who had been born there. Their meagre belongings were being packed up and they were getting ready to go home. There was no fraternizing but it was hard to remember what it was I was really supposed to be heading.

Q: Very interesting; of course that is what some of our people discovered on the mainland after the Japanese surrender.

Adm. W.: In any case in due course we finished the job we had been sent to do on those two islands, Ponape in particular.

Q: And other destroyers were busy doing the same thing elsewhere?

Adm. W.: I presume so although I don't really know. I can't recall what was being done, how the surrenders were being taken but a military government group in due course appeared with people who were formally charged with this sort of thing and they took over the administration, local administration in proper quarters ashore and they no longer needed the ship there to provide quarters for these people. So we were sent off. We continued on to China and Japan on that particular tour which, as I said, was my first sea tour.

Q: What was the destroyer's mission?

Adm. W.: We went on to join the Seventh Fleet, we were no longer on detached duty and we became part of the task force 77, and attached ourselves to a carrier in the main body of the fleet. We visited Shanghai, Hong Kong, Yokosuka, regular ports of call by the fleet. This was now visiting Japan and China right at the end of the war. I remember making a trip, when we were in port, to visit Nagasaki one of the cities targeted by the atomic bomb. My impressions of that are quite vivid and influenced my thinking in later years when I was so heavily involved in the strategic nuclear program. I have in my scrap book a photograph of myself standing in the midst of the ruins with a canteen of water on my hip, we weren't allowed to drink any water locally.

Q: You had a first-hand impression of the devastation.

Adm. W.: I also remember visiting Tokyo which had not been hit by an atomic bomb but it looked every bit as bad to me.

Q: Fire bombing?

Adm. W.: Absolutely black and it didn't look a bit better than Nagasaki did, the difference of course was that in the one case it happened in an instant, all the damage was almost instantaneous and the shock of that had to have been far greater than damage accumulated over a period of time but the total amount of damage was quite comparable.

Q: Perhaps this would call for some of your philosophy on the use of the bomb?

Adm. W.: Well, as far as the use of the bomb in Japan is concerned, I honestly believe that had the bomb not been used the Japanese would not have ended the war when they did, I believe there would have been many, many thousands of lives lost, both Japanese and Americans.

Q: It would have been an assault on the islands.

Adm. W.: Yes, no question about it and I think the war would have continued and it would have ended as it did in a US victory but not before many more thousands of lives had been lost, Japanese and American. So I agree with the use of the bomb as was done by President Truman. I also believe, and standing back for a moment with the view of a historian, that the fact there has not been an unlimited war between major powers in the 35 odd years since then is directly attributable to the fact that the nuclear weapons exist, that there is an arsenal in our hands and in the hands of our principal adversaries.

Q: Plus the example of when they were used?

Adm. W.: That's right. That is not to suggest that there have not been lots and lots of limited wars fought, with limited objectives, but when you look at the events cited by historians as approximate cause leading to major conflicts in the past, WW1 and WW2 and before that, unlimited major wars, you can see that the events that have occurred in the 35 odd years since the end of WW2 have been more than enough to have caused another war and we haven't had it. Quite frankly, I think it is the existence of these systems and these weapons and more particularly their delivery systems, the ability of those weapons to be delivered inescapably--in the hands of the United States of America but now, increasingly, in the hands of others. In my farewell address to the members of our office I called that particular point to their attention and invited them to think on it.

I think that is what explains much of the attitude we have had through the years to the Navy's responsibility for maintaining a dependable and invulnerable delivery system for strategic nuclear weapons.

Q: Do you have a copy of that address?

Adm. W.: Yes. Well, in any case, at the end of that tour some seven months later, the ship was returning to the United States.

Q: Bringing back the men?

Adm. W.: No, not at that point. Most of the people on the ship were reservists, they were all looking forward to going home. I was one of the very few regular officers on board and as such I am sure I was considered a precious resource. I was one of the very few that the navy could turn right around and send back out. After all the navy still had responsibilities in the Pacific but it was desperately short of people it could use to man the ships, officers were still being commissioned for the various programs, they still had obligated service as junior officers but officers with any kind of experience, even as little as I had at that time, were in very short supply. I was given a set of orders to go right back out and joining another ship at this time, the BORDELON, a second destroyer. I asked for leave and was given enough time--two weeks or a month--to get all the way back to the west coast to visit Los Angeles. I say, laughingly to tease my wife, that she was the best thing I had seen in so long when she was there on the dock, that my immediate reaction was to ask her to marry me. It wasn't quite like that but anyhow, when I returned to chase BORDELON down I was engaged.

Q: Was it as difficult to find the ship this time?

Adm. W.: Not as difficult to find but it was difficult to get to it. I knew where it was, I went out to Guam and from Guam (the ship was in Seventh Fleet already) went to Shanghai I went to Guam by transport, the USS WAKEFIELD which was going out to bring troops back home; it was virtually empty going out and carried a few military types like myself, quite a few dependents--wives and children who were going out to join husbands that were taking over occupation duty in the islands of the Pacific or in the Far East. From Guam I was flown by military transport to Shanghai and there I waited for the ship. The ship was going to make a port call there ultimately but I became impatient and was sent at my own request to Okinawa to intercept the ship a little sooner and that's where I caught BORDELON. While I was at Okinawa, being in a quonset hut there, we were visited by Eisenhower who was then already quite a public figure with a potentially budding political career.

Q: He wasn't yet Chief of Staff in the army was he?

Adm. W.: I don't recall exactly what his position was,

except he was a war hero, everyone knew him, he was Ike, he came to speak to the troops, and I just remember my impression of that, of seeing him from a distance. I joined BORDELON, which was a long hull, 2200 ton long hull destroyer; it was rigged up as a radar picket ship with lots of electronics gear aboard, some 20 odd officers because of the extra command and control features on it.

Q: What was your particular duty?

Adm. W.: I went aboard as the assistant chief engineer, assistant engineering officer which is the position I had had on HYMAN. Once you got into engineering if was sort of like trying to take another language, it was like Spanish, once they found I was qualified in engineering, that was what I was going to be doing. I continued as an engineer on BORDELON until one day all of the point system caught up with us and we went down from something like 23 odd officers to 7 in a period of about two weeks, all of these officers having their obligated time expiring.

Q: It was a crippling thing, wasn't it?

Adm. W.: Almost crippling; we were still with the fleet and we still had to operate with the task force but we had to spread our duties around and all of the unnecessary things had to go by the board and we could no longer afford the luxury of an assistant engineering officer so I was jerked out of that job and about half a dozen others; I was made the communications officer and the CIC officer and the signal officer and a number of other things, electronics repair officer.

Q: Tremendous experience.

Adm. W.: Jack of all trades, while standing officer of the deck watches one and three, getting no sleep at all. It was pretty harrowing but there was no thought of tying the ship up because we couldn't operate--we just simply made do. One of the things that happened as a consequence was, and this happened fleet wide and not just on our ship, that we couldn't operate all that electronics equipment because electronics was a technology, a capability that had grown up during the war and virtually all of the navy's capabilities were in its reservists; none of the regular officers had any background or experience with radar and fancy communications equipments and the like. An electronics holiday was declared in the navy at that time which said in effect we will just not worry about maintaining equipment that doesn't have direct concern with the safe navigation and operation of the ship. The ship has got to be able to stay out of harms way so we had to have the navigation radar working and had to concentrate on the basic communication equipment. Anything else, air search radar, electronic counter-measures equipments and all of these other things on the ship were just simply used until they broke and when they broke you quit worrying about them; at least they had such a low priority that we could never get around to them.

Q: It must have been very intriguing to you however--this electronic equipment?

Adm. W.: I'll tell you, I was so busy and so beset with constant fatigue from everything else that was going on that I didn't have much time to rejoice. It was so demanding just to keep that equipment operating that had to operate. Fortunately we still had a few technicians among the enlisted people and between them and myself and reading the instruction manuals, wielding soldering irons and screw drivers so we were able to keep the basic equipment functioning. When we got back to the states...

Q: You brought back a contingent then? At that point was that your primary purpose?

Adm. W.: Our primary purpose was fleet operations and we were at sea most of the time steaming with Task Force 77 and we operated at sea for weeks at a time, being replenished at sea.

Q: In and out of the Japanese mainland?

Adm. W.: Yes and steaming around the Guam area.

Q: You had to be very alert to mines, didn't you?

Adm. W.: You bet we did. We were looking for them all the time and we found quite a few and when we did find one we would sink it or blow it up depending on circumstances.

Q: When you went into a Japanese port you were cognizant of where the mines had been sown, were you not?

Adm. W.: I believe so. Again you must recall I was not necessarily plugged in to the cognoscenti in all of these things because I was a very junior officer doing what junior officers did which was trying to get through the day without getting into too much trouble. In any case we also made port visits as we had before, and after some nine months on that tour we returned and this time the ship was being reassigned to the east coast for overhaul at the Brooklyn Naval Shipyard. We made port in San Diego and I came up to Los Angeles to be married. A number of my shipmates came up to help celebrate that wedding and I recall how happy I was to see them because this being in the heart of enemy country, namely my wife's friends and family only, and in Los Angeles I desperately needed a few friendly faces. They provided almost more support than I could handle. That wedding is still a little bit of a blur to me.

Q: Was it a crossing of swords ceremony?

Adm. W.: It was a civilian ceremony although of course I was still in uniform as were all my friends. After a very short honeymoon I returned to the ship and we went on around through the canal to the east coast and Barbara drove across country with the wife of a shipmate and met us on the east coast.

Q: Was the ship still received as a returning hero?

Adm. W.: I don't recall that we were.

Q: I remember when the Missouri came back there was a reception for it.

Adm. W.: By this time, 1946, people were getting over the war. As part of the solution to the problem of how do we handle our electronics equipment although electronics talent has left the navy, they had a program to send naval officers to an electronics school at Treasure Island in California. The navy set up an electronics materiel school there of some six months duration and as that ship's electronics officer I was sent there to learn. That was a very good thing that happened since my wedding since the environment in Brooklyn was really not good at all, there was no housing available, construction had stopped during the war and there was no place to live. Barbara and I were sharing a part of a flat in Brooklyn and it turned out she had come down with jaundice, she was ill and things were pretty grim at that point. Then like a bolt out of the blue I found I was to be sent back to California for six months of school and she became well almost instantaneously. I wasn't about to go off and leave her in the hospital, so we travelled across the country, stopping in Carlsbad long enough for my father to announce that he had persuaded the local dealer to sell us a Ford car so we bought a 1947 Ford.

Q: They were in short supply weren't they?

Adm. W.: It was hard to get a car. You had to be on a waiting list forever but one of the advantages of coming from a small town where everybody knew us and in that little town I was a returning war hero, so it was possible to cut a few corners, pull a few strings. The local Ford dealer to whom I had sold Saturday Evening Posts as a child made it possible for us to get a car. We drove from there on to San Francisco and there for six months I studied electronics repair and maintenance.

Q: I trust you had better quarters there?

Adm. W.: When we arrived in San Francisco the only thing that was better was the climate. The only thing available for us to live in was some temporary quarters that had been built by Henry Kaiser for his shipbuilders, his shipyard workers. That was in Richmond, California on the open side of the Bay.

Q: That says a lot.

Adm. W.: We lived in what was literally a one room apartment.

Q: Tell me something about the course of study there.

Adm. W.: It was a crash course, I studied some fundamentals, some basics.

Q: Was it just junior officers?

Adm. W.: I would say junior to mid-grade up to about lieutenant, a lieutenant commander was a senior person there, but mostly there were lieutenants, lieutenants jg I was an ensign and I was an ensign for a very long time because promotions were extremely slow at the end of the war. Congress had passed a rule that said that any reservist who wanted to stay in could stay in at his rank, that, combined with the natural compression of the navy, the shrinking navy, meant that the senior ranks were more than filled up, there was a huge hump in officer ranks. Promotion prospects for people who came in at the back end behind the hump as I had, were very, very poor.

The course consisted of some basics, concentrated mostly on specific equipments and their theory of operation, their circuits, diagnostic techniques for determining what kind of faults led to specific symptoms and then correcting them with a great deal of technical work in which faults were deliberately introduced into the equipments and we were challenged to discover and correct them. The intent was to, as quickly as possible, get capability back onto the ships of maintaining and operating this elaborate, sophisticated for the time, equipment, which was part of my job on the BORDELON.

Q: I suppose much of it had been damaged in using it without full knowledge of its capability?

Adm. W.: I am sure that is true. In the shipyard it was all getting overhauled by qualified service technicians but the big question was were we going to be able to maintain and operate it once it got back in the hands of the sailors and the military. I did well in that course and finished first in that class which isn't terribly surprising because educationally I had the best preparation for that sort of thing. I don't think there was anybody else from the Naval Academy. I am mentioning that because it turned out to be significant later on in my getting selected for an assignment to the atomic weapon program.

Q: It served as giving you a new direction?

Adm. W.: I don't think so at the time but it later turned out to be significant. The reason is that when the navy leadership decided to form an atomic bomb assembly team in Alberquerque, New Mexico, the Sandia base in Alberquerque, to learn how to assemble atomic bombs for the navy as sort of an afterthought. When they assembled this team Admiral Parsons, who was in an influential position in the navy R and D program, at that time decided--sort of an afterthought too--to add to the team several ensigns--junior officers--who weren't really needed on the team but he thought it would be useful to get some officers introduced at a relatively early point in their career in the atomic weapon business sensing quite properly that it was going to be an important field for the navy in the future and that it would be useful to start thinking then about getting a few officers started that way. I think that was very foresighted of him and it was certainly critical in my own career. It turned out one of the first nuclear submariners and I, as you know, ended up as director of the navy's Stragetic Systems Project Office later on in our careers.

After completion of that course at Treasure Island in Electronics Maintenance I was ordered back to my ship on the east coast which had by this time completed its overhaul. When I arrived in Newport I found the ship had already departed for its next deployment which was in Northern Europe. It was going to England and from there into Scandinavia. The ship had left before I arrived so I was awaiting transportation to the ship. This was in 1947.

Q: Admiral Kent Hewitt was over there.

Adm. W.: The Secretary of Defense was Louis Johnson who said that his objective was to cut the fat without touching the muscle and he had cut all the fat with a pretty sharp knife and as a consequence there was no money left to give to the navy for sending someone like myself by commercial means to catch my ship. I had to wait for some other military means of transportation to ride on without expense to the government and there simply wasn't anything going over there. All of my personal effects were over there as they were sent ahead of me in time to catch the ship. I was left there with my uniform and a suitcase in Newport for several weeks.

Finally the navy gave up on it as a bad deal and they took the next best thing in my case, and the least expensive thing, which was to order me to another ship, one already on the east coast and within reach. This was a fine solution for the navy but not very good for me as my effects were with the ship in Europe and no way to get them back until many months later. In the meantime my wife was with her family in Los Angeles ready to wait out a long deployment which never occurred. I asked her to please come back as I had been ordered to a ship that was here on the east coast, the USS MALOY which was a destroyer escort with a turbo-electric drive that was functioning with operational development force, testing and evaluating sonars and undersea equipments.

Q: What new anti-submarine warfare equipment was available at that point?

Adm. W.: I can't really say because I was on the ship so briefly, only for about a month. I didn't know that was the way things were going to develop. I reported to the ship, it was manned by a mustang Lieutenant Commander, he had a mustang executive officer and I think one or two other officers, the rest enlisted. I was the only Naval Academy graduate on that ship and it turned out that I came aboard in the midst of a feud between the executive officer and the skipper. I don't really know why, maybe it was sibling rivalry, but they both seized upon me as their confidant.

That made it kind of unpleasant and I was very uneasy about that situation. It isn't the sort of thing that an officer particularly enjoys, being summoned by one or the other and told about the deficiencies of the other; they were both quite senior to me. Anyway it was an unpleasant environment and one I wanted to get out of.

Q: Were you operating out of Casco Bay?

Adm. W.: No, we were operating out of Newport, Rhode Island. The ship was a turbo-electric drive ship and this was the winter of 1947 which followed a particularly dry summer and fall; the water supply level in the State of Maine was very low as a consequence and hydro power was short and that was the principle source of energy for the power company in Maine so with a freeze coming on that meant no more water supply until spring the Governor of Maine appealed to the President for assistance and the assistance took the form of sending our destroyer escort to Portland, Maine to tie up to the dock and disconnect the main motors to plug our generators into a ship-to-shore transformer and spend the winter pumping electricity into the State of Maine. With this unpleasant command situation that we had on that ship and the very uninteresting duty--it was uninteresting in the extreme--we were literally chained to the dock and we were steaming full power which meant that the plant was operating around the clock and we were standing steaming watches. I had my bride in a very drafty flat in Portland which was pretty miserable being ill heated, living conditions were quite poor, the professional situation was unhealthy and my obligated service was coming pretty close to an end--the two years of required service after graduation from the Naval Academy in those days, so we decided that it was time for me to leave the navy. I sought an opportunity to be interviewed by a couple of firms and wrote out a resignation from the navy. At this particular moment they got a secret message addressed to the commanding officer, as the classified material custodian and as the communications officer on the ship in addition to my other duties, I opened it and found out that the subject was me and my stomach nearly fell right through the bottom of my britches because the only reason anyone communicated with the commanding officer of a ship at a secret level, the subject the communications officer on the ship, it had to be because he had lost classified material or it was compromised, or a registered publication had been lost or he was due for a court martial. I could just see it--Oh My God--well, the subject was the fact that navy had selected me to participate in this very new field--the military application of atomic energy and I could be expecting orders right away to go to Sandia Base in Alberquerque.

Q: How providential, had you actually filed your resignation?

Adm. W.: No, I had written it out but hadn't typed it yet, it was in preparation and we had made the decision to leave.

I couldn't have come at a more crucial moment.

Q: The reason I asked about Casco Bay was that you had said the ship was working for OpDevFor, weren't they operating at Casco Bay at that point with Vice-admiral Willis Lee?

Adm. W.: I think you are right, but again I was on the ship so briefly before we were ordered off to New Mexico that I never really became fully acquainted with it. The only operations of the ship that I recall were the operations associated with keeping the power plant going at Portland. We had run out of fuel in about a day and a half operating that way so every couple of days one of the officers on the ship would take charge of a small tanker that was assigned to us and take it down to Kittery-Portsmouth to pick up a load of fuel and bring it back up. I took my turn at that which was pretty bitter duty but it was kind of exciting because for a brief period of time I was in command of my own craft. I can remember the wind howling and the icicles growing out horizontally from the rigging in that little tanker.

Q: That was a moment of great discouragement, wasn't it?

Adm. W.: It was. I thought that this exciting navy that I had been introduced to with its exploits in the South Pacific, had certainly turned to worms, I could see very little ahead in the way of prospects, promotion opportunities were poor, the kind of duty we were involved in was not pleasant, living conditions were poor and I just thought it would be better if I left the navy and started another life.

Q: How soon after intercepting the message did you actually learn officially.

Adm. W.: That told me officially that it was going to happen. In fact I have even saved the letter all these years. I recognized at the time that it was crucial.

Q: Perhaps we should have a copy of that for the appendix too.

Adm. W.: So, we travelled across the country and in due course arrived in Alberquerque to join the team of officers that had been sent there to form the navy's first atomic bomb assembly team.

Q: Will you say something about the complexion of the team.

Adm. W.: The team consisted of 20 to 25 military--all officers. At that time the atomic bomb business was considered so highly classified and sensitive that only officers should be cleared for it, even though much of the work that was going to be done didn't really call for skills or responsibilities that were expected of officers nevertheless the security sensitivity did. These officers, most of them experienced specialists in electronics or similar background, with the exception of a couple of ensigns including myself, were there and just because we didn't have any enlisted men along didn't mean that we didn't have things to do that were pretty mundane such as typing letters and handling correspondence and so forth. It turned out that I was not only the most junior man there but was also capable of typing and knew how to punctuate, so I found myself doing more yoeman work. This was during the period when we were waiting for our clearances to come through, and we were taking courses in nuclear physics, mathematics refresher and the like so that when our clearances did come through we were able to start our real business which was training in learning how to assemble an atomic bomb and we were ready for that. The atomic bomb we were dealing with was called then and still is the FATMAN. This is the bomb that was the original implosion weapon, the plutonium bomb that was used on Nagasaki. A laboratory device really had been designed by the scientists at Los Alamos and was never intended to be a militarized weapon; it was designed and used by scientists and that was what they left us as their legacy when it was turned over to the military at the end of the war.

Just to give you an idea of what was involved: The process of assembling, checking out, preparing such a bomb for being loaded aboard an aircraft took from 24 to 36 hours depending upon the skill of the team doing it. The navy team set the record as we did it in 24 hours once. We literally had to assemble the bomb from scratch, testing each component and assembling it with other components in the sub-systems and then testing them and so forth. It was quite a laboratory operation. The idea that some day nuclear weapons would ever become so dependable and so well militarized that they could be screwed under the front end of a rocket and launched would have been an incredible thought at that time.

Q: But it was something to dream of? It was the ultimate?

Adm. W.: Oh yes. But in any case this was the weapon we were dealing with and those two years at Sandia Base went by very quickly. I was told, we all were, that our career from then on would be in this business--all of us. We could expect (this was advice from the Bureau of Personnel) that we could expect to stay in Alberquerque because we were so highly classified and so specialized we would stay in Alberquerque for the rest of our careers; we would be sent to aircraft carriers to assemble bombs in the event of a national emergency and would be flown off the carrier, but other than that we would stay and train and prepare ourselves at Sandia Base.

Q: You had to be guarded.

Adm. W.: We had so few bombs in the national inventory at the time and each one had to be treated almost like a laboratory device. That was the state of the business at that time. What we had no way of knowing was that our adversary the Soviet Union was rapidly acquiring a capability of its own. Conventional wisdom said it would take 20 years before anybody managed to duplicate what we had done during the MANHATTAN Project.

Q: But we didn't really know about Peenemunde then?

Adm. W.: What we really didn't know was what they had learned, what became public through the spy trials of Burgess, Klaus Fuchs and the Rosenbergs and the rest. This became public while I was there and everything changed.

Q: What scientists were there at the time?

Adm. W.: Sandia Base, which was really a military operation and was an army base run by the army, it was an Armed Forces Special Weapons project; the scientists as such were at places like Los Alamos which was only a short distance away, about two hours drive from Alberquerque. People such as Robert Oppenheimer who was a director of the Los Alamos Laboratory during the war had moved on and was a member of the Atomic Energy Commission and the General Advisory Board. Edward Teller who later broke away and formed the Livermore Laboratories because of his controversy with Oppenheimer over the development of the hydrogen bomb. I believe he was still at Los Alamos at that time. In any event momentous things were going on. Within the services there was a great controversy going on between the air force and the navy on rules and missions surrounding the atomic weapons. Again I was not a part of that, I was still much too junior. I was promoted from ensign to Lieutenant JG while we were there. I was learning how to assemble bombs and to play my role in it and to train others in learning how to do it. we had many distinguished visitors from Washington who were coming back to find out for themselves what this was all about, what was real and what was only apparent about the bomb business, whether it really was the ultimate weapon.

Q: Was Louis Strauss in the picture then?

Adm. W.: Yes he was. He was Chairman of the Atomic Energy Commission at that point.

In due course in spite of the predictions that we would spend the rest of our careers doing this sort of thing my tour was drawing to a close and I was being prepared to be sent back to sea again and I was asked where I wanted to go. By this time I had had quite a taste of scientific and exotic assignments and what I really wanted in the worst way was to some day go to a Post Graduate School and study nuclear physics. Of course I couldn't to it from there because I needed to get another tour at sea but since this was really my desire I looked around for a sea assignment that would fit that kind of a pattern best. What I hit upon was the USS NORTON SOUND.

Q: I suppose you really had to stay within that pattern didn't you? But you did have that freedom of choice?

Adm. W.: No I didn't have to and I did have the freedom of choice in spite of everything I had been told about how exotic we were and how special we were and how because of the unique knowledge we possessed that we would never be allowed out of the country again--we were told all of those things because of the risk of compromise of the information we had. In the meantime the spy trials revealed that that information was already inescapably lost and in the hands of the Soviet Union.

Q: That was a real blow wasn't it?

Adm. W.: It was indeed. I can still recall the shock of opening the morning newspaper and reading some of the revelations that were coming out during the spy trial, the trial of the Rosenbergs and the things we learned that the British spy Klaus Fuchs, that scientist who had been at Los Alamos all during the war and was feeding back all the time to the Russians. They were informed right up to the minute of almost everything we were doing.

Things were put back into an ordinary perspective pretty quickly and I was once again looking for sea duty and chose NORTON SOUND.

Q: That is a seaplane tender?

Adm. W.: An ex-seaplane tender; I chose it because it was involved, in fact it was the only ship in the navy that was involved in testing of guided missiles. That seemed to be a field that had the same kind of future in implications to the navy as atomic weapons did. I didn't at that moment foresee their early marriage, I just saw it as another interesting thing to do. I asked for it and was very happy to get the assignment to NORTON SOUND. As a matter of fact I think that Chick Hayward was probably helpful to me; he was the senior naval officer at Sandia at the time and I think I did consult with him and ask him to intercede and help me to get that assignment. I can't recall for certain whether he involved himself with it. While enroute from Alberquerque to Port Hueneme...

Q: Was that where she was stationed? She was largely off the coast there wasn't she?

Adm. W.: She operated in close proximity to Point Magu which is the Navy Missile Test Center on the west coast and Port Hueneme is right next door to Point Magu. Enroute there we stopped in my hometown Carlsbad and had a final holiday/vacation there with my parents before going on to Port Hueneme. It was at that time that my father passed away--while I was there. He died quite suddenly from a heart attack. This was sort of an end of a phase in my personal life.

Q: He must have been overjoyed at your development.

Adm. W.: In that family no matter what the kids did it was something marvelous and I am sure that my father and my mother, particularly my father, must have absolutely bored the socks off of all of his friends bragging about the exploits of his kids particularly his son. It was almost embarrassing, except that he did it in a way that I think was acceptable to his friends because he was so sincere about it. He honestly didn't realize, I am sure, that other men had sons of their own and would like to talk about them on occasion but I don't think they ever had a chance to get a word in edgewise. In any event he was beloved by his community. I was given emergency extension of leave to stay for the funeral and to wrap up his affairs, and the funeral said as much about him as anything else. Jewish families are very very few in that part of the state and the funeral services were conducted by the Presbyterian minister who happened to be one of my Dad's closest friends, and the church was filled to overflowing and they had to set up loud speakers on the lawn, the whole town shut down quite literally. The man was beloved by that community. I have saved through the years clippings, talking about him-- editorials were written all over the state. He wasn't a wealthy man, he was just a good man and a patriot and a man who had done more for his community than anyone could expect. In every sense of the word I think he was probably one of the greatest men I have ever known and I have tried to factor out my own bias when I say that although I know it is not possible.

Q: Wasn't it fortunate that you were there at the time, though it was tragic.

Adm. W.: Yes, it was almost as though someone was directing the scene and the events from afar.

Q: For the second time--Portland, Maine and then there.

Adm. W.: Yes, it was the last two years of his life that we were able to be so close to him in New Mexico. We were able every few weeks to get down to Carlsbad and spend the weekend. The distance wasn't so great that we couldn't drive down on Friday evening and back again on Sunday evening. Even though I was in the navy and had no right to see my parents who were way back in the southwestern town of New Mexico, we did for those last couple of years and we saw quite a bit of them.

Now, getting on down to the NORTON SOUND. NORTON SOUND had a very interesting role to play. It was the only ship in the navy that had any guided missiles on it and they were strictly for test purposes. We were sort of the floating White Sands Missile Range.

Q: You had the REGULUS 1, didn't you?

Adm. W.: This was long before REGULUS 1 was ready for testing; we were testing (TERRIER wasn't ready for testing yet), these were mostly test vehicles of one sort or another, that were things like LARK and LOON; LOON was the navy copy of the German B-1 buzz bomb; LARK was a liquid propelled surface to air missile that was used as a test air-frame for testing different kinds of seekers, radar seekers and the like for surface to air anti-aircraft use. We, on one particularly memorable occasion, took the liquid propellant rocket VIKING which was a large single-stage rocket modelled roughly on the German V-2. It was built by Martin and was used for high altitude tests, it could carry a payload to about a hundred miles up and was used primarily for experimental purposes. VIKING #4, the fourth such VIKING rocket--all the others had been tested at White Sands--was to be launched from NORTON SOUND and the reason for this was that the scientific payload that it carried was designed to conduct experiments, cosmic ray experiments, at the geo-magnetic equator. There is no way you can do that from White Sands it had to be launched from the geo-magnetic equator which, it turns out was one point off Christmas Island. So we were doing the job of taking that rocket down to Christmas Island and launching it.

Q: That, later, was the site of the ASROC tests.

Adm. W.: Yes and I think some of the early British atomic tests were conducted down there.

Q: How were your rockets launched? Did you have catapults?

Adm. W.: The surface/air rockets like LARK were, what we called from a zero length launcher. It is a launcher that has literally zero length but it flung the missile into the sky, gave it a kick, and the missile immediately took over with its own booster. I am not sure whether the LOON was launched that way or not exactly; some of them were launched with a short run on a rail. I was later involved with REGULUS and this was launched from a short rail.

Q: And then finally a catapult?

Adm. W.: Yes, from the aircraft carrier I think it was catapulted. In the case of VIKING it was launched vertically, it had a short rail run--just launched it straight up. At this particular time, for reasons which were never entirely clear to me, the navy placed importance on disclaiming any interest in military applications of the VIKING rocket.

Q: Wasn't this the time of the drive of "Atoms for Peace"?

Adm. W.: I am trying to recall--this was now, 1950.

Q: Louis Strauss was involved in that whole program and of course this was something General Eisenhower was interested in.

Adm. W.: The emphasis was on how the navy was simply supporting peaceful applications of these things and we actually publicly were disowning or disclaiming any interest in a military application of this rocket. In fact it was the same attitude that was attached to the early VANGUARD. You remember our efforts to put a satellite into the sky and we were overtaken by the Soviet SPUTNIK. In fact this was some seven years later but we as usual were heavily shocked into doing what was necessary for our own security. This was quite an event during that year and a half that I was on NORTON SOUND.

There is another impression I have of that tour that stuck with me and later had influence on some of the things that I did later on in the POLARIS program and that was the whole approach to guided missile testing. The guided missiles we were testing in those days were extraordinarily unreliable, they seldom worked properly and a failure was much more common than a success. In fact I wrote a treatise on the subject which is in my files but one particular event I recall very early in my tour on this ship--I was the assistant instrumentation officer which meant that I was one of those responsible for collecting data on each of these tests. One of the tests had been conducted and it had failed and the operations officer on the ship called us all together, everybody who had participated in that test, and, very much in the atmosphere of a witch hunt, he was trying to find out who possibly was responsible for that failure and I had the impression that he was treating it as if somebody had run the ship aground and he was going to find the culprit. I thought to myself, this is an extraordinarily poor way to do things because the only thing we have left after one of these tests is data--information--some of which is locked up in the minds of the people who had participated in the test, and if you are going to create an atmosphere that makes it sound as though whoever had any information especially if it is suggested they might have made a personal mistake they are going to be the last ones to speak up and give it. Now the environment one should want to encourage is one of complete candor and freedom and cooperation and desire to get information that could be helpful in understanding, learning and improving; instead of that he was in effect discouraging.

Q: He wasn't much of a psychologist, was he?

Adm. W. I thought he was an example of an operationally trained officer in a position of authority over technical people, which isn't necessarily bad if he is sensitive to understand his role. But he was playing his role very poorly and I made a mental note there that stood me in good stead later on. That was an impression.

Q: What about the relationship with Sandia at that time?

Adm. W.: There wasn't any really. Not with the NORTON SOUND. The base was exclusively concerned with nuclear weapons. There was no connection at all. The scientific and technical people that we were dealing with were defense contractors, the navy laboratories like the Naval Research Laboratory that was in charge of the VIKING experiment, they build the special cosmic ray experimentation and the like for the front end of that rocket. The Applied Physics Laboratory of the Johns Hopkins University was very much involved, the Naval Ordnance Test Station, China Lake people were involved, the people obviously from Point Magu including a German scientist by the name of Willy Fiedler--one of the paper clip scientists working for the navy at Point Magu and later on we met again in my career when he was with Lockheed helping design the POLARIS. Those were the scientific people. Sandia was, as I said, exclusively concerned with those atomic bombs and the only way we had of delivering nuclear weapons in those days was by aircraft, gravity bombs. Other things were on the drawing boards or in development and until the nuclear warhead itself could be reduced in size and simplified in design it was not going to be capable of being put on any other kind of a delivery vehicle than a manned aircraft where it could be carefully attended to and monitored.

It was from NORTON SOUND that I finally got my real heart's desire and that was an assignment to Navy Post Graduate School which was then in Annapolis, in preparation for taking a graduate course in nuclear physics.

Q: Before you go to that, what about the storage problems on the NORTON SOUND, safety in handling that type thing?

Adm. W.: That is kind of interesting. The LARK, which I said was a surface to air test vehicle, was a liquid propelled missile that used as fuel an oxidizer of red fuming nitric acid and aniline; these are both extremely toxic materials, they are hypergolic, they burn as soon as they come in contact with each other so they were carried in tank cars--small wheeled containers and we placed them as far apart as we possibly could on opposite sides of the flight deck.

Q: And hoped you didn't prove a conductor?

Adm. W.: We would fuel and prepare the missile for testing by running lines over from these tanks filling its oxidizer and fuel tanks respectively. In the case of the VIKING, this was fueled with alcohol and liquid oxygen and for that purpose, particularly for carrying the liquid oxygen the NORTON SOUND had to be fitted out with huge thermos bottles you might say, they are huge, well insulated containers in the ship that could take liquid oxygen and keep it cold at liquid oxygen temperatures. During the trip down to the equator from which we could fuel the missile and launch it, obviously we didn't fuel it until we were ready to prepare it for launching, at that time I convinced myself that liquid fuels were not the sort of things one wanted to be shipmates with.

Q: You knew that before you got to the POLARIS?

Adm. W.: Long before I got to POLARIS.

Q: The damage control on NORTON SOUND must have been highly developed too, wasn't it?

Adm. W. Yes, although I wasn't involved in that. We were quite conscious of the kind of materials we were dealing with. The ship, both in its crew and its officers were all highly selected individuals, all specialized people and some of the best people the navy had. Some of those people showed up later on in the POLARIS program, and our paths crossed again. For example, the officer who was involved in the launching and handling operations on NORTON SOUND was second in charge of launching and handling system development for POLARIS. I found that out when I got back to rejoin the Special Projects Office and I found old friends there.

Q: Who was that officer?

Adm. W.: That was George Halverson and he later became a flag officer before he retired. And there were others, Merrill Sappington was an officer who made his flag before he retired, he also was on NORTON SOUND at the time I was.

Q: Was J. B. Colwell on there?

Adm. W.: No he was not, I met him for the first time when he was Raborn's deputy on Special Projects. Of course the real reason that I later ended up in the POLARIS program at all, it turned out, was because of another officer who had been shipmates with me at Sandia Base, his name was Thomas Walker. Tom had been at Sandia and was caught with one of the original group that Raborn pulled in and gave hunting licenses to and told them to go out and bring in anyone he wished. Tom remembered the ensign at Sandia and said "I'll take him" and that is another part of the story that we will get to later. The interesting thing is how some of these people were contacted and the impressions were made early on in the career and this keeps cropping up. It is a little bit like a James Michener novel I think.

Q: It was a real fraternity too, wasn't it?

Adm. W.: It really was. There weren't really that many technically trained people in the navy.

So I was sent back to the Post Graduate School which was then in Annapolis. After some six months they decided to move the school to Monterey, California so we moved back across the country again from whence we had come.

Q: And you hadn't yet gotten settled in Annapolis?

Adm. W.: Having just gotten to Annapolis from Port Hueneme then back to Monterey. But that was a lovely place.

Q: This was to be two years at the school and then a year at MIT.

Adm. W.: The other way around, one at the school and two at M.I.T. The idea of being one year at the school was merely preparing us to be able to handle the level of classes that were going to be given at the graduate level in nuclear physics. Later on my impression was that I worked very much harder and was very much more strongly challenged academically by the work that I was given at the Naval Post Graduate School than anything I ever got at M.I.T.

Q: Various men have talked about that in that sense, Lloyd Mustin was one. He thought so too.

Adm. W.: I think that the navy was always over-corrected; they were so conscious of the fact that the people they were sending to schools like M.I.T. had been away from the academic life for a number of years and obviously they were rusty, had forgotten how to study, if they ever knew.

Q: And they had to make good.

Adm. W.: They wanted them to make good and they were older, on average, than their classmates who typically had gone directly from undergraduate work right into graduate school and were right up to the minute and if they were going to succeed they had to be prepared for it.

Q: Most of the navy men were married and had families starting at that point.

Adm. W.: Those were distractions you can bet and I did too. We were prepared, six months when the school was still at Annapolis and six months more when it was in Monterey. We lived in a lovely little place we rented in Carmel.

Q: What prompted the shift?

Adm. W.: I can't really speak authoritatively about that. I know that this was something the navy had wanted to do for a long time, to physically separate the Naval Academy and the Post Graduate School.

Interview No. 2 with Rear-admiral Robert H. Wertheim

Place: At his home in Annandale, Virginia

Date: Wednesday, 21 January 1981

Subject: Biography

Bt: John T. Mason, Jr.

Q: We are in the year 1951 and you have just gone out to the Post Graduate School in Monterey, California, for a six months period before going to M.I.T. Will you tell me about those six months?

Adm. W.: The six months began very happily with our moving into a rented cottage in the very quaint community of Carmel where my wife and our very young son and I lived while I commuted to the PG School. The classes were conducted in and around the old DelMonte Hotel and that whole complex has since been built up enormously. There is, as you know, a magnificent plant there now for the PG School. In those days it was much less, there was just the DelMonte Hotel and some temporary buildings. The classes were very demanding aimed, necessarily, at elevating the educational level of garden variety naval officers such as myself who had been out of school for a number of years, up to the point that we would be able to compete successfully against the underclassmates in graduate school in institutions such as MIT.

Q: Was there any hiatus between what you had just done at the Naval Academy in the first six months, was there any interruption in the course?

Adm. W.: No, the transition was remarkably smooth. The faculty as well as the students were all moved there over the Christmas holidays and we finished the term in December, movers arrived in a great caravan moving us all simultaneously from the east coast to the west coast. Those of us who lived inland, drove there and visited our parents or friends enroute and arrived on the west coast to meet out baggage. It was purely a physical move but the logistics of the thing had been planned like a campaign, and like so many of the WW2 campaigns, it went off exactly as planned. As a student, as opposed to one of the faculty or the staff, I wasn't involved in the planning process I could only observe the consequences of it and all I can say is that it was a tremendously impressive thing. I was concentrating on the personal logistics of getting myself and my family from one coast to the other. From the point of view of academics there was really no interruption, other than what we would have expected during a long Christmas holiday.

Q: That's what you expect of the navy however.

Adm. W.: But we don't always get it, nevertheless that is what is expected and it should be expected.

There we spent the second six months of the preparatory year of Post Graduate School. I call it preparatory because the courses we were studying weren't really graduate courses as much as they were upper level under-graduate courses in the mostly hard sciences-mathematics, physics and the like, and they were aimed to bring us up to the level that would allow us to compete successfully. Then in due course we completed that six months and again packed the old station wagon and with wife, child and dog we made another trip across the country, this time to Cambridge, Mass. to enroll at MIT in their graduate school in physics, at last into nuclear physics which I had so wanted to get into quite a few years.

That was an intellectual joy, it was mind stretching, it was exciting, my classmates were a number of years younger than I most of them being young men and women who had not interrupted their education when they completed their under-graduate studies, they had gone on right into graduate school.

Q: How large a contingent of navy people came on from Monterey?

Adm. W.: In my particular group, which was the physics group, there were only three of us for nuclear physics. There were other groups--we started out four and wound up three, that's not too bad, this was the physics curriculum that was sponsored by the Bureau of Ordnance. There were others taking physics there I believe, though I am not certain, that were sponsored by other agencies or activities in the navy like Office of Main Research had a program. Bureau of Aeronautics I believe had a program in Aeronautics.

Q: How closely were you monitored by BuOrd?

Adm. W.: Not at all. In fact we weren't monitored by anyone, we were there strictly as students and we reported to the head of the Naval Administrative Unit who looked after the ROTC students and those students such as myself who were there under navy sponsorship. We got a pro forma fitness report every year out of hand when you got your pay check. Got my pay checks and administrative matters but other than that we had no interface at all with the navy. You could tell us in a moment walking down the hall because we were always dressed properly with jackets, ties, and shirts whereas most of the students were slouching along in jeans, open collars and hair hanging down over their ears. I was often mistaken by my fellow students for one of the professors.

Q: That's understandable, that certain distinguished look.

Adm. W.: Well we were a little older and were dressed properly, but apart from that we were strictly students. To me, it was a pure joy to be studying in that environment and in the field in which I was so intensely interested. Interestingly enough, this was a period during those two years at MIT when the McCarthy era came to its climax, the ,50s.

You will recall the big climatic scenes and the army/McCarthy hearings and the like--that was going on while I was doing my thesis work at the Synchrotron Laboratory and my fellow physicists with whom I was working there, members of the faculty and other graduate students were very liberal and, even though my personal politics and preferences I always thought were very much on the liberal side themselves, compared to them I was a radical right-winger. I was certainly not pro-McCarthy by any stretch of the imagination but they looked at me with great suspicion. It took quite a while before they finally became convinced that I wasn't some kind of a paragon of right-wing evil.

Q: Tell me about the high points of that two years as a student.

Adm. W.: The high points were the work itself and the academics. I think I mentioned earlier--it is like training for the big game, preparing at the Naval Academy Post Graduate School for going to the civilian graduate school. We ran scared, in fact I found that the academics were relatively easier for me at MIT than they had been earlier. I had in fact trained right up to the hilt and I found it very easy to get good marks. Although there was still a lot of hard work and I worked very hard indeed, I enjoyed the academics and because I was doing well I felt I was on top of them. When I finally got into my own thesis work which was I mentioned was done at a high energy accelerater

Synchotron but which has since faded into the background and it no longer even exists at MIT. When you speak of high energy nuclear physics today you are talking about orders of magnitude higher than what we were then working with. Nevertheless at that time it was one the front edge of what was possible and my thesis work led to some very exciting things and I found that extremely stimulating. So much so that I was quite interested to see if I couldn't stay on and get a doctorate, which would have required another year of work.

Q: Was the navy amenable to that idea?

Adm. W.: The Bureau of Ordnance was not; the Navy as such had programs that led to doctorates, specifically those that were sponsored by the Office of Naval Research for instance, they did normally lead to a doctorate. When my physics professors approached me with the suggestion that I stay on for a doctorate I said, "Why don't you ask the Navy if they would do this? I would love to but I don't think that I carry much weight." They did, they enquired but the answer came back from the Bureau of Ordnance, "Thank you very much but he will be just as useful to us with a Masters Degree as he would be with a Doctorate and it would take another year or so. We would rather not."

Q: The reason I ask is because the navy is often said to be not very happy with Phds in their midst.

Adm. W.: In all fairness I have to say that the difference between a masters degree and a Phd for a naval officer, in carrying out his working purposes, it really doesn't make that much difference. Personal satisfaction of course in being able to achieve the ultimate degree but beyond that the value to the navy of the extra time spent away from duty had to be marginal I think, for most of our jobs. I was sorry to leave without it but on the other hand I understand.

Q: Did you work in tandem with the other navy fellows who were in your category--the two other men?

Adm. W.: No, of course the classes were the same but the thesis work which took up most of the last year there was entirely independent and I was the only one of us in that particular laboratory. One of the others was over in the Vandegraf Generator Building working on energy levels working out energy levels in obscure nucleii and I forget what the third was doing. Each of us was doing his own work.

Q: Can you tell me something about the thesis work?

Adm. W.: I ended up working with one of the associate professors at MIT on a project which was looking at the reaction products of bombarding certain nuclei with high energy photons. Photon is another way of saying a quantum of light energy and these photons were sufficiently high and sufficiently energetic to actually break up these nuclei, to break out pieces of them. What the professor had developed was a scintillation telescope, a device that would react to measure the charged particles being ejected from a nucleus, identify its charge and its mass. The experiment that I ended up conducting, using that telescope that he had designed, looked at such particles, specifically what I was looking for was charged particles with a charge of unity, in other words they were protons, a nuclei of hydrogen, of deuterons which also have charge one but have twice the mass, or tritons a tritium nuclei, all of them with charge one, being ejected from elements of varying mass numbers and tried to look for some kind of a systematic relationship there. In the process I was actually successful in doing this. It was very exciting to me because I had concluded some place along the line that I was going to end up with a negative report for my thesis, an experiment conducted which would be duly recorded, it didn't produce anything but at the eleventh hour and working late one night in the laboratory and putting my data together, I saw in fact what I was looking for--a systematic relationship which was very exciting. It was the first time I had ever done anything like that and gotten a small taste of what the giants in physics and chemistry had done through the ages. It was a tiny, tiny taste of it.

Q: Did that lead to something?

Adm. W.: It led to something for me, it led to my thesis which was exciting, and some new insight into the structure of the atomic nucleus. As to the mechanisms as to how the nucleus was glued together at least it suggested how these nuclear forces behaved. As far as leading to anything beyond that, no. That excited some of my professors there which led them to ask for me to stay on for some additional work but that didn't develop into anything.

Q: Was that famous Dr. Draper still there?

Adm. W.: Dr. Draper was still there, yes, although he was working in an entirely different world and I didn't even know about him then. Later I came to know him quite well. He was working with students in the aero navigation world and the inertial instrument world, inertial navigation, inertial guidance and so forth but that wasn't even a gleam in my eye at that stage.

Q: What a wonderful experience that was.

Adm. W.: It was indeed, it was a high light.

Q: How did your wife survive all of this, you didn't have much time for her and your family?

Adm. W.: No indeed. We had bought a house and this was our first house purchase--a little four-room house, not four bedrooms, just four rooms--out on the periphery of the community, on the Waltham/Lexington line just inside of Route 128, the beltway around Boston.

Q: The electronics area.

Adm. W.: Now it is, it wasn't then. We had a full basement four rooms upstairs and the basement was my area where I set up my desk for studying, my bookcases and so forth. Living was upstairs; we had to ration ourselves--one night a week, it could be either Friday, Saturday or Sunday night we would allow ourselves to do something other than my studying--all other nights I was incommunicado, I would come home from school, have dinner, then immediately proceed to the basement and study until all hours of the night, then off again at the crack of dawn for school. That one night a week we would do such extravagent things as maybe go out and play bridge with our friends or see a movie if we felt particularly affluent.

Q: You had only one son at that point?

Adm. W.: That's right. That basement was an experience, it turned out that it leaked and when we had heavy rains the water would come gushing in and that was really traumatic because I had all my books and papers and things down there so I was constantly fighting a leaky basement in addition to everything else but nevertheless we survived. Youth is a marvelous thing for surviving experiences like that. In the end the time came to think about what to do next. Armed with all this marvelous educational experience and the other background in technical fields, the guided missile experience on NORTON SOUND and the nuclear weapon experience at Albequerque, I proceeded to talk to my detailer in Washington.

Q: Did BuOrd have ideas?

Adm. W.: BuOrd at that time, I had an obligation to BuOrd to serve one or two tours ashore with BuOrd at the appropriate point in my career so I owed them for my educational experience and of course I was also obligated to the navy for two years of active service for every year spent at school so I had quite a way into the future committed to the navy in general and BuOrd in particular, but the next tour would be a sea tour getting back from shore duty. So, I went to see my detailer to see what sort of thing he might have in store for me. I remember this experience very well. I forget the rank of the detailer at the time but he opened up my record, examined it and he reacted with horror. He said, "You have ruined your career!" I was shocked because I thought that up to that time I had been doing just great, getting good marks at the school and having good fitness reports and all that sort of thing wherever I had gone. But he was horrified, I had departed so far from the norm--while my classmates were out getting good sea experience, tending nets or whatever it was they were doing, I was wasting my time with these cushy jobs ashore, which is the way he saw them.

Q: Exotic things?

Adm. W.: Exotic, and they didn't match his checklist at all.

His pronouncement at that time really, really shook me. I had never appreciated, until that moment, that I wasn't doing exactly what the navy wanted me to do. That started me thinking about what indeed I did want to do, whether or not the navy was the right career for me or whether there was some way of finding something that rationalized these things.

Q: It must have brought back some of the thoughts you had in Portland?

Adm. W.: Indeed it did but of course I now had six years of obligated service staring me in the face. But it started me thinking a little bit about perhaps becoming an engineering duty officer someplace along the line, getting out of the pattern that this detailer was thinking about, one that I was clearly no longer matching very well. I felt that I had gotten into this pattern through no fault of my own, I hadn't asked to be sent to Albequerque although I was delighted when that happened. I was responsible for having gone to NORTON SOUND, I had asked for that but after all that was a legitimate sea assignment; Post Graduate School, indeed I had asked for that but again it would not have been given to me if the navy hadn't thought it appropriate I felt, but this detailer said, not only was I ruining my career but had he been in that particular job when my application for Post Graduate School had come through he would never have allowed it to be approved.

Q: How inflexible can you be?

Adm. W.: I guess you can be pretty inflexible. That was a traumatic moment, nevertheless I found myself, in due course, assigned to the heavy cruiser LOS ANGELES. You will recall that up to that time I had been in only small ships, destroyer, destroyer, destroyer. He felt it was time I got on a larger ship.

Q: Did he think you would get back on the right track again by going to the LOS ANGELES?

Adm. W.: Maybe he had some faint hope that I might be able to rescue what was left of a shattered career. I went to LOS ANGELES in 1954; it was a heavy cruiser, an 8-inch gun ship and I was assigned as main battery officer because of my ordnance background I suppose. This was the second level below the gunnery officer on a ship of that sort. It was soon after I was on LOS ANGELES that the decision was made that LOS ANGELES would receive the REGULUS I which was the surface to surface missile and the only REGULUS that then existed. It is a cruise missile as we now know them, in those days we didn't think of it so much that way but it was basically a pilotless aircraft. It is almost identical in size and characteristics to the airforce's MATADOR, carries the same size warhead to about the same range--basically a small jet airplane. This installation fell under my supervision because I was the main battery officer and it would be part of the main battery, so I was given the job of...

Q: Were you a lieutenant at that point?

Adm. W.: Yes, I was a full lieutenant.

Q: Who was skipper of the cruiser?

Adm. W.: Jake Waterhouse. I might say that he passed away just a week or so ago, we will have memorial services for him shortly, he was a wonderful, warm human being and will be greatly missed by his shipmates and friends.

That was a very happy experience with a crew of officers the associations with whom was one of those rare ones that tended to stick, we have kept in touch with many of the shipmates on that particular tour for one reason or another through the years, when we haven't on other ships so much.

Q: Do they have annual reunions?

Adm. W.: Not really, it is just personal friendships and attachments that were made then.

Q: This must have stimulated you to have that kind of an assignment coming up because it wasn't outside of your specialized field.

Adm. W.: No, but I did have some guilt pangs because I thought about that detailer again--what's he going to think of this--I didn't ask for that either.

Q: But detailers of course do not stay forever, do they?

Adm. W.: I have become a little cynical about detailers--
and their primary function is to find people to fill jobs--
what they consider to be a normal, proper career pattern is
usually that which is necessary in order to fill a job, it
tends to be expedient in their interpretations, I'm afraid.
I have to wonder how many young officers' careers have been
influenced profoundly by what was, perhaps, a very temporal,
transitory need of a particular detailer.

Q: This might go off on a tangent, but hasn't the situation
changed somewhat now? Isn't it possible for a man to be a
specialist before shore duty and to come back to that
constantly?

Adm. W.: Yes. As a matter of fact the whole concept of
sub-specialization within the navy grew up since that time
and is now very much a part of the normal career pattern.
Today the navy encourages every officer to have a specialty
or a sub-specialty.

Q: Now back to the LOS ANGELES.

Adm. W.: In any case we installed REGULUS on LOS ANGELES;
it was the first such installation, it was kind of a grafting
of a capability onto a ship that was not designed for it--
adding a guided missile with a nuclear warhead to a ship
that wasn't designed for that purpose. It was kind of a
new thing for all of us.

Q: She didn't have to go into a navy yard?

Adm. W.: Yes she did. This was done in a yard availability but what I am saying is that such things as providing adequate security for the protection of nuclear weapons, meeting the requirements for the two-man rule and the like, and limited access. On a ship, in the hangar deck, which is where we kept the missile and its warhead, required us to do some things that were clearly expedients--locking doors, putting bolts on doors, stationing marine guards. The hangar deck on a heavy cruiser was not designed for limited access. It was designed for quite the opposite, for ready access. I remember the trauma of attempting to meet these security arrangements in the face of an irate first lieutenant who said, "By God, nobody is going to keep me out of any part of any ship, of any part of this ship. I and my damage control teams have to be able to get in to where we want." He armed himself with a set of bolt cutters and as fast as I would add padlocks he would snip them off. We had to have an understanding which we ultimately worked out. The installation was jury-rigged really.

Q: What about launchers? What kind did you have for the missile? This had to be installed also?

Adm. W.: Yes, the launcher was also a jury-rigged arrangement, it was the same design launcher that had been used or was being used for launching from aircraft carriers--launching the REGULUS from aircraft carriers, it was a rail launcher and the missile would be winched up into position on the launcher and then the launcher rails would be elevated by hydraulic mechanism; the whole thing had been built by the Naval Aircraft Factory which no longer exists (in Philadelphia) and when the thing was elevated, the engine was cranked up as it had to be before launching. Visualize if you will, in your mind's eye, a small jet airplane up on rails that were elevated high into the air and pointing up on an angle of 35° or 40°, supported by two arms extended vertically and as the ship would roll this whole mechanism would sway back and forth, wave around in the breeze so to speak up there, with the jet engine whining and with the high explosive in a nuclear warhead and jato bottles ready to be ignited--the whole thing was a disaster waiting for a place to happen.

Q: Pretty vulnerable in a storm?

Adm. W.: Not only vulnerable but it was probably more hazardous to us than it would have been to any enemy. That was the installation we had initially. Later we had that launcher arrangement replaced with one that was a much safer arrangement, one that had things under much better control, rails that allowed the missile to be moved from the hangar deck up to the launch deck and under positive control all the way. Nevertheless we actually made a deployment to the Far East with that missile and with live warheads and I guess, in a dire emergency, the government could have actually called upon us to launch it, God forbid!

Q: What was the range of the REGULUS?

Adm. W.: I believe it was about 500 miles but of course the control system from the ship would not have allowed it to control a missile for anything like that range. We had a radar that would allow us to control it basically to the line of sight, to a target within the line of sight. The principle means of controlling REGULUS however was with a chase plane, another aircraft that would fly along with it and control it and cause it to dial on its target, so in that particular role it really became just an auxiliary means of delivering a bomb. If you think of one airplane controlling the delivery of a weapon on a target it isn't terribly different from if that airplane had carried the bomb in the first place. This simply allowed it to be done remotely and from some distance away and therefore more safely and perhaps better able to penetrate.

Q: It was something in transition?

Adm. W.: Yes, it was not by any means the invulnerable ultimate weapon that we later came to think of our ballistic missiles as being a delivery system that could not be intercepted but rather just another aircraft to carry the bomb.

Q: You must have had very direct lines with BuOrd while all this was going on?

Adm. W.: The controlling bureau was the Bureau of Aeronautics they developed REGULUS, a very reliable weapon for its time, not terribly capable. It was also installed, in addition to the LOS ANGELES, on certain aircraft carriers and on some submarines. Some of the submariners who were earliest caught up in the guided missile business would have tales to tell about their experiences with REGULUS.

Q: That was considered a real break-through, wasn't it, to get it on a submarine?

Adm. W.: That is clearly the ideal launching platform because the notion of a submerged vehicle that could carry the nuclear weapon within range of the target, undetected was very attractive. Of course it had to surface as the missile had to be moved out from its hangar and serviced and launched from the deck and the submarine was exposed for a fair period of time in order to carry out such a launch. Then of course it also required another aircraft to control the missile once it was launched.

Q: How frequently did you have launchings of the REGULUS?

Adm. W.: we had a number of launches while I was aboard not too frequently, the missile itself was recoverable, it wasn't expended when it was launched. After a test flight the chase plane would take control of it and bring it to a landing strip with lowered landing gear and it would actually land and be reuseable. Some of these missiles had been used over and over and over again, just like an aircraft.

Q: That became then the sole purpose of the LOS ANGELES?

Adm. W.: No, I can't say that at all. It became an auxiliary or supplemental function of the LOS ANGELES. The LOS ANGELES was still basically a heavy cruiser with its principle role being shore bombardment or other targets, fleet targets or shore targets suitable for its armament. The REGULUS was added on at the expense of its seaplane carrying capability which really had marginal utility in any event, so it was added on without taking anything else off.

Q: Did you have a double-headed hat at that point, did you continue as gunnery officer?

Adm. W.: I was main battery officer, I was made battery officer, reporting to the gunnery officer and I continued that, yes. I was responsible for the heavy 8-inch gun battery as well as the REGULUS, and a number of other duties that are typically assigned, watch duties and so forth.

Q: As you look back on that experience, can you say what you actually learned from REGULUS that was useful to you in the development of your career.

Adm. W.: Its difficult for me to come up with anything specific. I did accept the idea that there was a way of marrying the guided missile and a nuclear warhead, which up until that time were separate worlds. The nuclear bomb was one thing and the missile was quite another and here was the first real marriage of the two that I had been exposed to, a relatively successful although a quite immature marriage, one that I was to have an opportunity to improve on.

Q: REGULUS was ordered out of commission and production in 1958 which was two years after you left but I suppose from your description of it at this point, there was good reason why it was.

Adm. W.: The reason of course was POLARIS. REGULUS I was to be followed by REGULUS II, a much higher performance version of the same thing, a super-sonic version of REGULUS. That system never really got into production or fleet use primarily because in the meantime POLARIS had been developed and was going to be successful and was a far, far superior delivery vehicle for a nuclear warhead on a land target. Because of the success of POLARIS the demise of REGULUS was forordained. The same thing happened in the air force. You recall the much heralded cancellation of programs such as NAVAJO which was a long-range intercontinental range guided missilem cruise missile, that the air force had developed. This was also never put into service use and was prematurely terminated because of the successful development of intercontinental ballistic missiles.

Q: Wasn't there in the navy however, a residue of regret that REGULUS was cancelled?

Adm. W.: Sure it was. It was a successful one, a reliable weapon and there were people who still were skeptical as to how dependable POLARIS could ultimately be. There is always regret at giving up something that really works well and REGULUS worked well.

Q: I thought there was a reflection of that in the CNO at that time,--his regret?

Adm. W.: Yes, quite true but nevertheless I believe the CNO at that time was Admiral Burke, was it not?

Q: Yes.

Adm. W.: Admiral Burke was the strongest advocate of POLARIS and POLARIS could never have gotten going or been anything like what it has become, without his strong support. Even though there was great regret in his mind I am sure he knew what the right thing was to do. If we could have afforded all of those things it would be different, but one has to be somewhat brutal at times about things we kill. An analogy might be gardening--if you are a gardener you know that the time comes when your young plants are coming up, one must pluck, not prune; you don't snip back all the plants equally you pull some of them out so the others can grow. This was the case I think for REGULUS. REGULUS had to be killed in order for POLARIS to properly reach its ultimate position.

Q: Your sea duty came to an end in 1956.

Adm. W.: That's right and during that time on the LOS ANGELES I had made the decision that I would bite the bullet and become an engineering duty officer. I felt that my interests and that of the navy were best served by my becoming a technical specialist rather than continuing to attempt to keep my operational tickets properly punched and at the same time keeping up to speed in the world of technical management that I really wanted to concentrate on.

Q: That really was a level-headed decision wasn't it?

Adm. W.: Well it was a risky one. It was one that was made against good advice--well-meaning advice. I was encouraged to do this by virtually no one. Most of my colleagues at the time, my peers, strongly advised against it. They said that you have a limited probability of reaching high positions in the navy, of reaching your full potential in the navy, you will probably top out as a commander, maybe a captain at best. It just isn't the way for you to go. Basically what they were saying was flattering, they were saying in effect, "you've got the potential for competing for senior rank, if you stay on track and becoming an engineering duty officer will put you off the track." Especially in the field I was in which was ordnance. There was then and still is a ship engineering duty and aeronautical engineering duty but ordnance engineering duty was a very tiny group of officers, a very elite group however the members so seen by their peers. They were seen as a group of officers who didn't necessarily fit very neatly into any of the other categories, it was a group that had been created during WW2 and continued afterwards as a convenient repository for a few people that didn't fit very well. There were some exceptional officers in that group but it was a very small group, it was marginally viable because of its size and the Bureau of Ordnance, unlike the Bureau of Ships, was really run by unrestricted line officers. The role of the ED was not clear in that group. In the case of the Bureau of Ships, the chief of the bureau was an engineering duty officer and the bureau itself was a technically managed group. Ordnance was always seen as a proper role for unrestricted line officers in what we have later learned to call a sub-specialty of ordnance. Nevertheless I had the feeling that whether that was the right career field or not for me, my experience to that time and my own personal preferences were such that it came closer to fitting my pattern and my interests than anything else.

Q: And you didn't want to be distracted by the constant shifting back and forth from sea duty to shore duty?

Adm. W.: I just didn't see how one could be a professional engineer or a technical manager in the navy and at the same time maintain all of the operational tickets, in a sense how could you do that without losing your amateur standing in addition to your other duties. You couldn't, the length of a career just wasn't long enough to do both of those jobs right. I was so impressed with the suggestion that was made by Admiral Parsons when he said let's send two or three ensigns into the Nuclear Program, when he first got involved in it at the end of the war, because it is going to be important some day and we ought to have some people who are really experienced in it. I don't know that he necessarily had much brief for ordnance engineering duty as such, I felt that the navy really should have a few people in that category.

Q: He probably would have been led to that?

Adm. W.: He might have, I like to think he did. In due course I asked for it, it was approved and effective upon my transfer from LOS ANGELES to shore duty. That shore duty was to be the Naval Ordnance Laboratory at White Oak, Maryland. That laboratory had a small group under Commander Jim Dare who was one of the original officers working under Parsons. He had gotten his masters degree in nuclear physics in the same program that I had followed, he was one of my predecessors in that program and he had set up the group of physicists at NOL to do some pioneering work in the navy on nuclear physics.

Q: Were they largely academics over there?

Adm. W.: I think it was a mixture of civilians and military and they wanted me to go there. Of course I was eagerly looking forward to that because it would be in my field, it would be at an ordnance laboratory, everything seemed to fit and I was quite happy with that prospect. Then, lo and behold I got a letter saying they weren't going to do that at all, that other decisions had been made. I even saved this letter as I found it interesting.

Q: Was it a detailer again?

Adm. W.: In this case yes, it was a Personnel officer from the Bureau of Ordnance. It came to Los Angeles and explained to me that they had slated me for NOL at White Oak, Maryland but a far stronger assignment developed. It goes on to say, "As you may know the most urgent priority program in the navy today is the development, with the army, of intermediate range ballistic missile. A group of officers under Rear-admiral Raborn are being gathered together to push this crash program."

Q: Hadn't yet called it SP?

Adm. W.: They did call it SP but if he used that expression I would not have known what he was talking about. He went on to say, "A highly competent group of technical officers with outstanding service reputations are being called on to man this detail. Your name was brought up and you were selected." It turned out that what really happened was that Raborn had been given a blank check by Admiral Burke, and told that he could have anything he wanted, within reason, any people he wanted--just name their names and this project carried the top priority in the navy. So he had gathered around him a few, highly competent, people, naval officers that he knew well to form the nucleus of the new group and he effectively turned to each one of them and told them, "Name anybody you want." One of those officers was then Commander Tom Walker, who later became vice-admiral Walker. At the time I think he was Lieutenant Commander Walker at Sandia Base. His job under Raborn was to organize a test organization, a group that would be responsible for testing missiles. He was in the Personnel shop at BuOrd looking over the list of names of people he might want to ask for when quite by accident somebody mentioned my name in conjunction with my being reassigned from LOS ANGELES to White Oak, and he said, "Oh, I remember him, he's a good officer, I'll take him." He remembered me as ensign JG during the time back at Sandia Base, so when I reported to the Special Projects office and was duly shown into Tom Walker's office he told me what the job was that he had in mind for me. It turned out that he needed a Progress Officer, an officer who would be responsible for keeping the progress charts up to date that were displayed in the management center for Admiral Raborn and his top staff to keep track of the status of the program. I was sick, I was literally almost physically ill and I said, "Tom, this is a terrible thing to do to me, you don't realize that while I greatly appreciate your asking for me, I consider it a great honor to be asked to join this group, you don't realize that since I have seen you I have done other things. I have gotten experience in guided missiles, I have now a graduate degree in nuclear physics. I am no longer the officer that you knew back at the base. I want to do more than that. This program that you are involved in doesn't have any of that in it. The missile that carries the warhead is the responsibility of the army. The navy doesn't even have any responsibilities except to take that missile aboard a surface ship, so there really isn't anything here for me to do. How about reconsidering and letting me go on back to the NOL assignment?" Tom immediately recognized that this wasn't a good assignment but he said, "Look, I agree this is a wrong thing to do but we need good people in this outfit and there is bound to be something you can do here." So he took me up to see the technical director, Captain Greyson Merrill, who was later relieved by Levering Smith. Greyson Merrill was an aeronautical engineer, a distinguished officer and Captain Merrill said, "Right, we'll find something for you to do, you'll be on my staff." So my initial assignment, after that brief hiatus getting started was being on the staff of the Technical Director.

Q: And you gave up the charts?

Adm. W.: I gave up the charts and was given a lofty title, Special Assistant for Nuclear Applications. That sounds marvelous until you realize there really weren't any nuclear applications, at least for the navy. Later, not too much later, we had some very big ideas about this, but at that point my job was primarily a rather glorified executive or staff assistant to the technical director. He took me with him on all of his trips, I made trip reports and kept track of his conversations, ran special errands and tasks for him. It was exciting business but it was on the fringes, it was on the periphery of it.

Q: This was only in the first few months wasn't it? As I remember it got underway in December of 1955 and this was now June 1956.

Adm. W.: That's right. The group was barely organized and barely started.

Q: And it was still burdened with the relationship with the Army?

Adm. W.: Exactly. I have saved from those days, a picture of the missile that we were actually going to be putting aboard ship. A picture of the JUPITER--you will notice the frost is on it, it is full of liquid oxygen, the same fuel and oxidizer that we had used on NORTON SOUND in launching VIKING, the thing that was such a hazard. We of course now were dealing with how could we live with this on board ship, a naval vessel that was to carry a number of these missiles. The idea of being able to do that on a submarine was a gleam in our eyes but it seemed very remote indeed with those hazardous fuels. I remember the exciting times with Captain Merrill making trips down to Huntsville to visit with Dr. Wernher von Braun (at Huntsville, Alabama) and General Medaris who was the army officer, Admiral Raborn's counterpart in running that part of the program, and meeting with those people who were famous even then. That's where I was when some of the momentous events of the late summer of 1956 occurred, specifically the famous meeting at Woods Hole for Project NOBSKA. This was a meeting for focusing on undersea warfare, at which Dr. Edward Teller had gently criticized the navy for planning its nuclear weapon capability around nuclear technology of the mid-1950s for the weapons system that wouldn't become operational until the 60s, why not plan for a capability that would be more contemporary for the time, and he specifically projected that the nuclear warhead that we were thinking about for JUPITER and for the air force ICBM program and the like could be reduced in size without significant reduction in yield dramatically by that period, he predicted--I think these numbers have long since been declassified, but the warhead weights of some 1500 pounds or so of that period, could be reduced to something like 600 pounds.

Q: Were you present at that meeting?

Adm. W.: No, I wasn't present, I was in NSP at that time. The news of this came back like lightning.

Q: I remember Red Ramage (V-admiral Lawson P. Ramage) telling me, he was present and he rushed back to Washington to relate this to Admiral Burke.

Adm. W.: The implications of that were absolutely striking, though that is a poor, a weak word for what those implications were.

Q: Just opened a new horizon.

Adm. W.: A whole new horizon. We had already started, in the navy, thinking about solid propellant motors for JUPITER. In fact we had authorized and the navy had approval for developing an alternate propulsion system for JUPITER so that the JUPITER system could one day be put on a submarine.

Q: Weren't there two young men working in Virginia on this whole project for solid propellants?

Adm. W.: Probably there were but the major work was being done by a contractor--Aerojet General Corporation--and the navy's number one expert in solid propellant rocketry was Levering Smith who had just left, a short time before, a long tour of duty at NOTS-China Lake, Naval Ordnance test station at China Lake, California, as the associate technical director and was Commanding Officer of the Naval Unit at White Sands. So Levering Smith was sent for by the navy and assigned to Special Projects office. He reported there in the summer of 1956 within a very few weeks of the same time that I was. His job was to take charge of the development of the solid propellant motor system that would take the JUPITER front end, the JUPITER guidance system, the JUPITER payload, warhead, nose cone, the whole bit, and allow it to be safely used on submarines. The submarine of course would have to be especially designed for this purpose. It would have been a huge submarine carrying a very few missiles, but that was the ultimate weapon as far as the navy was concerned. This was the situation when the word came back to us from Woods Hole about Teller's criticism. As it happened I was the only officer in Special Projects office who was available and had the requisite technical background to be given the job of tracking down what all this really meant, what lay behind it, is it really feasible. If it is feasible, what would it mean in the size of the payload? In other words not only the warhead but the aero-ballistic thermdynamic protection that it would have to have around it to allow it to survive re-entry into the earth's atmosphere at hypersonic velocities, the arming and fusing system needed to cause it to function properly at the appropriate altitude, and so forth. I was given the job of pursuing that issue and all of a sudden everything fell into place. The right guy at the right place at the right time, fantastic, just absolutely fantastic.

Q: That's about the third time we can call it providential.

Adm. W.: You can call it providential if you will but I can't begin to tell you the sense of excitement that that carried with it. Only one little problem, I was about three ranks too junior for my associates. My counterparts in SP were at least commanders; my counterparts in the airforce were airforce colonels or generals and they had huge organizations of very prestigious scientists working for them; Ramo-Woolridge Corporation that has since become Thompson-Ramo-Woolridge, and Aerospace Corporation, respectively; big prestigious industrial organizations. Here I was a lieutenant, albeit a senior lieutenant.

Q: Raborn didn't have the authority to say 'raise your right hand'?

Adm. W.: Raborn, to say the least, was an inspiration; he took the view that if anybody was assigned to his organization it automatically meant he was the best in the navy. He went around, bragging to everyone who would listen to him about the fantastic team that he had and their tremendous talent and ability. He said it so often he even got us to believing it. Talk about having the support, trust and confidence of your superiors, there is no question about it; very few of us really stop to think about the risks of all this, in other words that we might be getting into deep water and carrying the whole navy along with us on our shoulders; we were just convinced that whatever we wanted to do would be done. That was what was happening in the fall of 1956. I was still on the staff of the technical director and I recall making a trip with him and Admiral Raborn up to MIT in the fall of 1956 to approach Doctor Draper

(Charles Stark Draper) with the proposition of taking on the job of developing the guidance system for this new small missile that we had in mind, because not only did the warhead have to get much smaller, there were noises coming out of Dr. Draper's organization that the guidance system could indeed also be reduced in size dramatically and this would be necessary if we were to fully exploit this new technology, this new possibility. So we approached Dr. Draper and that was one of my last trips as aide de camp to the technical director. Dr. Draper, as I am sure you know, accepted that assignment.

Q: It didn't take much to persuade him, did it?

Adm. W.: Not a great deal, he was pretty excited about it too but he did place some conditions on us which we were happy to accept.

Q: Such as?

Adm. W.: He said, as I recall that conversation, that in the past some of his developments of his instrumentation laboratory had been turned over to industry--for production-- and industry had attempted to improve on it in the process of producing it and had fouled it up horribly and he wanted to have final say, yes or no, to any change that anybody proposed to make in any of the designs that came out of his laboratory when they went to industry for production. The instrumentation laboratory was not a production organization it would require industrial support in order to produce and of course he was given that assurance that he would have complete control over the industrial support contractors to make certain they made no changes in his designs unless he approved them. That worked out very well and still does to this day. We still use the Draper laboratory name in the navy program and they still have complete control over change in the industrial support.

Q: No hitches in that arrangement at all then?

Adm. W.: I am sure there were a number but in the end it made for a smooth transition from the development organization to the production organization. The Draper Laboratory is now a beautiful organization and they have done a beautiful job for the navy over the years.

Q: How did Raborn function in this area? He was an aviator and didn't have this technical background.

Adm. W.: Well, Raborn had a good technical background although his principle role was as entrepreneur. He was Mr. Outside. He was the face to the public, the face to the rest of the navy; he recognized I believe, quote correctly, that opposition to POLARIS if it was going to arise in the navy would come out of the aviation community, they would see this as a threat somehow to their plans for big aircraft carriers because to need a big aircraft carrier you need a big airplane and with a big airplane you need a big payload and what bigger payload was there around than an atomic bomb and if the submarine delivering atomic payloads on land targets, deep inland, was to become a reality then somehow one would have to deal with this potential opposition from the aviation community in the navy. As being a distinguished naval aviator himself, Raborn turned this around and successfully sought and gained the support of the aviators by playing out that one of the roles for POLARIS would be to suppress defenses. You visualize the POLARIS being launched on anti-aircraft, or those fields that would otherwise launch fighter aircraft and then the big Sunday punch coming in from the carriers at sea.

Q: So he superimposed this idea?

Adm. W.: Sure, so that they would be better able to penetrate inland without opposition because of the much higher speed of the ballistic missile and it could be delivered deep inland in a matter of minutes, whereas it might take hours for an aircraft to reach the same target; the targets defenses would have been beaten down and the aircraft would then fly in unopposed.

Q: I suppose you could call that an incisive kind of an argument?

Adm. W.: Well, I think it was an expedient argument and it worked. He had some opposition within the navy, I suspect a fair bit of opposition could have been generated because just as today, a strategic role for the navy is seen by many as diverting sources that would otherwise be applied to general purpose forces which are important to the navy. The navy has no real requirement, as a navy, for this strategic mission, strategic bombardment role, unlike an airforce, our airforce whose creation and establishment as a separate third service at the end of WW2 was built around the notion that a strategic bombardment was a unique role, that justified the service around it. In that sense the airforce requires a strategic mission whereas the navy is sort of the other way around. If you want to put a strategic missile delivery system at sea in a submarine you require a navy but the navy has no requirement for that role--it was around for a couple hundred years before anybody invented it. So there was potential opposition within the navy that was successfully charmed out of the way by Raborn or bulldozed out of the way if you like.

Q: He also made it quite well known that he carried in his pocket that letter which gave him carte blanche.

Adm. W.: Indeed he did and one can't possibly give enough credit to the Chief of Naval Operations, Admiral Burke, for his success, his far sight, his wisdom in putting the interests of the country above the narrow interests of the navy in getting the POLARIS program started. I think that evidence now available to us would show that the navy never really suffered from this, that the navy's budgets have grown commensurate with its increasing responsibilities over time. At that time, you will recall, the three services were getting budgets that were roughly comparable in size, for a long time the navy has gotten more than one-third of the pie.

Q: It was the best kind of public relations as far as the population at large was concerned, they began to know about the navy.

Adm. W.: Indeed. I have saved a copy of Life Magazine that glamorizes Admiral Raborn a little bit.

Q: He had plenty of his own natural glamor.

Adm. W.: It has pictures of him at home playing the organ, and marching aboard a submarine with a determined look on his face to participate in a test launch, and so forth. Raborn did an absolutely fantastic job of generating public support and keeping the navy in line. He was an inspired choice.

Q: And keeping the Congress in line.

Adm. W.: Oh, my God, yes--keeping the Congress in line. It was an inspired selection by Admiral Burke to have picked Admiral Raborn. Of course, what isn't as well known is what went on inside the organization. Admiral Raborn just literally inspired us all by trusting us all. He expected we would all do fantastic things, he expected that we would literally work our tails off, that we would work all hours of the day and night, that we would have the support of our families, that we would make our industrial partners literally that--partners, he told us that when we travelled to visit one of our contractors we were to get to know them and to know their families because they were going to be expected to work just as hard as we were. The same thing was true the other way around; he frequently would get our families together to tell them what we were doing and how important it was and how important it was to support their husbands and fathers.

Q: That was true of the factories throughout the land.

Adm. W.: Absolutely, he was an absolutely inspirational leader, an intuitive leader, he was doing the right things at the right time. The people who were really doing the work, people like Levering Smith and others, could quietly go on about their business. They had the resources they needed, they had the support of the authorities they needed, largely because of the charisma and the inspiration that came out of Raborn.

Q: Did your staff people have a weekly injection of this charisma at these famous Saturday meetings? Will you tell me about them?

Adm. W.: Yes indeed. The meetings were just literally that. Every Saturday morning we would have a staff meeting and at that time, late '56 and early '57, the staff was small enough that we could all meet in one room--SP was not very large. We would go over in detail where we stood on all the critical areas, it was management by exception in the sense that we were not reporting things that were going according to plan but rather those things that were departing from plan by one means or another so Admiral Raborn could quickly spot the areas where he needed to inject himself. He made that very clear that he wanted to be involved when things were not tracking as they should so that he could get whatever outside help he needed or provide whatever decision or authority that needed to come from his level.

Q: Who got the job of keeping the charts?

Adm. W.: Not me. I had by that time a job that took all of my time and attention.

Q: Did your job put you in touch with the manufacturers directly?

Adm. W.: Yes, I guess this would be a good time to talk a little bit about how that job actually started out.

In January of 1957 we formally organized a group we called our Special Task Group. This consisted of several committees, one for each of the several major subdivisions of the weapon system; each committee was given a task by a steering committee which was overseeing the entire exercise, to prepare tradeoff information which would allow sensible decisions to be quickly reached on the basic envelope parameters

of the new POLARIS system. By envelope parameters I am
talking about the basic outline of the system, the dimensions
of the missile, its weight, its performance, tradeoffs
between those dimensions and the submarine whole diameter,
the effect on the submarine as a function on the number
of missiles to be carried, basic decisions as to interfaces
between guidance and fire control and navigation and so
forth. There were subcommittees in each of these major
subsystem areas, launching and handling, fire control,
guidance, missile, navigation; and each of these committees
was given tasks to perform to bring back these tradeoffs
among the various parameters which could then be balanced
by the steering committee to arrive at the fundamental
decisions so that those envelopes could be frozen and then
the various groups could go off and perform their development
tasks, more or less not independently of one another but
in parallel so that the Bureau of Ships could develop the
submarine at the same time that others of us were developing
the missile so that the guidance system could be developed
while the payload was being developed while somebody else
was developing the propulsion system so that they would all
come together at the end, and fit.

This was a three-month exercise, it began January 1957
and I was given the job of heading up what they called the
Re-entry Committee which was one of these groups. My committee
was concerned with the tradeoff between the size of the warhead,
the corresponding size of the heat shield, the aerodynamic

and thermodynamic protection for the payload, its arming and fusing system and the like and its interface with the missile. Then, how to provide adequate safety and at the same time assure appropriate reliability. I assembled the team of people from government laboratories and industrial support--contractors. Interestingly enough the individual that was first sent to us from Dr. Teller's organization--the Livermore Laboratory--was a young scientist, then only 28 years old, by the name of Harold Brown who was later to become better known in other parts of the world. In any event, this group represented the Livermore Laboratory, the Naval Ordnance Laboratory, which was going to be working on the arming and fusing systems for us, the old NACA (National Advisory Committee for Aeronautics) which was a predecessor organization to NASA, they sent us a couple of individuals, our Sandia corporations sent a member and I had a couple of members from our industrial contractor Lockheed. I remember the very first meeting of this group.

Q: How many did you have? Quite a collection of brains.

Adm. W.: There must have been a dozen of us altogether, I was the chairman. This was a collection of brains but these people were not well known in this business. The big names in this business, people like Dr. Theodore von Karman and Alexander John Allen and Eggers who were famous for doing pioneering papers on hypersonic re-entry into the earth's atmosphere. Names of people like that were still floating around, Dr. Arthur Kantrowitz of Avco-Everett Research Laboratory, was well known. Big names were not represented on my committee, these people that I had represented prestigious organizations but weren't well known people. In any event I sat them all down and we discussed at our first meeting the task that lay before us and how I wanted to approach it. After that first meeting I went back to my little cubbyhole of an office, I had sent them all off to do various assignments and they were to report back in two weeks when we would have another meeting, and I was followed back to my office by Dr. Lloyd Wilson who was one of the men from Lockheed. Dr. Wilson was actually a thermodynamicist from St. Louis University who was on sort of a sabbatical, an industrial sabbatical with Lockheed at the time. He had gotten caught up in this thing just as I had and he said, "Lieutenant, what you are trying to do here is awfully important," and I said, "I know that Dr. Wilson," and he said, "But its so important you really ought to have famous people in it who really know what they are doing." And I said, "Dr. Wilson, I don't want people who know what they are doing, I want you." It was a spur of the moment comment and I guess I thought I was being funny but it turned out and (he told me later) that nothing I had ever said, before or since, impressed him that much, what I had in fact told him was that I wanted an innovative new approach to a problem not to be in any way constrained by previous conventional wisdom and that, in fact, is what we did.

Q: With younger people?

Adm. W.: A fresh approach. The conventional wisdom for the design of a ballistic missile, payload--the nose cone, was to have the Atomic Energy Commission develop a warhead off on one side, the Department of Defense and its contractors would develop a protective heat shield, an aero-ballistic shield, they would have agreed between them ahead of time where the attachment points would be, how the loads would be carried and shared, what the electrical signal interfaces had to be, so that they could each separately do their thing.

Q: Sort of parameters?

Adm. W.: That's right, so that ultimately when the two came together and they had bolted it in place then you would have a complete system. To give you a feel for this, that 1500 pound warhead, the same warhead that was being used on all the ballistic missiles of the time, was properly protected and shielded and encased, the whole system ended up weighing twice that, between 3200 to 3500 pounds. That in turn reflected itself in the size of the missile that had to carry it. Now our job was not only to shrink the size of the warhead to the level approaching that that Dr. Teller had promised but we also wanted to cut every ounce of weight out of that front end that we possibly could; the smaller we could make the payload the smaller the missile could be. I was convinced there were great efficiencies to be achieved in the design process if we could somehow or other get the warhead designers and the heat shield designers working together. One of the main reasons the two were being treated separately was because they were two entirely different organizations, the Atomic Energy Commission and the Department of Defense, they were separated not only physically but even legally; there were laws keeping them separate.

Q: And by all sorts of restrictions, weren't they?

Adm. W.: That's right. And physics caused many of their difficult problems. Bomb physics required that the mass distribution around and in close proximity to the nuclear payload itself be very carefully controlled, otherwise if there were asymmetries or discontinuities it might affect the way the bomb functioned. The way that was solved in the conventional design was keeping them physically separated by several inches and that led to a separate structure. If you will think of an egg inside of a crate, the egg is protected by its own shell but it is again protected by the crate itself. What I had in mind was can't we somehow get together and make an integrated design, one that would integrate the warhead case, which itself is a very substantial structure but is there primarily to perform bomb physics, and the aero-ballistic heat shield so that one could support the other and the integrated system could be reduced in size and weight. That was what I really was thinking when I told Dr. Wilson that I didn't want the conventional experts, I wanted people like himself who didn't really know anything.

Q: Were other teams comprised of younger experts, people who were not famous?

Adm. W.: Yes and no. Some were and some weren't. As I said I was junior by at least two ranks, to anybody else in a comparable position in the organization. Commanders and captains headed the other teams; people like Dr. Draper who were very famous, well-known people, his team was working on the guidance system. There were some people who were well-known and there were some others who weren't. Basically the navy team was composed of younger, innovative people who had not, up until that time, been totally caught up in the big airforce and army ballistic missile programs. Even our industrial contractor, Lockheed, was selected primarily because they were the only aircraft company, we now call them aerospace companies, that hadn't already been involved in these programs.

Q: Chrysler had been cited first, had it not?

Adm. W.: Yes, Chrysler had been picked by the army as their industrial support contractor for the JUPITER. General Electric and AVCO had been picked by the airforce for their front end work, General Dynamics - CONVAIR - for work I believe on ATLAS and the Martin Company for TITAN, and Douglas for THOR. When we looked around for somebody to help the navy, we started with Chrysler because when we were working with JUPITER it seemed to make sense, so both army and the navy would have the same contractor. But when we broke away to do POLARIS it was so different from the JUPITER solid propellant, a new missile altogether, we didn't think that Chrysler was really the right contractor and that's when we went to Lockheed and Aero-Jet for the motors.

Q: When these committees were formed, was there any idea of an over-all date when all of this would come together?

Adm. W.: Yes, we started the thing out, the idea was we would do POLARIS, the solid propellant missile in about 1965, something like that.

Q: Ten years.

Adm. W.: Might have been 1963, whether it was '63 or '65 I can't really recall. I think '63 is right. In the meantime we would do the JUPITER on an earlier schedule, on the surface ship, to be followed by the submarine application later.

Q: There was a certain amount of reluctance to going back wasn't there.

Adm. W.: Well, it seemed to be the prudent path. By the end of 1956 the navy had been redirected to the solid propellant, the small solid propellant missile we called POLARIS instead of JUPITER. We were in effect divorced from the army at that point, altogether. As I recall the goal was like 1963 for an operational capability and that is the program we were all working on when we finished the trade-off assignments. In March of 1957 our Special Task Group completed its work and it was I believe the fall of 1957, October, when the Soviets launched their SPUTNIK. That resulted, among other things, in the acceleration of the schedule.

Q: That was a super injection wasn't it?

Adm. W.: That's right. In December of '57 the program was accelerated by three years to 1960 as an objective. That caused a rather considerable dilemma. As I told you, we had set some ambitious goals for ourselves, I can tell you first hand about some of the things we were trying to do in the payload area, the re-entry area, the same sorts of things were happening elsewhere in the system. I told you that we were attempting to develop a payload or a warhead that wasn't yet in hand, using a design approach that had never been tested and it was quite a departure from the standard approach to such things, all of which was forecast to be available on a 1963 schedule. If we had for example, taken a 600 pound warhead and designed a re-entry vehicle in accordance with the conventional approach we would have had a total system weighing on the order of 1350 pounds, that was the initial design approach that was suggested, using the standard procedure--egg in a crate. In fact we set ourselves a goal for an integrated design carrying 600 pound warheads that would weigh only about 850 pounds which was an indication of how adventurous we hoped to be.

So when they accelerated the program from 1963 to 1960 we were then faced with a very crucial decision as to whether or not we could stick to our original objectives on a 3-year earlier schedule or whether we would have to back off and be a little more conservative. In fact we chose to just take more risk and to work faster and harder.

Q: It was the prevailing spirit.

Adm. W.: Yes it was. In some areas there was a deliberate acceptance of reduction in performance, the missile itself for instance. When they accelerated it by three years we couldn't achieve the same range, the original range objective in the particular size missile selected was 1500 miles; when they accelerated the program Admiral Smith who was then the technical director only committed to achieving 1100 miles on the 3-year earlier time scale. Ultimately of course we did get the 1500 miles and we got it sooner than 1963 but nevertheless the acceleration was accomplished by judicious backing away from some of the performance objectives. For instance reliability was not as high as we had set for ourselves because we didn't have time to do all the testing we needed to do. We did many things in parallel that we might otherwise have done in series, sequentially. In the warhead area we accepted a warhead yield which was perhaps a bit lower than we would have had, if we had had the three more years to work on the problem.

Q: I suppose always with the reservation that another model

would come out eventually?

Adm. W.: Oh yes, it was our intention, in fact it was specifically spelled out in the requirements that there were certain minimum objectives that were to be achieved in the initial operational capability which were then to be upgraded to certain ultimate objectives--follow on systems. So we were always thinking about growth within this envelope to a greater capability.

Q: Were the decisions arrived at by these various component groups subjected to an over-all scrutiny by the whole steering committee?

Adm. W.: Yes, that is what the steering committee was set up for. It was set up as sort of an overseer of the work of the subcommittees. As I said, this was a three-month process and when that steering committee effectively blessed the selection of the parameters it ultimately spelled out the POLARIS system--sixteen missiles per submarine for instance, of such and such a diameter to come out the launch tube. Initially we didn't know whether or not it would be possible to launch a missile bare under water so there was enough room allowed in between the mount tube, which is the structure of the ship, and the missile itself so that a capsule could have been put around it to keep the missile dry until it got out of the water, the capsule would then fall away and the missile would be launched. Things of that sort.

Q: Can you repeat the story of the Figure 16?

Adm. W.: That story has been told so many times.

Q: I know, but I'd like to hear it from the horse's mouth.

Adm. W.: I'm not necessarily the horse, I might have been one of the mules. The person who could best tell that story is Admiral Levering Smith who in fact was right at the heart of that. I do recall very well that from a purely engineering and technical standpoint the payoff was a very weak one between the number of missiles carried and the size and cost of the submarine. By that I mean, that once you paid for a submarine and built it to carry any missiles at all, the cost of adding more missiles for that submarine was relatively low and there wasn't any obvious number to cut off, whether or not one carried eight, twelve, sixteen, twenty-four or even thirty-two missiles. In a submarine there was no obvious break point where the submarine suddenly became very much more expensive or very much more difficult to maneuver or whatever--it was going to be a big submarine in any case. Once you paid the price for the nuclear power plant, the crew and the various equipments necessary to sustain them the attainment of the additional missiles didn't cost much. Those were the technical and economic facts of life, so the choice was ultimately made on other factors, operational and I might even say emotional. The STG members, I think had they been allowed to express themselves publicly, would have opted for a larger number of missiles than sixteen because of those technical and economic reasons. In fact, it never went on record what they recommended because Admiral Smith wisely chose not to ask them to. He had their individual votes sealed and given to him and he read them privately, then he took them to Admiral Raborn, I am now repeating the story, this is second hand as I wasn't there when this actually happened; they discussed it and they realized that there was such strong opposition from the operational community for the larger number of missiles.

Q: Twenty-four?

Adm. W.: Yes, twenty-four, which was really the number I think, that the bulk of the membership of the STG would have recommended, that they chose to pick the smaller number. So sixteen became the number selected, it was said there was no systems analysis or the like that dictated that number however I found it amusing that when the Soviets got around to building their ballistic missiles, lo and behold the YANKEE was build with sixteen missiles on it, the French built their ballistic missile submarines with sixteen and so did the British; so each of them must have concluded that when they did their studies, there was no obvious reason for picking that number but the Americans had picked sixteen so maybe they knew something that had influenced this choice.

Q: Did you have anything to do with Electric Boat?

Adm. W.: Of course the office did; I did not personally. In fact the Electric Boat Division of General Dynamics that actually built the GEORGE WASHINGTON and many of its successors, was under contract with the Bureau of Ships. Bureau of Ships was a partner with SP, SP and Admiral Raborn controlled its funds and the relationship was very much like a contractor, in other words, we did not attempt to tell the Bureau of Ships how to build the submarine and in that sense Electric Boat was Bureau of Ships' contractor. We interfaced with Electric Boat but it wasn't anything like an intimate interface as existed with our own contractors.

Q: Will you repeat that about Carl Shugg and others at Electric Boat?

Adm. W.: I am sure that they saw Admiral Raborn and SP as the team's quarterback, really running the show but we can't overlook the fact that there were very strong directors of that part of the program such as Admiral Rickover in the case of any nuclear powered vessel and the Chief of the Bureau of Ships and his submarine people who were strongly directing that aspect of the program, namely the submarine and its interfaces. The SP controlled the interfaces. Admiral Raborn and we in SP did that and still do directly and dictate the interfaces, by that I mean the dimensions, the tolerances, the electrical inputs and outputs, the optical inputs and outputs between the ship and the weapon system. Those become imposed on Electric Boat or any other of the contractors from the submarine area as contractual requirements.

Q: I suppose there are elements of that which are likely to impede the whole breakdown more readily.

Adm. W.: Oh sure, and those become give and take in the course of development. One always encounters unplanned problems that require renegotiation if you will, of those interfaces, but you can have only one quarterback on any football team and the ultimate decision has to be made by someone and that one in the case of this program has always been SP.

Q: You had very able cooperation from BuShips in Jimmy James didn't you?

Adm. W.: Absolutely, and he was the one who characterized his relationship with Raborn as one of Raborn's contractors. It was that very healthy relationship that I think made the program possible, made its success possible. Without it it could have been a shambles. We had everybody pulling with and for SP at that time. Again I have to come back and say that an awful lot of the credit has to go directly, where it has always been provided, to Raborn for that kind of inspirational public relations, external relations.

Q: How much did Admiral Burke inject himself or was it apparent in the whole thing?

Adm. W.: It wasn't apparent to me at my level, I am sure it was very apparent to people like Admiral Raborn. But we knew we had the navy's support, there was no question about that and that could only have come from the top. I only found out about that letter that Raborn carried around in his pocket some years later.

Q: He told me about that, he was very proud of it.

Adm. W.: I would like to tell a little story about a true experience during this exciting time, the period right around the time of the acceleration of POLARIS. I think it will illustrate the atmosphere inside SP as well as outside it as well as anything can and at least as I perceived it. One of the decisions we had to make when we accelerated the program in the re-entry area was whether or not we were going to be able to build the re-entry body out of beryllium which had originally been our intent--use of the relatively exotic metal beryllium was planned by us for use in the primary structure of the nose, the re-entry vehicle, as well as some of the other aerodynamic structure.

Q: Was it available in this country?

Adm. W.: Beryllium ore was from overseas mostly, there was some beryllium ore in this country but it hadn't been developed. It came mostly from Brazil and Africa. Beryllium was relatively rare and was used primarily as an alloy with copper for certain specialized purposes. Pure beryllium had never been used as a primary structure for an airframe or anything of the sort. We had selected it because first of all for its thermodynamic properties, it had a very high heat capacity and thermal conductivity, very much like copper in that regard, which was being used by the airforce in the design of the heat sink for the ATLAS and the TITAN. But it was also very much lighter in weight, its density was very low so that it offered the weight saving we were after. The problem with it was, as you have already suggested, that it was relatively rare, we weren't all that sure we could come by it, nobody really had much experience in fabricating it in these large shapes. Anyhow, that material had been selected by us.

Q: Again an innovative thing?

Adm. W.: Yes it was innovative, nobody had ever done that before. When the program was accelerated we had the difficult decision as to whether or not we could stick with this use of beryllium on an accelerated schedule. After having a stormy meeting with my co-workers and getting all the facts and figures together as the head of that joint group, I was still the chairman; I say joint group because the Atomic Energy Commission and the Navy were working under my chairmanship and of course the manufacturer was under contract to us,--I decided that we would go for broke and try to build this thing out of beryllium on the accelerated schedule.

Q: What were the objections from the other members of the

committee?

Adm. W.: Risk primarily, and cost. It was very costly and it would carry implications to the Atomic Energy Commission because, as I told you, we had gone with what we called an integrated design in which the heat shield and the physics package, the warhead, were integral, so a decision made on the primary structure would affect not only the cost to the navy but also to the AEC, and their laboratories. So I said we would do it and having rendered that decision I went home--back to Washington, this meeting had been held in California--and I was no sooner back there when a telegram arrived from the AEC addressed to the director of Special Projects and pointing out their objections to this course of action, saying in effect that it was costly and citing other objections and asking that it be reconsidered. The message, since it concerned re-entry and the mail room knew who was doing what to whom those days, sent the message to me for a reply.

Q: Was this from the chairman?

Adm. W.: It was from the Atomic Energy Commission, I think the San Francisco operations office, but the laboratory representatives had been very uneasy about my decision and they were uneasy about their ability to convince their bosses and in fact they hadn't been able to when they went back home and that telegram resulted. Anyhow it came to me to prepare a reply so, I prepared a reply which in effect said,

"Thank you for your message, I appreciate your concern however the decision will stand and we are counting on your continued support and cooperation," something of that sort. I sent it up the line and it was duly released just like that. In fact, I think it was released by Admiral Smith, I have spoken to Admiral Smith since and he maintains he really did understand what he was signing, but I still like to think that Admiral Raborn had created an environment and Admiral Smith supported it fully which said, "We have given you your responsibility, we are depending on you, we trust you to do what is right and we support what you propose to do." Anyhow, my friends on the AEC told me some years later that when that message got back to them they became convinced that I really had all the authority that I claimed I had had. That when I made a decision it was in fact committing our organization. Of course I never had any such authority.

Q: Not on paper?

Adm. W.: Not on paper but from then on they supported me as they never had before simply because they assumed that I was speaking for the navy. Some years later we got around to straightening them out on that, but only after the program was successfully completed.

Q: You, in effect, carried that letter in your pocket too?

Adm. W.: In effect, that's right. That sense of trust and inspiration that Raborn exuded, and Admiral Smith also, the two of them. Its awfully hard to put into words exactly the environment that that created for those of us who were working down in the trenches.

Q: There have been other, so-called, SP projects in the navy since then but none carried that kind of authority.

Adm. W.: No, I don't think so and I sometimes wonder if that's a good thing. I can't imagine that the twenty-five years could have gone by without at least one other project justifying that kind of an organization and that kind of authority. Certainly one can agree that every project should not have it but certainly there must have been at least one other in that time.

Q: And its certainly true there can only be one at a time, there couldn't be more than one operating.

Adm. W.: There is only the danger I think, that an organization set up as SP was and run the way SP was will abuse its authority and will carry it to extremes. Or, alternatively it will allow Parkinson's law to take over and grow all out of size, become an empire. Somehow or other that hasn't happened.

Q: Was it perhaps because this was SP, but it was in the public eye, it had to be by the nature of it as it was developed in industry. The Congress was terribly cognizant of the whole progress and so this itself, in addition to the high caliber of the people involved, was enough to hold it in line. Is that feasible?

Adm. W.: I think there is a lot of truth in that. I think also there is another factor that applied then and has continued to apply in the years since and I have alluded to it before--that is the sense that SP was trying, and still is, to do its job within the navy, a job which has really served a national need rather than a navy need and that it has to be very, very careful never to go beyond its bounds, to take claim on more resources in the navy than absolutely necessary to do its essential job. By resources here I am not just talking about money I am talking about critical skills, people, as well as industrial capacity and funds. In that environment there is a self-discipline required of the leadership in SP not to allow itself to become more than it needs to be in the navy or we will lose the support of the navy which is absolutely critical to our ability to do the job. Again I have to contrast that with the situation in our sister service, the airforce where I don't think that such inhibitions are nearly so strong.

Q: Then there is the reverse of the coin you describe and that is that it couldn't possibly become parochial else it would not be effective either.

Adm. W.: That's true. We have to fit, not only in the navy, but specifically we have to fit within the submarine force because we need the support of the submariners. They could potentially be called parochial, I suspect we have to be with them but at the same time not allow ourselves to be exploited.

Q: There is another very significant story--the decision on the front end for the POLARIS A-3 which was to be the ultimate one.

Adm. W.: Yes, as I mentioned the original POLARIS, which we called POLARIS A-1, when the program was accelerated that initial capability was minimal, it was that which could be achieved in the shortest period of time and so POLARIS A-1 had limited capabilities. POLARIS A-2 substantially improved on those capabilities getting the range of the missile up to something like 1500 miles but basically the POLARIS A-2 was simply an improved version of the original missile, it carried the same front end for instance, my part of that missile was unchanged from POLARIS A-1, similarly the guidance system was the same. Most of the changes were in the motor and in the missile structure. The real next full generation of modernization within the POLARIS system was POLARIS A-3. This missile was to meet the ultimate objectives of the POLARIS program, a missile of some 2500 nautical miles range which would greatly increase the operating area available for patrol by the submarine. It was to have a warhead carrying a full megaton of yield whereas the original POLARIS had only half that. It was a general motherhood statement in the operational requirements that said it was to have minimum vulnerability to counter measures.

Q: What was the approximate date for this POLARIS A-3?

Adm. W.: POLARIS A-3 was undertaken in 1960 with an objective I believe of being operational in 1965.

Q: The GEORGE WASHINGTON was all ready?

Adm. W.: Oh yes, GEORGE WASHINGTON was already on patrol and a number of her sisters but the program was continuing to expand, the submarines were coming off the line at a steady rate--they were in construction and weren't coming off very much yet and in 1960 GEORGE WASHINGTON had just barely gotten on patrol but we were looking downstream to a new capability which would be deployed in 1965 and by that time there would be a number of submarines at sea but were then still in construction.

The Re-entry Committee, the group that I was heading, was faced with rather a singular problem or set of problems in meeting our part of the requirement. Specifically, that one megaton yield was a problem because in 1958 the Soviet Union and the United States entered into an unformalized but nevertheless implicit agreement to stop nuclear testing. There was no one megaton warhead that had been tested in the size that we wanted. To commit to that would in effect be committing to putting a warhead on this missile that might not ever be tested in its full yield. The Atomic Energy Commission advised us that they would be willing to certify such a warhead, that the extrapolation was not great from things that they had tested, and that they should be able, with high confidence, to be able to give us such a warhead.

Nevertheless I was uneasy because I felt that it was entirely consistent with some past experience that the best intentioned scientist could end up making mistakes and that we would not discover it until too late.

Q: Had the ARGUS project contributed any knowledge to you?

Adm. W.: No, that was not in any way related.

Q: Quite different I know but I wondered?

Adm. W.: What we were dealing with was the design of nuclear explosions, not necessarily their upper atmospheric effects but rather the actual design of nuclear explosives. In particular we were dealing with the level of understanding of those things which might permit a design with adequate confidence, without a final full-scale test. At that time this was out of the question and I was just not convinced that that was possible, or at least prudent for a system that was going to be as important as POLARIS. What then was the alternative. It turned out that the AEC had tested a smaller design, a device, of about 200 kilotons (2/10ths of a megaton), which was really the design that they intended scaling up to a megaton.

Q: Therefore their confidence?

Adm. W.: Yes. I felt much more comfortable with using the device that had actually been tested. If we used that much smaller warhead we could carry more than one of them in the front end of the missile and it turned out--you do the arithmetic--if you could carry three of those and properly space them in a triangular pattern, the effect on the ground the area covered on the ground approximated that of a single one megaton warhead.

Q: Can you say thus MIRV was born?

Adm. W.: Thus multiple re-entry vehicles were born. I was attracted to the notion of going with three warheads on a single missile. Largely because of this nuclear testing issue that allowed us to use a device that had already been tested and therefore did not depend upon whether or not this nuclear test moratorium would continue, but also because it served the other purpose that I mentioned that concerned minimum vulnerability to counter-measures. If one not only deployed these warheads so that they had maximum, optimum coverage on the ground when they detonated but they were also spaced relative to one another during re-entry into the earth's atmosphere, they were spaced properly and a potential anti-ballistic system could not attack them simultaneously, they would have to be attacked individually, which would multiply by a factor of three the difficulty of the defensive system designer. To my way of thinking that was one way of responding positively to the boiler plate in the operational requirement that called for doing something about minimizing vulnerability to counter measures. I saw this approach, while highly unconventional for the period, as one of having considerable attraction. Besides which, it was novel and I was still young.

Q: So it met all these requirements?

Adm. W.: Exactly. I didn't know how this was going to be greeted by my masters in SP. The conventional thing would have been to agree with the Atomic Energy Commission that they would scale up the size of a single warhead, we would have a conventional front end and away we'd go. Surprisingly enough this idea received a warm reception from Admiral Smith who was then the technical director when I took it to him; it also served another purpose that he had and that was that he was facing the problem of putting enough propulsive energy into this POLARIS size missile to reach 2500 nautical miles. In order to do that not only was he going to have to put in a great deal more energetic propellant but he was also going to have to lighten up all of the non-propulsive elements of the missile--reduce the weight in the motor case, in the nozzles and the other structure and the like and he saw this immediately as a way of simplifying the design of the second stage motor it permitted the design to be made as a single structure without so-called thrust termination ports being built in. One can separate the warheads instead of having to terminate the thrust of the second stage motor when it reached the appropriate velocity, one could simply eject these re-entry bodies off to the side and let the last propulsion stage just fly on out until it burned out. It simplified the design of the motors and at the same time it met some other nice objectives. The problem with it was various, for one thing it multiplied by three the number of warheads that were going to go into the POLARIS system which put us in competition with the other services for warheads, it irritated the dickens out of the army because the army was, at the time, trying to get approval for putting NIKE ZEUS, the anti-ballistic missile system they had designed, into production; in the JCS the NIKE ZEUS had failed to get approval because the navy had opposed it along with the airforce but the navy had opposed the army's plan to put the NIKE ZEUS into production as not being necessary. I can recall talking to one army general on the joint staff who was irritated with us for coming up with this approach and meeting a need to penetrate the Soviet anti-ballistic missile system, and he said, "How can you argue that it is necessary to penetrate Soviet anti-ballistic missile systems when you (the navy) oppose the army's developing such a system or producing such a system on its own?" I managed to convince him that it was still prudent to provide that kind of capability for the future.

Q: That's where parochialism comes into the picture.

Adm. W.: Exactly. The airforce wasn't all that wild about the navy's design for the front end; among other things, the airforce was working then on MINUTEMAN at that stage and it wanted to use that extrapolated warhead design, the larger untested design, so it couldn't very well accept an argument that said it wasn't prudent to extrapolate.

Q: Yes, but the basic merit of the proposal, why did it fall through the crack with them?

Adm. W.: Actually as it turned out there were officers in the airforce who saw the merits of it and who supported our going that way. In fact they even undertook investigations on their own to find out whether there were not some advantages to the airforce in going with the multiple re-entry system. They set up a special project in New Mexico it was called CLAW, Clustered Atomic Warheads, in which they were actually investigating what benefits might accrue to the airforce by going in on that approach. I had to be very careful there, obviously it was more than one airforce opinion, just as there was more than one navy opinion. What I am describing to you was a period of time which was the first time that I, at least, ran into significant opposition and had to actively participate in convincing people outside of SP that the technical approach that I and my committee had selected for various reasons that we thought were good and sound and prudent were not automatically accepted.

Q: This was largely outside of your own service, was it not?

Adm. W.: Yes, largely outside of my own service. That was

the first time I ran into the very new Office of the Secretary of Defense. It was new in the sense that it was new with its influence. Mr. McNamara had just come in with Mr. Kennedy and he set up a team of people in the office of the Secretary of Defense to not only dispose but also to propose ways to go in defense procurement. I remember running into one of the bright young men over there who saw one of my briefing charts and demanded to know precisely how each point on the curve had been derived mathematically and he caught me completely short because I had just simply taken that from one of my contractors and was using it, uncritically. It looked sensible to me so I was using it, I couldn't derive it.

Q: And he felt he could?

Adm. W.: He felt that to understand it he had to be able to derive it, he took out his pencil and paper and wanted to calculate it. This was one of the curves showing the value of three versus one warhead in the ballistic missile penetration role. I learned a valuable lesson from that, I have never since used any graph in any presentation that I have given that I didn't know at least how it was derived even if I couldn't do it myself. I think that's a valuable lesson.

Q: A lesson for historians too.

Adm. W.: I'll leave that for you. That's another story

and suffice it to say that before POLARIS A-3 became operational the Soviets resumed nuclear testing with a vengeance and we learned a lesson about trusting them in this country. I think that occurred but not always a permanent lesson.

That's the story that lies behind the first use of multiple re-entry vehicles on any ballistic missile. The POLARIS A-3 is a multiple re-entry vehicle system and was the first such. None were the MIRV because the I in MIRV stands for Independently guided. And that, by the way, when it did come it also came on the version of the fleet ballistic missile system and that is POSEIDON, which is another story.

Q: That is a very significant one that you have told me.

Note: The typist inadvertently omitted 30 numbers from the on-going pagination. The next number used is 171.

Interview No. 3 with Rear-admiral Robert H. Wertheim

Place: At his residence in Annandale, Virginia

Date: Friday, 23 January 1981

Subject: Biography

By: John T. Mason, Jr.

Q: We continue the POLARIS story and your involvement with that in the very early days going back to 1956 and there are several other segments that perhaps you want to deal with; for instance, the PERT system.

Adm. W.: I have a perspective on the PERT system which I am certain is not completely balanced.

Q: And somewhat different I imagine?

Adm. W.: It may be somewhat different because it was a view from the trenches as opposed from the outside or from on high. First of all let me create for you the atmosphere in which we were working at the time. We were a relatively small team of naval officers and civil servants working on a project of importance quite comparable to that that had been pursued for a fair bit longer by our sister service the Airforce and to a lesser extent the Army in their ballistic missile program. The airforce had vast publicity and public recognition of the programs they were undertaking with their intercontinental ballistic missiles, ATLAS and TITAN and their intermediate range ballistic missile, THOR as well as other programs of air breathing missile programs. These ballistic missile programs had a great deal of publicity and it was well known that the airforce was mustering the great talent of the nation, the scientific talent of the nation in the form of Ramo-Woolridge Corporation who had hired the finest scientists in the country for them, and many others. This made it easy I think for the public and Congress to accept the billions of dollars being spent by the airforce--to accept that they were being well spent. We in the navy had a different problem, we didn't have any glamorous scientific names although Admiral Raborn did his best to make the most of the few that he did have. He seized upon the very well known Dr. Draper's name when he agreed to support the program--the guidance development and a few others. He did have a small embarrassment with the front end of the program as all he had was this lieutenant but he managed with that. He compensated for that in part by misrepresenting me as a scientific whiz kid masquerading as a lieutenant. He quite correctly represented his technical director, Captain Levering Smith, as the finest scientist in uniform, which happened to be true but not well known as it turned out by most people because of Levering's very quiet, retiring way. Basically he lacked something, or at least he seemed to feel he did, and this need was ultimately filled, in my view, by PERT--Program Evaluation Review Technique (I believe this is what that acronym stands for)--a scheme to develop by a consultant for S.P. a scheme for systematically laying out a program plan, breaking it into its essential elements, introducing it into a computer program which would then produce and identify critical paths and help identify, by use of the computer, the progress along the way, limiting weak links you might say, in the plan showing what was dominating the program path and what were the most likely outcomes as far as time required where one might be able to shorten where one might be in trouble if the time were extended. It was really a sophisticated planning process but Raborn saw fit to represent this as a means for modern management by the use of the still somewhat mysterious electronic computer--that is mysterious to the general public. By much publicity and much tub thumping I think that Admiral Raborn was able to communicate an impression that we really weren't depending upon just a bunch of garden variety of naval officers and civil servants to run the navy program but rather we were doing it with the aid of sophisticated computer technology.

Q: Isn't that interesting; he did succeed because, I being a part of the general public, associated that this was the paramount thing with the project.

Adm. W.: Speaking from the vantage point of one who was working with the program I can tell you that as far as my part of the program was concerned, PERT had absolutely no input at all.

Q: It didn't really help at all?

Adm. W.: No, not at all, we made no use of it at all. Nevertheless we were constantly badgered by the people who were putting the PERT system together and trying to keep track of how things were going, for inputs--when are you going to start this and when will you complete that and how long will it take and so forth.

Q: And then PERT was concerned about those charts that you mentioned earlier? You would have been involved with PERT had you been relegated to that job.

Adm. W.: Exactly. In all fairness PERT is a splendid discipline, in my view, for forcing people to think a program all the way through from beginning to end. It is particularly useful in an R and D program, one in which one is proceeding in the face of considerable uncertainty, planning, identifying, critical paths, planning alternate routes around them in the event one gets into difficulties and so forth. But once the planning process is complete the value of PERT thereafter for actually managing a program is considerably less. It was represented not just as a planning tool but rather as a management tool, in that sense I think it was somewhat misleading.

Q: Was it not taken by industry also, in other areas?

Adm. W.: Yes, because as I said, it is a valuable technique properly used; I think it was represented as being more than it really was. But that is not to take away from it the fact that it was really something useful.

Q: Was it helpful to any of the scientific elements? Did it help any of the people involved immediately in the program?

Adm. W.: In my opinion, no. I think that PERT never told any of us who were really on top of the job, anything we didn't already know. It may very well have been useful to Admiral Raborn, it certainly was helpful to him in representing his program and presenting it. It is used even today in laying out program plans but virtually not at all in managing them.

Q: What about Pehrson as a person working in this area?

Adm. W.: Gordon Pehrson?

Q: Yes.

Adm. W.: Shall I be very frank? I think Gordon Pehrson also was very helpful in selling the program because he had a marvelous personality, a great deal of charisma, he could charm the socks off anyone; he was dynamic and had terrific charisma. I characterized him since as a tremendous first impression maker, but there wasn't an awful lot to follow it up in my opinion. He would give us all a pep talk and we would walk out of the room full of enthusiasm and then we would turn to one another and say, "Wait a minute, what did he say?" and no one could remember.

Q: An intangible impact?

Adm. W.: That's right. In my opinion, and this again reflects my own biases, I like to judge people for what they actually accomplish and to my way of thinking, in a program of the magnitude of POLARIS that takes time, it takes a great deal of time. Gordon, in my opinion, was superficial, people like Levering--the kind who stayed the course and saw it through from beginning to end--deserve every bit of praise and recognition for what was actually accomplished. POLARIS was done by people like Levering Smith, not by Gordon Pehrson.

I will pick up now and say a few more words about POLARIS, and the technical and programmatic aspect of it. The POLARIS A-3 front end, as I indicated earlier, was highly unconventional compared to the POLARIS A-1 and A-2 which used a single warhead even though that single warhead was in itself an unconventional design, it was an integrated design which permitted a much more efficient front end in terms of payload carried for the total weight involved. Nevertheless POLARIS A-3 was, with its multiple warheads, very unconventional but as I also indicated to you we were driven to that at least in part, by our very conservative view, toward the use of a nuclear warhead which might not have been testable under a nuclear test ban. By choosing the multiple warheads we were in fact selecting nuclear warheads which had been fully tested in their full yield.

Q: Had you explored in any sense your own reasoning for this, the background to it; were you influenced perhaps by the torpedo episode in WW2--the fact that the warheads hadn't actually been tested too thoroughly. Did this have any bearing on your feeling that you wouldn't like to embark on something that hadn't actually been tested?

Adm. W.: It probably did, now that you mention it, although it is hard for me to recall precisely all of the factors. There is one characteristic of any expendable ordnance, whether it is a torpedo or a bomb or a shell or a guided missile, if by expendable ordnance I mean ordnance which in order to be fully tested has to be destroyed--the item tested is destroyed in the process--one tends to become very conservative about departures from the test configuration in other words, everything one knows about the operational inventory had to be extrapolated from the test results of an item which was destroyed. All your confidence has to be based upon your ability to control the configuration and to be able to say to yourself that there is absolutely no change in what was tested and what I have in the inventory. That makes one very, very cautious of allowing any change which even remotely could affect the reliability of the device to creep into the system. So, in contrast with an airplane, let us say, that can be flown over and over again, or a guided missile of the sort like REGULUS which could be flown, landed and reflown, the POLARIS, and in particular the front end of the POLARIS like the part that carried the nuclear warhead, we tended to be extremely cautious about allowing any deviation or any departure from the configuration tested. So, yes that's a long answer to your question, the answer is yes we were influenced.

Q: It is interesting to observe that you had A-1 and A-2 before A-3 came along, but were they not necessary for this development although it wasn't entirely dependent upon them it was also dependent upon the treaty and all the rest. Is this what catapulted it?

Adm. W.: Nuclear warhead technology was moving very rapidly during this period and, as I indicated to you, the evolution of the smallest thermo-nuclear bomb went from the 1500 pounds which was the state of the art at the time that we got into it, to the 600 pound; going back even further as you will recall the first atomic bombs were 10,000 pounds but the 1500 pound weight that we were working with when we had the JUPITER program that the army and the airforce was dealing with in their TITAN and ICBMs was projected to go down to 600 pounds by Dr. Teller and that is what catapulted us into the POLARIS program. By the time we were ready for POLARIS A-3 we had available a tested nuclear device in 200 pounds weight--this was the device around which the multiple re-entry vehicle concept of POLARIS A-3 was conceived. POLARIS A-3 can be seen then as a combination of exploiting advancing nuclear technology which made the small warhead available, concern for an arms control environment which might not allow us to test a new version of that same design.

Q: That was indeed a driving force?

Adm. W.: It was a very major driving force. A longer range, less well identified concern for future anti-ballisitic systems, which made it attractive to provide multiple targets rather than having a single warhead that could be shot down perhaps with a single anti-ballistic missile; being able to multiply the magnitude of the job and thereby complicating the role of the defensive system designer, was a third concern--as I think I alluded to in an earlier conversation with you. Happily this particular design, this particular concept, reflected back into advantageous design options for the missile itself which Captain Levering Smith, at the time, welcomed. It allowed him to simplify the design of his thrust termination system for the POLARIS A-3, so all of those factors combined and what was seen as a very unconventional design approach in fact had elements of great conservatism in it.

Q: I assume from what you have said just a little while ago that there was no great change in the personnel, the scientific personnel who worked from the very early times on POLARIS, you mentioned the 20-year medal and so forth, most of the people stayed with it, there wasn't a great turnover?

Adm. W.: That was perhaps one of the greatest strengths and still is one of the greatest strengths of the navy's ballistic missile program--its continuity. We have been successful through the years in attracting and holding key people, not only in the program management headquarters itself but also in the industrial contractors that support the program.

Q: That's quite an achievement. What is the essential driving force that has made this so?

Adm. W.: When POLARIS began and a Special Projects office was created it was seen as just that--a Special Project. It was a special organization to do a special job, namely to carry out the highly accelerated development of a completely new concept.

Q: And it also implied a terminal date?

Adm. W.: It implied a beginning and it implied an end. The original intention was that when the system was successfully deployed at sea the development team would disband and presumably turn the job over to the regular bureaus and offices of the navy to manage as an ordinary, normal weapons system from that point forward. In fact, as that date approached, the terminal date, it became increasingly apparent that there really wasn't anyone that it could be turned over to.

Q: Was that the attitude on the outside also? Did BuOrd feel that way?

Adm. W.: I think you would find that that was a view that was shared generally within the navy, that this isn't really just another weapons system, it doesn't fit neatly into the navy's scheme of doing things. The bureaus and offices of the navy are not set up to handle this particular weapons system, the Fleet Ballistic Missile System as it was named really was unique. It needed to be separately cared for, from cradle to grave, and so the Special Project Office that was set up to develop it became ultimately the Strategic Systems Project Office with lifetime, cradle to grave responsibility for the system and its successive successor modernizations. While the first generation of POLARIS was indeed a completely radical new concept we were creating something new from nothing, every successive generation since has been an evolutionary improvement, both versions of the original system and it has built upon what we already had, it has incorporated lessons learned not only from the development of the predecessor systems but also their production and the operational experience in its support at sea, as well as improvements in the technology that have become available through the years since.

But, in order to apply lessons learned one needs to have the people who learned the lessons and that's where continuity comes in. The conventional wisdom says that the best way for the Department of Defense to acquire new systems is to decide what it wants, write it up in a request for a proposal, fire it out to the world at large, allow competitive American industry to come in with their best ideas, bargain for the best possible price much as one would go out and bargain for a new automobile between competing dealerships, and whoever finally comes in with the lowest number is the lucky winner. In fact the analogy is very poor. That is a very poor analogy to the successful management of the Fleet Ballistic Missile Program through the years. A program such as that has been successful and had a history of improvement and increasing effectiveness through the years because we have not thrown away what we have learned and the precious experience gained but rather have kept the team together. But at the same time we haven't allowed that team to grow, we haven't yielded to the temptation to build an empire or to expand and take on diversionary functions, which opportunities have been numerous through the years. There have been many, many opportunities.

Q: It is generally the way of the world to do that, but not necessarily the way of the navy.

Adm. W.: Not necessarily the way of the navy and here I must give credit to Admiral Smith primarily for resisting the temptation to take on additional functions which he, quite correctly in my view, recognized would be distracting and would tend to dilute the concentration on the primary mission of this organization and would perhaps ultimately cause it to become a threat to the navy's way of doing things, to the detriment of the national role, very unique national role that the navy was playing in providing a sea based deterrent system, that leg of the triad. So he resisted it and I resisted it when I was at the helm. The team still is small and many faces in that office are faces that have been there for many years and very importantly, the industrial support organizations, with few exceptions, are still the same ones that started the program.

Q: Now to get at that aspect of the continuity, dealing with individuals in terms of personnel in the organization, what has inspired the men there to remain and not be tempted to go out commercially and make an awful lot of money?

Adm. W.: I won't pretend that the complete ballistic missile system and the contracts that they have had with S.P. through the years have been anything but commercial successes from their viewpoint.

Q: That is in terms of industry but I mean in terms of personnel within the organization itself.

Adm. W.: Within S.P.? I can speak for myself of course. I feel that it is very difficult for one to spell out all of the things that go into creating a sense of satisfaction in a career. Certainly, I think I have discussed this with you earlier--the sense of doing something important, the sense of doing something that is appreciated by one's peers, of having overwhelming national importance and value, and even more than that--international significance.

Q: And that stands for survival.

Adm. W.: That's right. And, also being in an organization which allows you to be effective, to see the results of your own work. Let me create, for a moment, a picture of a stereotype of an individual working in a functional role within the navy or one of the navy's offices or bureaus--by that I mean he is performing a certain function but not for a particular project necessarily, but for many projects--just aeronautical engineering or logistics or something of the sort, he is repetitively doing the same sort of thing over, and over, and over, he does not necessarily have any personal identification with a product or with a project end objective. He is performing a function. That's the typical job. Within the project office, the Strategic Systems Project Office, formerly S.P. it is quite different. Every individual in the office, whether he is performing a function or anything else has a direct identification with the end objective, we are all focussed on that goal and the goal may be the development of a POLARIS, or a POSEIDON or a TRIDENT, its production in a timely manner to get to a particular, a certain series of shipyard commitments to get a ship to sea in a particular time or, once at sea, to maintain it and support it so that the weapons system is reliable and ready, etc. Any failure to meet these objectives by any individual within the organization will have an effect that will be promptly seen and measured, so, we were all committed and identified with the end product in a way that simply can't be matched by any organizational form other than the project organization. Now project organization is not the normal way of doing business, we have many projects in the navy as do the other services but very few, in fact it is hard for me to think of another project that is organized vertically the way SSPO is with cradle to grave responsibility, and with a full range of capabilities within the project office to accomplish the missions.

People tend to be happy in that environment I think, they tend to be fulfilled, they tend to be satisfied professionally and personally. They wake up one morning and suddenly realize they have been there ten years or even twenty years and enjoying themselves every minute.

Q: There is a hiatus in your biography. I assume that you left this particular job in 1960, did you not?

Adm. W.: We got the formal go-ahead for POLARIS A-3 in 1960.

Q: Did you remain with it for the next year before you went out to China Lake?

Adm. W.: Yes. I left for China Lake in July 1961.

Q: The year from 1960 to 1961 you still were occupied there with the Special Project.

Adm. W.: Yes, that last year of my first tour in Special Projects Office, during that year the GEORGE WASHINGTON was successfully used to test for launching the first POLARIS missiles, we burst upon the national scene in consciousness, all the papers were full of it, and the excitement and the trauma of sweating out those initial tests and seeing them successful, meeting our initial commitments to deploy the system much earlier than had been originally planned, all of that happened during that period. At the same time, as I have mentioned, we were planning for the next generation of POLARIS A-3 and I was very busily engaged in trying to win acceptance and approval for my scheme for the front end of the guided missile, with the full support of my bosses. I was carrying papers back and forth to the Pentagon and to the Atomic Energy Commission and to the staff of the Joint Chiefs of Staff and all the other actors in the drama who have to approve anything of that sort. After all we think of POLARIS and each of its generations since as being navy weapons systems but any system that carries a nuclear warhead is also an atomic weapon system and from the point of view of the law, which created the original Atomic Energy Commission and successive versions of those laws since and successive reorganizations since, any such program has to be a joint Department of Defense/

Atomic Energy Commission or successive agency, approve it and as such there are formalities one must go through--formally request the chairman of the AEC to make a joint development with the Department of Defense for such a system. I was spearheading those efforts, which were necessary, in order to gain approval for the next generation development.

Q: That must have taken you up on Capitol Hill as well, did it, and was the Joint Committee in existence at that time?

Adm. W.: It was but I did not make any Congressional appearances at that time, that was all handled at a higher level, it was done by people like Admiral Raborn who was really almost the single voice outside of the navy for the program.

Q: Did you have to really be terribly convincing with some of these elements or were some of them reluctant to accept the new ideas?

Adm. W.: Oh yes, there was a great deal of reluctance as there always is, to doing something that is radically different. That is proper, one should be reluctant to depart from a known and proven path to accept something radically new.

Q: Can you recall what kind of objections they raised and on what were they based?

Adm. W.: It is always just a little bit vague just to start characterizing some else's motivations. I can only talk about impressions that I had. There were some legitimate technical concerns, they were about whether the effects of three multiple re-entry vehicles delivered from a single missile, if it would in fact approximate a single much larger yield weapon, which of course was part of the proposition that I was advocating. There was technical concern about whether or not there would be mutual interference among the warheads, if one of them would detonate and somehow or other sanitize or defeat succeeding warheads, whether they would be far enough apart to avoid mutual interference.

Q: Is that a scientific point of view or a lay point of view?

Adm. W.: Those are scientific concerns, technical concerns, and one had to pursue those and satisfy one's self. One had to be satisfied that in fact the spacing of the bodies one from another would be adequate so that a hypothetical anti-ballistic system warhead detonating near one of them would not in fact affect the others. This item was a part of the scheme to space them far enough apart so that they couldn't be affected and would require three successful intercepts rather than just the one. There was technical concern about our ability to separate these warheads from the parent missile without ruining the accuracy of the system so that they would not be so far from the target--scattered so far from the target that they would be ineffective. Those were technical concerns. There were economic concerns about the cost of the three warheads whereas before we had had only one for each missile. There were political concerns about whether or not one could safely extrapolate without testing. As I indicated before that was not entirely a technical issue, there was some politics involved in that, the airforce had chosen to go the other way--to accept an extrapolation in their design for MINUTE MAN. There were other political concerns, I have mentioned that the army was desperately trying to get approval from members of the Joint Chiefs of Staff to go ahead with their own ballistic missile system called NIKI ZEUS and they were concerned about the navy's lack of support for that proposition and to have the naval officers show up on their steps after the navy had voted against them, the production of an American anti-ballistic system, to have another naval officer show up and say we would like you to support our proposition of designing the next generation of navy ballistic missile with anti-ballistic considerations very, very high on the list of concerns. They'd say that is inconsistent, you are talking out of both sides of your mouth at once, concerned about the Soviet's anti-ballistic system but unwilling to support the production of a US anti-ballistic system.

Q: Did the concerns also go beyond our own situation and think in terms of potential treaties with Russia?

Adm. W.: No, that wasn't really a concern at that time. The only involvement with Russia was the test ban and that was an unwritten agreement, one of these unilateral test moritoria which was not spelled out in any kind of a treaty.

Q: But a presidential sort of agreement, wasn't it?

Adm. W.: Yes it was a presidential decision to stop testing, the Soviets were to stop testing, it was sort of an expectation that as long as we didn't test they wouldn't test. In fact we later were straightened out in that regard when the Soviets resumed testing and resumed testing in a way that made it clear they had been planning to do so all along. They took advantage of our moratorium to catch up and we learned from that I trust. Nevertheless these were all conflicting elements that I was involved with in one way or another during my effort to convince the Office of Secretary of Defense and the Joint Chiefs of Staff and the Atomic Energy Commission staffers that our proposed approach for POLARIS A-3 was indeed the appropriate choice.

Q: In a personal sense it was a logical and a good development for you to have to go beyond your application to the project at hand and deal with the ramifications.

Adm. W.: It was a very important development in my education.

Q: That's what I mean.

Adm. W.: You see, up until that time everything I had been doing I had the sensation that I was doing it with the full support of the whole world; there wasn't a single person in this entire western world that wasn't behind me and was willing to accept what I was doing.

Q: That was a kind of scientific naivety, wasn't it?

Adm. W.: Indeed it was. For the first time I suddenly realized that it was necessary not only to decide on my own behalf what was the most sensible thing to do, but it was going to be necessary to convince others.

Q: Another thought occurs to me, may we go back--in talking about the continuity within the S.P. and the tradition that has been developed, you now have some knowledge of organizations elsewhere in the world, in the U.K. perhaps, and perhaps you have knowledge of what goes on in Russia; do they have the same kind of continuity in their development in this area?

Adm. W.: In the case of the U.K. their POLARIS system is a carbon copy of our own, as a matter of fact it is more than a carbon copy, we sell them the weapons system. They build their own submarines and they build the warheads to put on them but they are constrained to meet the same interface criteria that we meet in our own system and as far as the weapon system itself is concerned they buy it from us. The organization they have set up therefore, is not the same kind of development organization but it is a counterpart organization to our own. As a matter of fact that is spelled out in the POLARIS sales agreement between the US and the United Kingdon, that they will set up a Project Office.

So they have attempted to parallel it in that regard but it isn't really a good analogue because they haven't really developed a weapon system like our own but rather evolved one from us. In the case of the Soviet Union, I can't represent myself as an expert on the way they manage their research and development but the impression I have is that they do much more of this sort of thing, organized the way we do than the way we do here in the US. In the Soviet Union they tend to have design teams married to industrial support organizations--factories or plants--and they concentrate on working on one product line forever.

Q: The complete unit?

Adm. W.: Sure. You will find one team has worked on a class of missile systems, generation after generation after generation, they design it, they produce it, they support it, they move right on to the next version and do the same thing. They don't all go into production but the same team will stay together. They do more of that sort of thing than we do. Our Special Projects Office and its successor organization remained an anomaly within the navy but that would be much more typical a form for the Soviet organization.

Q: I suppose you can say in our case that it is voluntary on the part of the individuals involved, whereas in Russia it would not be voluntary; and there they are an elite group recognized as elite with all the privileges that go with that kind of thing.

Adm. W.: That's right, and as a matter of fact the difference between voluntary and involuntary assignment of people brings me back again to the subject of a nuclear test moratorium and other kinds of arms control agreements. What we must keep in mind I believe, in our case we choose to restrict ourselves on what we will do in the way of testing for instance, that will influence the caliber of people willing to stay and work in our nuclear laboratories on nuclear designs. Our scientists tend to lose interest in doing things that can't be tested so they tend to drift off and do other things. A nuclear test moratorium for a protracted period of time, in my view, would impact on our ability and capability of our nuclear laboratories. There is no such risk in the case of the Soviet Union, nobody is going to drift away from anything unless the Soviets want them to. In fact they can be required to stay put and be prepared for the next move in whatever their strategy might be. So there is this difference in a free society where people are free to choose what they do and one in which they are not. We have to keep that carefully in mind.

Q: Therein seems to be a weakness on our side.

Adm. W.: Of course it is a great strength on their side but its a weakness if we allow ourselves to be lulled into wishful thinking. We should be very realistic about what we agree and don't agree. I think we have learned, I really do think that the kinds of agreements that we are negotiating these days with the Soviet Union reflect a great deal more pragmatism and realism than they used to.

Q: Now we are about ready to go out to China Lake. You went out there in August of 1961 and became assistant head of Weapons Development in NOTS.

Adm. W.: Yes, in NOTS. That's right. I had decided that with POLARIS deployed successfully and POLARIS A-3, the second generation of the front end at least, approved to go ahead it was time for me to go do something else. I had spent five years in S.P. and it was time for me to go.

Q: Did you feel you had reached a plateau in S.P.?

Adm. W.: Oh yes.

Q: And there was a new missile coming on?

Adm. W.: I thought it was somebody else's turn and there was a very fine officer available who had a comparable kind of technical preparation, his name was Commander Alexander Julian, Jr. He was a year senior to me and had taken the same course at MIT as I had and he was an aeronautical engineer of great distinction and had a great deal of background in the weapons program--nuclear weapons program-- and when it was clear we could get him to take this job I felt it was a good time for me to move on to something else. I had just been selected for commander and I felt I was ready to take on new responsibilities. I felt what I would really like to do was to step out and take over a project of my own rather than continuing to work on a piece of the POLARIS. In going to China Lake, this was a decision that was made in part for me by the advice of people like Levering Smith who had spent many years of his own career at China Lake and he recognized NOTS as the premier navy laboratory, one which was unique in that it not only did the research and development but also had the test ranges to permit testing of the weapons that were being developed and it was loaded with some of the navy's top scientific and technical talent. After some conversation with the then technical director at China Lake, Dr. Bill Maclean (of SIDEWINDER fame), and he was very encouraging and appeared to be very anxious to have me; I agreed and it was so ordered.

When I arrived at China Lake, as I indicated, I felt that coming in as having demonstrated myself as a successful manager in a highly technical area that I would be greeted with open arms and promptly escorted to the most prestigious and difficult technical management job that the place had and would have the whole thing turned over to me amidst cheers, throwing of flowers into the air, with banners and the like; but in fact nothing like that happened at all. I was greeted warmly, given a very nice set of quarters for myself and my little family.

Q: Had you a second son by that time?

Adm. W.: Yes, our second boy was adopted in 1954, both of

our boys were adopted, so we had two young sons who were very much involved in school. The environment was perfect for raising a family, the community was a closed one, there was a fence around the place and everybody lived on the station.

Q: Was Admiral Thomas Connolly there at that time?

Adm. W.: No, that was after he was there. The senior technical military officer there was Admiral Carl O. Holmquist (a captain then who later went on to be Chief of Naval Research as rear-admiral). The living conditions and the ambience could not have been more pleasant, technically I think I was greeted with some reserve and that reflected the fact that the technical officers at a place like China Lake performed one of a couple of roles, one is that junior technical officers might very well come out there and get involved in projects as a regular staff member, more senior officers as I was by then (as commander) either were in an administrative function or flew airplanes for testing weapons or provided liaison with the operating forces. The laboratory itself was really run by a permanent civilian scientific and technical staff with these officers providing the glue that connected the place to the navy. I came in, obviously, looking for one of the kinds of jobs that the technical staff was there to perform. After sort of initially bruising myself by attempting to do what clearly was not in the cards for me to do, I backed away and realized that I was going to have to earn my spurs, I was going to have to win a place.

I couldn't expect to demand it by virtue of my own past accomplishments.

Q: As an outside observer I would say that was probably a lesson in humility, but you have a great deal of humility within your being anyway so you must have accepted it.

Adm. W.: I've got a great deal to be humble about, as we all do really. Yes, it was a lesson in humility, it was also a very important lesson. I think, as opposed to starting a program and being responsible for creating something from the front end, to march into a new organization that is mature is quite another matter and one needs to establish one's self, to win a place, and that takes time and a little bit of sensitivity (which I also had to acquire, or reacquire). I tried to do that and I did find an idea, one of several there, one that I thought was attractive. It was to take that SIDEWINDER, that you referred to earlier, and make of it a relatively inexpensive limited capability weapon for defending small ships or ground based units from relatively low-flying aircraft. The SIDEWINDER is designed as an air-to-air weapon to be launched from one aircraft at another. There was nothing to keep it from being launched from the ground or from a small ship and so there were people there--I can't maintain this was my idea--it was an idea that had been around for a while, to have the SIDEWINDER launched from the ground or a ship as an anti-aircraft weapon for defense units that otherwise might have no independent air defense of its own. I found several other civilian engineers there who wanted to work on this thing with me. I put together a small team with the approval of the weapons development department chief.

Q: Was he very pleased with this development?

Adm. W.: Oh sure, they were happy to see me interested enough in it to want to take it on. I put this team together and we tried to work out the capabilities, representing the capabilities and limitations it would have, to where there were central technical matters at issue. We attempted to design experiments that would raise those questions that would establish facts where there were none, data where there was none.

Q: This is what's called the CHAPARRAL?

Adm. W.: This is the CHAPARRAL. I gave it that name by the way and I think you would be interested in why.

Q: Yes I would.

Adm. W.: I felt that while the idea I was working on wasn't necessarily new, it had been considered and rejected for one reason or another before and if I was going to give it a fresh start it really needed a new name. The navy made its missiles typically after birds (not always, the SIDEWINDER wasn't a bird), a bird name wasn't particularly inappropriate but this particular bird was going to be a ground based bird and being a native New Mexican I decided that the Road Runner and the Spanish name for the Road Runner is Chaparral, so I said let's name it CHAPARRAL, that sounds exotic and it would come across as something new and it would also be somewhat descriptive. So that's what we did. I'll not bore you with the details--I failed utterly to convince the navy that they should put this system aboard.

Q: What major objections did they raise?

Adm. W.: The objections they had were, first of all the SIDEWINDER being an infra-red seeking missile would not be effective under certain weather conditions--fog or cloud cover or the like when one couldn't really see the target aircraft, also it would be most effective only when the aircraft was going away from you and you could see the hot tailpipe or hot engine parts and it wouldn't necessarily be as effective when launched against an aircraft that was attacking and head on to the ship. It was characterized as a limited capability system which of course it was but it was also very simple, and it was also going to be very reliable and one that would be certainly a great deal better than nothing which most of these small ships that we were concerned about had, at that point.

Q: The small ships you refer to were what?

Adm. W.: Mine layers, mine sweepers, auxiliary ships of one kind or another. From my viewpoint I thought of a large number of small ships on a particular operation, each equipped with some capability like this. A very simplified form not requiring radars or any other fire control installations, and this would be a considerable threat to an attacker who might otherwise feel free to come in and go after them or to go after other ships in the vicinity. The navy itself didn't buy it, but the army did. Ultimately the army equipped itself with the CHAPARRAL on land based weapons carriers.

Q: Such as tanks?

Adm. W.: I think they were mounted on track vehicles and the like--they were quite portable. The marines I believe also used it. It is still being produced, there are still items in the budget for CHAPARRAL, a large number of them were produced and used by the army.

Q: And the navy has never been tempted to change its decision.

Adm. W.: The navy always wanted something better, they wanted a radar capability rather than just infra-red capability which added complexity to the system and added cost to the system and at that point the reviewers and the critics were able to say, if we are going to spend that much on it, if it is going to get that complex there is something better that would cost us just a little bit more and we might as well go first class. As a consequence we have got nothing.

I was maintaining that having some capability if less than complete was certainly a great deal better than nothing.

Q: How far had you and your team gotten in the development of this?

Adm. W.: The development was relatively simple, it was mostly an application and a concept; we had conducted some critical tests, primarily target acquisition tests conducted out on the test range where we simulated the system on the back of a truck, took the system out into the desert and invited aircraft to come in and try to find us while we were trying to look for them. One of the issues was whether or not we could see them before they could see us and that sort of thing. We had done all that, we had prepared proposals, concept proposals which I had taken back here to Washington and presented to the Bureau of Ordnance.

Q: Who was head of the bureau?

Adm. W.: I think it was P. D. Stroop.

Q: It probably was, Freddie Withington had gone by then. He was so enthusiastic about SIDEWINDER that he had jumped up and down.

Adm. W.: Anyway, this was only one of several projects that I worked on. I had a couple of others as well but that was the principle one.

Q: What were the others?

Adm. W.: Well there another scheme but it was quite a bit more exotic, it had to do with the generation by an explosive charge of an electro-magnetic pulse; the scheme being that if one could generate an intense pulse of electro-magnetic energy comparable to a lightning strike you might think, if you did this by a combination of treating a very strong magnetic field which would be suddenly collapsed by an explosive charge and you could generate an intense pulse of electro-magnetic energy which could then be used to cause damage to electrical devices, sensitive electrical or electronic devices at some distance, or alternatively it could be used to generate an unique signal that could be heard and perhaps understood if it were coded in a certain way, at great distances. There were a number of possible utilities for this thing--code named TARANTULA, for no good reason, but here it was again a scheme that was a derivative of some of the things that were done in the design of atomic weapons and I had involved some of the people at Livermore Laboratory that I had known in the earlier POLARIS program, had gotten them interested in it as well, and we were trying to work together in China Lake and the Livermore Laboratories on that scheme, so that was going on. I was also involved in the committee that was working with the chief scientists of the old Special Projects office, thinking about future sea-based deterrent systems, they had a small team thinking ahead on this.

Q: You hadn't severed your connection actually?

Adm. W.: No I had not and I was very pleased and flattered that they wanted me to participate in that and so I attempted to do that on a part time basis. All of these things were going on and, as I said, in spite of the inauspicious beginning in my tour at China Lake, once I learned how to work within the system I found myself thoroughly enjoying my tour. But I can't begin to pretend it was anything like the challenge and excitement that went with POLARIS. I was feeling that I was doing something useful and I certainly was living in a pleasant environment and enjoying every minute of it.

Q: How far did this project go with the electric impulse that was the idea?

Adm. W.: Not very far, because we came into very serious technical problems with it. The problem was basically one of impedance matching to an antennae. I believe that that problem has since been solved although I haven't been close enough to that part of the world to say for sure. Schemes like this are being used today to generate energy that is used to create a power supply for intense pulses of laser energy, but at that time that was the key technical problem—how to couple a very low impedance source to a relatively higher impedance antennae efficiently. We were wrestling with that at the time we left. I was at China Lake for only a year. Had I stayed longer we might have done more.

Q: Is it related in any remote sense to the Communications System that the submariners have been working on--the underground thing for communicating with submarines throughout the world?

Adm. W.: Are you talking about the ELF (extra low frequency), yes and no; not anything like ELF per se although the signal that would have been generated by such a device would have been very, very low frequency and would penetrate sea water in the same way ELF does but it wouldn't be capable of carrying a coherent signal transmitting a message that way. What one would hope to do was make it by setting off several such explosions spaced in a certain way, it might be a code that would represent a pattern that would represent something rather than actually communicating a message directly which of course ELF is capable of doing. So there is a relationship but not very close.

I came away from China Lake with a much clearer impression of the role of the Navy Laboratories in general and that one in particular, especially in its very special capabilities that they provide to the navy, what they can do for the navy and how they could best be used. I could not have had this understanding any other way without having been there. I am a little bit sorry that the facts of my career prohibited my getting there while I was even younger and more junior when I think I might have been even more effective. Nevertheless I am grateful for that assignment and I think that

China Lake will always be a very special place to me. I think the navy laboratories, and China Lake in particular, can afford to do things that private industry cannot do for the navy. Private industry cannot tackle extremely high risk projects on their own, there would have to be some reasonable assurance of success I believe before any private industry would be willing to spend its own money on it or before it would be in a position to make a proposal to the Defense Department for funding.

Q: It is more closely related to its stockholders of course than is the federal government.

Adm. W.: It must be. There has to be a reasonable assurance that there is a good chance for a payoff. Through its laboratories the navy however, can undertake a certain number of very high risk projects, technically high risk I mean, and they can actually at a place like China Lake, conduct critical experiments; there is plenty of real estate there, facilities are there--shops where one can build almost anything and take it out on the range to test and see if it works or not, the talent--the breadth and depth of the talent there--is unique. So there is something very special that a navy laboratory can do, and in addition to that, the largest roles these days of the naval laboratories is to support the offices and bureaus of the navy in certain special ways. They tend to be funded directly by functional groups or project offices to do certain specific tasks.

Q: They are strictly navy, by that I mean they are not available to airforce or anybody else?

Adm. W.: Oh no, they are available to anyone who wants to fund them; they are industrial funded, many of them, that is they do what they get the money to do and they will accept tasks from anyone within the navy, or the airforce, NASA or the Department of Energy, occasionally they will do things for private contractors if they are interested in the things the contractor wants to test and he doesn't have a place to test. If he wants to use the government facility he can arrange for the use of the facilities. The prototype, the concept can be design built, tested, and proven entirely at China Lake before the navy needs to make a decision as to whether or not it wants to take the next step and fully develop the engineering for production. It is also capable of doing many, many other things. These are impressions I carried away with me from that place.

Of course I made friends and contacts there that have stood me in good stead for the rest of my career.

Q: They have too a continuing personnel.

Adm. W.: That's right, and by the way they have a continuing personnel turnover. A difficulty the navy laboratory has is in keeping good people. The government offers quite attractive entering salaries for engineers coming out of college, the work they can make available to them is extremely attractive.

Instead of being buried in the bowels of a company someplace in some laboratory, they are able to participate in a variety of things and move up rapidly; advancement is rapid within the government civil service up to a level of about GS-12, promotion opportunities beyond that level tend to become very restricted because there simply aren't very many openings beyond that and that is the point at which many of these young engineers choose to depart the government. That is a mixed blessing, it is bad because we lose a lot of people, but on the other hand it is good because we seed private industry on which the navy depends so much for its technical support with people who have had the right kind of education and training, and brought up by the navy. That is another role, less heralded but an important one, served by these laboratories.

Q: In your time there, was there any residue from the academia of WW2?

Adm. W.: I can't really say there was. Most of the big names had long since departed and gone back to other worlds by that time.

Q: Shall we now turn our attention to the Department of Defense?

Adm. W.: Yes, as I said I was uneasy about my role at China Lake, it was pleasant but I was impatient for responsibility and I could see it wasn't going to come very quickly. In the meantime, with President Kennedy's election and his movement of a new team into the Pentagon headed by Mr. McNamara and with other names like Mr. Hitch, Alain Anthoven, and Dr. Harold Brown. As I believe I had mentioned, Dr. Brown had been on our team from the very beginning and when he was looking around for people to staff his Director of Defense Research and Engineering he asked me to join him. In fact he had asked me while I was still at S.P. but at that time I said no, I wanted to leave Washington as I had been there long enough but after a year at China Lake I was ready to reconsider. So when I received a telephone call from Washington saying, "Are you ready to come back, we want you in the Office of the Secretary of Defense," this call came from that office from a naval officer whose name I do not recall, he was on duty there but had been asked by Dr. Brown to send for me, I said, "Yes, I'll come." That was 1962. We were told to get back as quickly as possible. I bid a quick farewell, jerked my kids out of school, threw them all in the back of the station wagon along with the dog and the whole family moved as quickly as we could back to Washington and I went to work in the new office of the Secretary of Defense. That was a cultural shock too, of a different kind.

Q: I imagine it was, and a contribution to your education.

Adm. W.: It really was. I told you about the humbling experience I had at China Lake, I had a different kind when I got to Washington. When I presented myself I was shown to my new office which was about the size of a very small hat rack somewhere; it had just barely enough room in it for a desk, a safe, and a chair.

Q: This was in the Pentagon?

Adm. W.: Yes, in the Pentagon, on the inner side of the E-ring. I searched out and ultimately found my civilian boss, Dr. Richard Montgomery who was the assistant director for Strategic Systems. I was replacing another naval officer who had retired and had departed before I arrived so I never met him but my position was military assistant to the assistant director for Strategic Systems and he in turn worked for Dr. Brown who was director of Defense Research and Engineering. I was going to be used in somewhat of a dual role. As a naval officer I was going to be asked to keep in touch with the navy for the office of the Secretary of Defense in my area of interest and also as an experienced engineer in Strategic Systems which was the role of that office. I was going to be asked to perform professional duties having nothing to do with the navy. In fact I found myself involved in many respects more with the airforce than with the navy. But when I first arrived and was given that tiny office I had some mixed emotions. I well recall the cultural shock I had when soon after I arrived my new boss asked me to undertake an analysis,--a relatively arcane subject--it was to attempt to quantify the potential merits of providing a commander in charge of launching missiles in a nuclear strike, with information about the success or failure of each missile as it proceeds through its powered flight phase. Missiles in those days were not as reliable as they have since become and there was concern that we would have to target more than one missile against a target to be sure of attacking it successfully, and if the launching commander knew that the missile had successfully gotten through guided flight and was in its ballistic trajectory then he would perhaps be able to more efficiently use his assets, he wouldn't need to launch a second strike; or, conversely, if he knew one had failed during powered flight he would know that he needed to launch a second one. So, then the job I was given was to attempt to quantify what merit and value this would have as a function of the reliability of the device that was reporting back to the commander and so forth. Anyway it was not a very complicated job nevertheless it was one that was important. I proceeded with this assignment--back to my little cubbyhole, looked around for the staff that was going to assist me in doing this. Obviously everything I had done up until that time I suddenly realized that I had done it with the help of a staff, whether I was in S.P. when I could call upon help from industry or other engineers in civil service, and when I was at China Lake there was a team of people I could call on--all of a sudden I realized that he meant, literally, me--there was nobody else in that little office and nobody else I could call on. I stared helplessly at my slide rule and my book of tables and I thought he really meant me, personally. I seriously considered suicide but looking out the window saw that the drop to the next floor wasn't all that much. Again I learned, as I had before, that you have to do some things yourself. I did it and it worked out all right. It again impressed on me how much we depend on other people if we are really going to do anything of consequence, but there are times when you have to do it yourself. Anyhow that was my introduction to the Pentagon and to my new staff position.

Q: What sort of send-off did Dr. Brown give you?

Adm. W.: I saw very little of Dr. Brown personally, during my tour of three years there. I went into his office on several occasions when it was appropriate that I communicate something directly to him but most of the time he was quite remote and I was dealing with people at lower levels. Of course my service contacts in the airforce and the navy helped. It was an interesting three years, a very exciting three years and I think we could fill up several reels of tape talking about all the things that went on during that time, but I don't think that appropriate. But to pick one or two, one of the first things that I was involved with was the decision to cancel a program called SKYBOLT. SKYBOLT you may or may not recall, was a scheme for mounting a ballistic missile on an airplane, a B-52 aircraft. It was a ballistic missile, it was air launched and it was being developed by the airforce but, significantly, it was also planned to be used by the

British on their bomber fleet. They had a fleet of bombers that they intended to maintain current and capable into the future by giving it this capability of launching SKYBOLT. SKYBOLT was a technically ambitious project, challenging, complex, and costly. In due course the decision was made within the Office of Secretary of Defense for reasons which were represented primarily as being based on technical difficulties. In fact I have to say that it was also based perhaps even more significantly on the fact that we could no longer justify it economically for our own purposes. However it was on technical grounds that the decision was announced that this project be cancelled. This came as a tremendous jolt to our British friends because this was their central....... the heart of their plans for modernizing their nuclear capability.

Q: How long had it been going along?

Adm. W.: It was in testing, it was about in the same point of development that POLARIS A-3 was at that time. It was actually in flight test and it was failing flight test, just as POLARIS A-3 was failing at that stage, but nobody was talking about cancelling POLARIS A-3. There was no question but that it would survive and be made to work and that was that but if you are not sure you really need something then the technical difficulties become insuperable--that was the case for SKYBOLT. In reflecting the US sensitivity to the British concern at their loss of this system, President Kennedy was going to meet with Prime Minister Harold MacMillan of Great Britain in Nassau shortly following that decision. One of the items on the agenda, not the only one but a key one as far as we were concerned, (our office) was a discussion of alternatives that he was going to offer the British, one of which was POLARIS. One of the jobs that I was given was to help my boss in preparing background papers for the president to take with him to Nassau on the POLARIS option. We stayed up all night one night working on these papers attempting to describe the POLARIS system, what it would cost the British, what the strategic implications might be, what the scope of such a program might be. I guess that went into the president's briefcase and in due course that was the choice the British made--to replace SKYBOLT with POLARIS.

Q: Quite a change wasn't it--from the sky to the sea?

Adm. W.: Yes, and there were bitter internal political battles I am sure, not only in our government but also in the British government. As between the Royal Airforce and the Royal Navy, in effect what this said was that for the British, who could afford only one means of weapons delivery, nuclear weapons delivery, as opposed to the TRIAD of the US, this meant that the key role for nuclear weapons delivery was shifting from the Royal Airforce to the Royal Navy for the long term future as indeed it has. It was greeted with mixed emotions by the Royal Airforce.

Q: Yes indeed. They had become the paramount one as a result of their experience in WW2.

Adm. W.: The details of the POLARIS sales agreement which spelled out exactly how this agreement was to be administered that is between the two countries, were worked out in the months following but not by the Office of the Secretary of Defense, it was turned over to the Navy and the State Department and their counterparts in the U.K. to be worked out. By then Admiral Raborn had left and Admiral Gallatin was heading Special Projects Office so he and Admiral Smith and others on the US side, people in the International Security Affairs office in the Pentagon and the State Department, the lawyers and accountants and so forth were working with their British counterparts in a series of meetings to put together what ultimately became the U.S./U.K. Sales Agreement. That was formally signed I believe in 1963.

Q: There had to be some change in the AEC set-up, had there not?

Adm. W.: No, I think the Atomic Energy Commission was still in place at that time--the Atomic Energy Act was still in place. The agreement was that the British would build their own atomic warhead. Now there was a separate agreement between the US and the UK for cooperation on atomic affairs, called the 1954 Agreement on Cooperation. That was an entirely different channel of cooperation and within that channel the US and the UK worked on helping the UK develop a warhead.

So there was that channel for cooperation, as well as the POLARIS agreement itself, for the remainder of the system.

Q: Do you know if there was any temptation on the part of the British government or the RAF to pursue research on SKYBOLT on their own?

Adm. W.: That was an option that was given them, to allow them to continue the project on their own. I don't think that was an attractive option because, instead of sharing the costs in a relatively minor way with the US they would then have had to bear the entire costs and that obviously was not attractive.

Q: No, they were in very bad financial shape.

Adm. W.: Also, they would have been bearing all the risks and this would have been done in the face of the US decision on its own behalf, to cancel the program because it was too difficult, so it wouldn't be a very auspicious beginning for any project.

Q: Besides they had the temptation of the submarine and the POLARIS.

Adm. W.: Also, they appreciated that the nuclear powered submarine, ballistic missile carrying submarine, was really the premier weapons system, especially for them, a nation that could afford only a small force, to have one whose pre-launch security and survivability was so much better than any aircraft could possibly have or any land based system could possibly have. I think that even today if you asked most Americans even airforce officers, if we had to give up all but one leg of our triad, which one would you keep; they would all say POLARIS or the fleet ballistic missile system. Certainly that is the conclusion that the British reached and they have, as recently as this past year, ratified that decision when they decided to modernize their force with TRIDENT as opposed to going with something else like the cruise missiles or some other alternative.

I dwelt on the POLARIS sales agreement because that began a relationship between Special Projects Office and the United Kingdom which continues to this day and has served not only the UK well, I believe, but it has been a factor in so many of the relationships with what I think most people would agree, is our staunchest ally over the years, and also has cemented relationships in many respects between our two navies and has given us a common project on which to concentrate. I think that the warmth of the relationship and the intimacy of that relationship has been substantially increased by virtue of this program over the years.

Other things that were going on during those three years that I was on the staff, that may be of some interest: There was a great deal of concern during that period for anti-ballistic missiles. It was a major concern, the US was developing its ABM systems, the Soviets were shocking the world by illustrating that they were very far along.

Q: That really was the source of the concern, wasn't it?

Adm. W.: You bet. It was certainly the major driver in the arms race because it meant that whatever one had in the way of ballistic missile capability it might not be adequate if some unknown numbers of those weapons were going to be shot out of the sky and what would you do about that? One thing you would do was buy a lot more of them, another thing one does is spend a great deal more on research and development to work on devices to defeat ballistic missile defenses, but it became a big driving force behind new defense expenditures. Mainly it was a threat to the deterrent--our ability to deter an enemy who might believe rightly or wrongly, that he had the capability of blunting a retaliatory strike--this was intolerable, we couldn't live with that so we, in the Office of Strategic Systems--in Offensive Systems in the Pentagon--were very concerned about getting projects started in both the airforce and the navy aimed at assuring ability to penetrate Soviet ballistic missile defenses. In the airforce we started a thing called the Advance Ballistic Missile Re-entry Program, which was working on technology, penetration devices, decoys, jammers and that sort of thing; the physics of re-entry looking for ways of defeating an enemy that might be attempting to make certain it could identify the warhead coming in, from all the rest of things that might be accompanying it, shooting at it, ways of becoming less visible, less identifiable, ways of coming in more quickly, ways of confusing or otherwise defeating the critical elements of the defensive system. In the navy we urged navy to propose ways of improving POLARIS, capitalizing on the capability that we had built into POLARIS A-3 specifically, also POLARIS A-2 to a lesser degree but primarily POLARIS A-3, to defeat enemy defenses. The three warheads was certainly a step in the right direction but we were concerned it wouldn't be adequate; you would have to be able to draw more than three intercepters for each missile, if one was to defeat a proliferated anti-ballistic system so the navy came up (under urgings from the Secretary of Defense office) with proposals for removing one of the warheads and replacing it with penetration devices of one kind or another and modifying the remaining two warheads to make them still more difficult targets and we called this entire system, that was to go on the front of a POLARIS A-3 the ANTELOPE system. I mention this because ANTELOPE was an exploitation of a capability that we had provided for in the design concept of POLARIS. It became clear to some of us right from the start that this game of defense, offence, counter defense, and other counter measures, is almost unending and that the only sure way of penetrating a defensive system whose characteristics are largely unknown to you or unknowable to you, would be by providing more targets than the defense can handle and making certain that the targets are indistinguishable from one another, that in effect each decoy carries a nuclear warhead. If one could provide more targets than the other side had defensive missiles and each target is real and therefore could not be distinguished from any other, each could be accurately placed on its target, then and only then could one be certain of penetrating, so the concept of what we now call MIRV emerged. The navy's proposal was to build a big missile that would fill up all the volume within the submarine launch mechanism--to fill up that entire space that I told you had originally been reserved for putting a capsule around the missile and later found not necessary for that purpose, then was used for shock protection but still more than needed, that volume was available to let the missile grow in size.

Q: What is that area in the submarine termed?

Adm. W.: It is the mount tube, that's what we call that section--the launcher. But we could carry a bigger launcher and allow the missile diameter to grow from something like 54 inches to 64 or 65 inches in diameter and the weight of the missile could virtually double. At first approximation we could double the amount of payload that could be carried to a given range and with the progress that had been made in the warhead end--nuclear warheads very much smaller in size and weight were now becoming available from the atomic laboratories. There was a big controversy going on within the navy about how one would exploit this greater payload capacity. There was a strong contingent within the office of the Chief of Naval Operations in particular which said rather than going for many small warheads that might be the way to go if we were interested primarily in assuring defense penetration, what the navy should do would be to have a few very large warheads on this big missile and therefore compete effectively with the airforce for the ability to attack very hard targets--Soviet ballistic missile silos for instance--military targets. Without great accuracy, which the submarine missiles did not have, the only way to assure that you could kill a hard military target was to overwhelm it with explosive power. So, there were those in the office of the CNO who were strong advocates of big bangs, and of course you couldn't carry very many of those so the growth to them was let's go to one or two, or at the most three, very large warheads.

Q: Were they also the advocates of the big carrier?

Adm. W.: Probably, quite probably yes. There was a natural tendency to feel that there was a competition between the navy and the airforce--anything the airforce was able to do the navy ought to be able to do--if it was carrying big bombs that meant big carriers, if it was carrying big warheads on their missiles that meant that's what we should do with that growth volume that was available in the POLARIS submarine--build a big missile so we could put a big warhead on it. That wasn't the way we saw it in the office of the Secretary of Defense, we saw that big, extra payload carrying capacity as primarily a way of assuring deterents in the face of proliferated and undefinable, technically undefinable, future Soviet ballistic missile defense schemes. They constantly surprised us, they kept coming up with new things that they would test and our own scientists kept postulating other things that they might do and we could have no way of knowing what they were doing, that would constantly defeat any cute tricks that we might invent for penetrating defenses.

Q: It must have been very frustrating time?

Adm. W.: It really was. In the end the navy actually proposed a scheme for carrying a few large warheads on a big missile and it was turned down by the office of the Secretary of Defense, the office in which I was a staff member. Then and only then did Levering Smith have an opportunity to come forward with another proposal and it was called POLARIS B-3 and this was multiple warheads.

Q: Not yet the POSEIDON?

Adm. W.: Not yet, it was POLARIS B-3, multiple warheads. Dr. Brown, in conversations with Levering Smith, urged that the system be given greater accuracy so that the smaller warheads could become competitive with larger ones as far as their effectiveness was concerned. He felt that Mr. McNamara would not approve any new system that did not have some improvement in accuracy in the submarine based systems; he also urged that warhead configuration use the maximum possible number of warheads on each missile. So this was the scheme that was called POLARIS B-3 and I woke up one morning, I remember very well, reading in the newspaper that the president had just announced his approval for a new project called POSEIDON. I had never heard the word before but it turned out that POSEIDON was the name that had been given to POLARIS B-3 and it was renamed POSEIDON for political reasons. The political reasons were that the administration was being heavily criticized for not having started anything new. As I recall from my days at China Lake, whether you call it CHAPARRAL or POSEIDON there is some value in taking an old idea and giving it a new name.

Q: What was the date of this pronouncement?

Adm. W.: This was in 1965.

Q: So this was Johnson?

Adm. W.: It was President Johnson who had inherited the mantle from Kennedy but was being criticized for never having started anything of his own. Kennedy was criticized as well for not having started anything.

So, it had doubled the accuracy of the POLARIS, it had doubled the payload of POLARIS, it had a front end specifically configured to assure penetration of yet to be defined and designed ballistic missile defenses. That payload was made modular and flexible in the sense that we could remove warheads from it if one wished in order to increase the range of the missile. By decreasing the weight up in the front end one could give it a little more range and therefore the system would have more flexibility to respond to changes in the threat to the submarine itself by giving it more operating area.

Q: Was ALPS in existence then? The automatic launching business--automatic loading positioning system.

Adm. W.: I am not familiar with that. What you are referring to is the technique for loading missiles into a submarine.

Q: Yes.

Adm. W.: Yes, that was basically a part of the front, original POLARIS system and it has continued to be used for the POSEIDON and TRIDENT as well, as part of the launching and handling system.

The reason I am going into such detail about the flexibility of the front end of POSEIDON is that in order to do all of these things--give it the modular capability of being able to respond either to a change in the anti-submarine warfare or the anti-ballistic missile threat of the future, and to provide accuracy that was missing in the earlier versions of POLARIS--was that it meant each warhead had to be capable of being separately released, separately guided, to a target, and lo and behold this was given the name by someone, not us, as MIRV--multiple independently targeted re-entry vehicles. It became a symbol of things evil by those who were fighting to cap the arms race. They were those who proposed that the right way of constraining the next generation of arms was to never test them so there was great pressure being brought on the administration, later on (I am now jumping ahead in my story), not to test the system. If we didn't test it obviously no one would use it and then we wouldn't have this re-escalation. Of course that was a lot of wishful thinking because MIRVs on land based systems, on an ICBM which is capable of being targeted by another ICBM, then is potentially de-stabilizing because it means if you launch your ICBM first you might be capable of knocking out more than one of his ICBMs with each one of yours. Therefore there is a tremendous incentive to launch first and therefore it is de-stabilizing. But multiple re-entry vehicles on submarine based missiles do not pose that kind of a threat at all because submarine ballistic missiles are not used to attack other submarines and without enough accuracy to threaten the other side's land-based systems they are not threats to them either. So they are no more than they are represented to be, a means of assuring a continued deterrent, the ability to retaliate with competence in spite of whatever the other side might do, whether it is anti-submarine warfare or anti-ballistic missile systems. Nevertheless the navy with its POSEIDON system got swept into the same bag with the airforce and we were labeled MIRVs as if it were some kind of a singular beast with a morality all its own. So that's another story. However, all of these things were going on during that three-year period while I was in DDR and E.

Another thing that was going on while I was in DDR and E was that I was growing a little older and as the end of my three-year tour approached, which was 1965, it was also my twentieth anniversary as a naval officer. I was graduated as you will recall, in 1945. So, I had a big decision to make, it was time to decide whether or not to retire, take advantage of the navy's generous twenty-year retirement option, or to stay on. The temptation to leave was overwhelming because in the office of the Secretary of Defense as well as in my earlier tour in S.P. I made all kinds of contacts in government and in industry and, rightly or wrongly, people had the idea that I would be interested.

Q: They were reaching out?

Adm. W.: Sure, there was plenty of time to start a new career, so I was considering that. I didn't really see any options or alternatives that were very attractive to me in the navy. I was an engineering officer, the career opportunities for people in my category, particularly for ordnance engineers which was a very small community, were quite limited so I was tempted to think about leaving.

Q: You still had your active contact with Levering Smith however?

Adm. W.: Yes, I did and I recall going over to see Levering

and discussing this with him in 1965. I had always sort of thought of Levering as my father confessor, the officer within that community in whose judgment I put the greatest trust and value, he was thoughtful, considerate, and a tremendously accomplished person. I discussed it with him and after some thought he told me a couple of things, one that Admiral Gallatin would be leaving in 1965 and that he, Levering, was going to move up to take over as director; and secondly that as a consequence of the general shifting of people within the office and from that the head of the missile branch would be open and available and he said, "You have been instrumental in conceiving this thing that we now call POSEIDON, how would you like to come over and take charge of managing the development?"

Q: That was a decisive question.

Adm. W.: It was that. All of a sudden I was being offered the opportunity to do what I had always lusted after doing ever since I had had a taste of the program as director of the warhead re-entry vehicle development, to take over the entire missile and I would be coming up for selection to captain very shortly. So the choice was get out then and make a new career in industry capitalizing on reputation and contacts as they existed then, or stay in the navy family and in particular continue a career that I had so enjoyed up to that point. I didn't really have to think very hard about that.

Q: Were you aided and abetted by your wife?

Adm. W.: Sure. Barbara has always taken a singularly uncomplicated view of things. She says she just doesn't want to live with somebody who isn't excited about his work and interested in what he is doing. So whatever I wanted to do was going to be fine with her, within reason. We had a nice comfortable home, the kids were in school here. I never thought I was going to become a permanent Washington resident but we learned to become one. Most of all, I think Barbara must have sensed what was really the fact and that was there was nothing in the world I wanted to do as much as that job. So in 1965 I came back and relieved my friend Alex Julian who had relieved me some four years earlier when I left for China Lake. He in the meantime had moved up in the office and had succeeded to the head of the missile branch and I relieved him as head of the missile branch. He went across the river and relieved me in the office of the Secretary of Defense.

Q: A little game of musical chairs. Do you want to go back to those three years in the Department of Defense and say something more about it? Did you get involved in the inevitable studies and so forth that were always desired and demanded?

Adm. W.: Sure. That was the biggest product of the place-- paper and studies. The function of that office wasn't really one of designing or inventing but rather one of weighing and evaluating alternative proposals and concepts which were competing for all the scarce resources.

Q: That's more in keeping with the concept of the Department of Defense, isn't it?

Adm. W.: Yes, that's its proper role I think. But in that period, under McNamara, the office of the Secretary of Defense was a very powerful institution--much more powerful than it had been before or it has been since. It had more to say about how the military dollars were going to be spent than ever before. The services chafed under this, there was a great deal of unhappiness on the part of the airforce, navy and army about these young whipper-snappers and the whiz-kids in the office of the Secretary of Defense who were imposing their computer mentality over the experience and judgment of older, wiser heads. This intellectual conceit or whatever, of the OSD staff reflected in part the style of Mr. McNamara himself who, in his dealings with Congress, managed to irritate an awful lot of people.

Q: But you were able to meet them on the same level, intellectual level and this made a difference didn't it? Didn't this wipe out your stripes and make them not so significant any longer?

Adm. W.: Yes it did, of course people over in that arena at OSD there was very little concern for a person's rank in fact most people weren't even aware of it. We worked exclusively in civilian clothes in a civilian office, for civilian bosses and whatever stature we had was more the consequence of our ability to persuade others or to function in that environment as an individual rather than by virtue of any number of stripes or bars.

Q: I would imagine that many of the studies that were inaugurated and developed had real value especially if they were used to determine a course of action. Did they all do this?

Adm. W.: It is generally conceded now that McNamara and in general, his systems analyst chief Alain Enthoven, Ter Hitch, his controller, came in with impression that modern systems analysis permitted quantifying all strategic and military issues; all of the problems the Defense Department had could be quantified and choices could be made on the basis of hard, computer print outs, and that military judgment as such was considerably less important than had been represented in the past. You might say this conceit irritated an awful lot of people, it irritated the services, it irritated members of Congress, many of whom had been in those positions in the Congress for many years and had had insight and knowledge and understanding of military programs and needs far beyond anything that these youngsters could possibly have. The reason I am dwelling upon this is because when finally the time came for a new administration and Mr. McNamara departed the scene, the reaction was in fact, over-reaction.

The pendulum, as is characteristic of pendulums everywhere, swung too far in the other direction in rejecting McNamars'a excessive dependence on systems analysis--we went so far as to throw out the baby along with the bathwater.

Q: Some of the personnel remained however, did they not?

Adm. W.: Not many. Most of the key people left.

Q: One of the large factors I think, might be the idea of the package concept of a project?

Adm. W.: Yes. And that leads me into a relatively important subject that was important to S.P. and to the navy. I was caught up in the middle of it when I came over and took that new job in S.P., I came from OSD, and that was a total package procurement scheme. One of the things that Mr. McNamara maintained could be improved in defense procurement was the idea of requiring competitive private industry to bid for the whole job and then to assume the responsibility for the entire job--by that I mean if a new weapon was desired the contractors winning the contract would be hired to develop it, to produce it, and to deliver it as a total package-- sort of like a turn-key operation.

Q: In contrast to a fragmentary approach?

Adm. W.: In contrast to much heavy involvement on the part of the government in the process of developing, in effect the sharing or partnership procedure wherein the two worked hand-in-glove, which is I am sure you realize, precisely the way the navy had operated on POLARIS and could never have gotten there any other way; but this was being attributed by some as the source of cost over-runs, excessive development times, other kinds of disappointments in programs—this was being attributed to excessive government involvement; too many changes being invoked by the government—if one would only turn the entire job over to private industry they would go ahead and do it right and to get the best possible price for it one would negotiate a contract that was a fixed price contract and once that was settled the contractor would simply be required to deliver the end product and bear any losses that were entailed but that was his look-out, that was a business man's risk when he makes a bid. That was the environment in 1965; that was the environment in which the now famous, or infamous, C-5-A contract was negotiated. I think later on this became a cause célèbre, Mr. Proxmire made a great deal of it and many others have too, for good reason, the program was full of disappointments and ended up costing a great deal more than anybody expected it to, Lockheed almost went under over it, and certainly the airforce got considerably less than it had bargained for but it was done strictly in accordance with the Total Package Procurement Rules as they then existed. That was exactly the same time period when POSEIDON was to be undertaken, so we in the navy were faced with the job of coming up with a mechanism for somehow or other giving at least lip service and hopefully more than that to the new procurement rules without losing the things that we considered to be absolutely essential to the success of our way of doing things.

Q: What an incredibly difficult situation, riding two horses.

Adm. W.: It was incredibly difficult. How were we going to be able to use the contractor family that we had so carefully built up and trained and educated and who were responsible for the existing fleet ballistic missile system that was operating, its logistic support, its engineering support and we were now going to modernize it with the next improvement of that system, which itself was not a completely new system, it was in many respects merely an iterative improvement in certain things. The missile was new, there were other parts of it that were just improved versions of the same thing to go into the same submarines, and so forth, using the same logistic support organization. We ultimately were able to persuade the people in the office of the Secretary of Defense, by then I was no longer there, I was in S.P. but I knew them all over there having just left; we persuaded them that we would take the largest piece of the new system, the new missile--the motors for propulsion system--and compete them, break them out and carry on a competition for them as opposed to simply awarding to the motor manufacturers who had been responsible for POLARIS. We did this for a variety of reasons. We felt, first of all, we could accept the risk that went with that as long as we still had the missile prime contractor responsible for those motors, the missile prime contractor being Lockheed and responsible for the management of the competition and ultimately for the sub-contracting to the winner of that competition, that we the navy could hold Lockheed responsible even though the motors themselves had been awarded on a competitive basis. To get in the notion of total package procurement we invented a contract form that we gave a name--Operational Systems Development Contract--it was in fact a contract which covered the entire engineering development and initial production phase of the new system. Unlike previous contracts for POLARIS, it was not a cost-plus fixed fee level of effort kind of contract but rather a completion type incentive contract wherein the contractor's fees or profit was going to be determined on the basis of quantified (measureable in other words) performance, against schedule, objectives, missile range and accuracy and so forth, his performance against cost objectives, not only cost of development but also cost in production, all of these things were carefully spelled out in advance, agreed to, and defined in such a way that the contractor could make his trade-off decisions in such a way as to have the best possible outcome for him simultaneously knowing that it was also optimizing the results from the point of view of the navy.

Q: They had to keep within the parameters?

Adm. W.: Yes, keep within the parameters and to recognize the fact that no development program is without surprises and without unknowns; we knew that we were going to run across unplanned and unexpected problems, we couldn't tell the contractor in advance how to make his decisions but we wanted to define the contract in such a way that we would make his interests and the interests of the government coincident, we did not want to be adversaries under any circumstance we wanted to be partners as we had been in the past. Of course we also insisted upon and had the flexibility to change the contract at any time and in any way we saw fit.

Q: But he couldn't?

Adm. W.: He could ask for a change but he couldn't invoke one. By this means, drawing up a much more definitive contract with specified objectives in it, priorities spelled out in the terms of the incentives, the arrangements in the contract, by breaking out a portion of the program to be competitively awarded, we were able to convince the office of the Secretary of Defense that we were meeting the intent of the Total Package Procurement scheme while at the same time preserving what was most important to us in what we had demonstrated was a successful acquisition program.

Q: They did see that point?

Adm. W.: They saw it and accepted it, to their credit. Ultimately, when POSEIDON development program was completed successfully, the program was finished within a few per cent of its original cost goals and met most of its performance objectives, exceeded others.

Q: This was an innovative sort of thing in terms of the McNamara thesis, was it pursued in other directions afterward?

Adm. W.: After much unhappiness and many reservations about it, we fell in love with it in S.P. and convinced ourselves that in fact it had a lot of merit--that Operational Systems Development program concept of contracting in multiple incentive form to carefully identify all of the trade-off and the priorities ahead of time which was advantageous not only to the government but also to the participating contractors. It took a lot more work at the front end of the program to define it that well but it was time well spent. We convinced ourselves that really, given our choice in the future, that is the way we would prefer to work and in fact we did.

Q: Was Defense happy with that variant too?

Adm. W.: Well, Defense has a short attention span, once an issue has been resolved they go on to other things and until that issue is re-raised by Congressional interest or by some other means; if the service comes crying back asking for more money or more time or permission to be released from certain obligations or commitments earlier made, baring things like that, generally speaking they lose interest in it.

So POSEIDON quietly went on its way and was in fact a highly successful program.

Q: Going back to our launching pad here, the studies that were inaugurated in those days in great numbers, it is often said that some of them were after the fact. Did you find that in any case to be true?

Adm. W.: Surely. A case in point was that SKYBOLT cancellation they decided because we didn't want the SKYBOLT any more we were going to have to cancel it, but you can't just cancel it for that reason because the very logical question could be raised--if you didn't want it any more why the hell didn't you recognize that a year ago and we could have saved a lot more money. It was therefore necessary to invoke something else and so, after the fact, technical difficulties were invoked. But I also pointed out that there were no more technical difficulties in POLARIS A-3 and nobody for a moment suggested that it be cancelled; those were considered to be challanges, not problems. Another example, the TFX, the very famous joint service airplane, the arguments, the analyses that supported a common airplane for both airforce and the navy as opposed to allowing each to proceed on its separate way. I can't help but believe that a lot of that was hokey, it wasn't really objectively done. The decision was made ahead of time, Mr. McNamara wanted it that way and his staff knew to put together the analyses necessary to support his prejudgment. It happened from time to time.

Wertheim #3 - 237

Q: You must have another illustration or two.

Adm. W.: No others really come quickly to mind during those years.

Q: Most of the things you were doing there in those three years?

Adm. W.: Yes, most of the things were interesting and maybe even fascinating to a very limited community of scientific and technical experts dealing with exotic vulnerabilities that ballistic missiles might have, things that might somehow threaten the confidence that one could have in them. After all what we were doing in effect was basing our national survival on the confidence that our national leaders and the national leaders of other nuclear powers had in the certainty that these weapons could be delivered if they were ever called upon. Anything that suggested a threat to that confidence, however obscure, was something we had to deal with very directly and with a great deal of energy. People were constantly inventing things, when I say people I am talking about the scientific academic community but in particular the very highly specialized technical community that was privileged to have access to highly classified information, people who were members of scientific advisory committees of one kind or another. This was particularly true of the airforce's scientific advisory committee.

Q: A kind of brainstorming they were engaged in?

Adm. W.: Possibly. Any threat, any suggestion that wasn't completely understandable was a threat. For instance, one could postulate that there would be some obscure nuclear effect which was not fully appreciated that would scramble the brains of a missile in the first few minutes of powered flight before it released its warheads and would cause it to fail; it wasn't enough to prove that effect was there, one had to do the opposite, one had to prove that it wasn't there and proving a negative is very, very much more difficult. If you couldn't prove that it wasn't there then you had to come up with a scheme for defeating it whether or not it really existed.

Q: You were getting all sorts of imaginary potentials then?

Adm. W.: Yes, and many of these things were untestable, unprovable. As I said, there was a group of people and we sometimes referred to them as the West Coast Mafia, or the wise old owls on the tree limb who sat there and went "Who, Who, Who, What, What, What, and How, How, How," and they made it almost a profession to suggest problems that were difficult to deal with but these things had to be dealt with because once suggested and left unanswered they became a basis for doubt and doubt was our great enemy.

I well recall one meeting of this Airforce Scientific Advisory Committee and I was present as a member of the office of Secretary of Defense and presentations were being made by representatives of the airforce and the navy involved in the designs of these missiles and they were describing the technical approaches that were being taken to deal with one of these exotic threats that had been admitted by members of that committee earlier. It was very expensive business responding to this, it called for a very specific re-design of certain elements of the weapons system--costly retro-fitting and so forth. The presentation was being made by Dr. Burnett of the TRW Company who was the project leader for MINUTEMAN. While he was presenting his story about how they were designing MINUTEMAN to overcome this hypothetical problem, one of the members of the committee I noticed, was busily working as fast as he could and paying no attention to the speaker at all while working on the back of an envelope; every now and then he would nudge his fellow member on the other side of him and point to something he had written on the envelope, they would argue vigorously and he would go back do some more work, some more calculations, paying no attention to the speaker. Finally he finished his calculations raised his hand in the middle of a sentence, interrupted the speaker and said, "Pardon me Dr. Burnett but have you thought about thus and such?" and he then presented the idea he had been working on. The answer of course was "No." After all it had just been invented on the spot and Dr. Latter (he had been doing all these calculations) said, "Oh, that's very worrisome." I couldn't stand it and I said, "Dr. Latter if that is so very worrisome to you, why is it that you look so happy?"

Q: It occurs to me when you are talking about the scientific field, the missiles and so forth, you have here the use by the scientific community, of experience, of previous concepts and their use, you have this built up and this runs contrary to the attitude that has been relayed to me at least, in the Department of Defense at that time, the complete denial of experience in terms of the military, so how do these two jibe? Was it simply because it was scientific, was it accepted by the bright young men?

Adm. W.: You have to realize that this was a very exotic area and a very specialized area that I was involved with. Nobody in the military or elsewhere could maintain that they had experience with the use of ballistic missiles because they had never been used and hopefully never will be--these big strategic weapons systems. They were designed to be launched in extremis and into an environment of other nuclear weapons being burst with mysterious effects which were quite untestable and couldn't be demonstrably shown to exist or not to exist, possibly in the face of enemy defenses which again could not be tested realistically; so no one could maintain that he had experience--operational experience. We could say we were experienced in the development of such weapons.

Q: Development and production.

Adm. W.: And maybe even in their operational deployment,

and support and maintenance but nobody was a user in the classical sense,--unlike tactical systems and general purpose weapons systems.

Q: I see the distinction certainly, the one is almost sacrosanct.

Adm. W.: One of them was ideal, the strategic systems were and still are almost ideal for the ideal environment for a technical dilettante to come and muck around and to indulge his fancies. As I said we are constantly faced with having to disprove the postulate rather than the opposite.

Interview No. 4 with Rear-admiral Robert H. Wertheim

Place: At his residence in Annandale, Virginia

Date: Tuesday, 27 January, 1981

Subject: Biography

By: John T. Mason, Jr.

Q: As a continuation of your discussion last time, when you went to the Department of Defense in defense research and engineering, in September 1962, a major event was developing very rapidly in the Carribean and that was the Cuban missile crisis. The Russians by their efforts in Cuba were apparently making a determined effort to change the strategic balance of atomic power in the world. That I suppose has been ascribed to their motives in rapidly building up the Cuban situation from July of that year, on. What impact did it have on your cubicle?

Adm. W.: Since the business that I was in and continued to be in was that of weapon system acquisition rather than operational employment the developing crisis situation such as the Cuban missile crisis had no immediate bearing on our acquisition policies per se.

Q: No, but on your thinking.

Adm. W.: It certainly had a huge impact on the whole field of strategic weaponry of which I was a part. It is hard to ascribe motives to anyone else and in particular to an inscrutable foe such as the Soviet Union and Mr. Khruschev but it appears to me, and I presume this is a view shared by others, that he was attempting to move missiles secretly into Cuba to gain a strategic advantage over the United States on the cheap. In other words, without actually developing and deploying large numbers of highly capable weapons on his own capable of reaching the United States from the Soviet Union.

Q: He didn't have those.

Adm. W.: Then he didn't have those so he brought these short range weapons into Cuba.

Q: They were the MRBMs?

Adm. W.: That's right, and he was caught with his hand in the cookie jar and in a showdown with President Kennedy he came off second best and went home with his tail between his legs, which was a short-term, highly significant victory for the United States.

Q: Short-term reaction however, on his part wasn't it?

Adm. W.: It was indeed. There are students of history who

say that his defeat in that confrontation ultimately was a major contributor to his being displaced in the Kremlin. That may or may not be so but certainly a lesson was learned by the Soviets in that exercise and if one applies the normal lead time that is necessary for the research, the development, the production and deployment of a new system, if one takes new systems that ultimately appeared in the Soviet inventory of long range missile systems, strategic weapons, delivery systems and that goes back in time--the amount of time we believe it takes from the point a decision is made until a new system can be deployed--one can be led to the conclusion that the decisions to make those acquisitions had to have been made some time in the immediate aftermath of that Cuban crisis. One can infer, this strictly by circumstantial evidence, that the Soviets made a determined decision shortly after the Cuban missile crisis and presumably profiting from that experience, to make a massive build up of their strategic weapons and that over time that this is in fact what we have been seeing. They have continued that and have pursued it with dogged determination and overtime; they have overtaken the United States and it is well known and frequently reported in the press and elsewhere that by most measures, but not all, the Soviets have overtaken and surpassed us in these areas today.

Q: Now look at the other side of the coin, were there any direct results of this incident in our own camp? Did it set in motion any new ideas that were brought to fruition?

Adm. W.: In my little world it is difficult for me to identify any new strategic weapon developments that were specifically related to the Cuban missile crisis. There were certainly determined decisions to continue the developments that we had under way at the time but I can't identify anything specific that we did in our office differently because of the Cuban missile crisis.

Q: They had those KUMAR missile launching boats down there — did we retaliate with anything in that area?

Adm. W.: Again, not strategically. The KUMARs are tactical really, short range surface-to-surface missiles, so the answer has to be no, in my limited view.

Q: Another area I wanted to ask about was the development of satellites. Did they concern you?

Adm. W.: There is a very close relationship between space applications and the strategic world because satellites can perform many functions that are critical to the strategic capability of a country. For instance, for communications, for navigation, and very importantly for early warning and intelligence gathering. Satellites were being developed and exploited for all of these purposes during the period but again that was being done by a different office from the one I was in. The only space program with which I was directly connected and concerned was the navy's navigational satellite program, the so-called TRANSIT program. TRANSIT is an idea that was developed by the Applied Physics Laboratory of the Johns Hopkins University, when certain scientists at that laboratory in observing SPUTNIK, the first Soviet satellite which was the first earth satellite of any kind that was successfully launched (since they beat us to the punch) noted a distinct Doppler shift in the tone being transmitted by that satellite and that Doppler shift led them to believe that tracking the satellite would be possible by use of that information. In other words, the rate of change in the tone of the satellite could be related to the velocity relative to the observer on the earth and from a known location on the earth one could determine the orbit that the satellite had to be in--quite precisely this way. Then, in a flash of insight these scientists realized that the reverse could also be true if one knew the orbit of the satellite quite accurately, then the observation of the Doppler signals from an unknown location on the earth could locate the observer and that becomes a very precise way of navigating. It was seen very quickly that this could have tremendous importance to the submarine ballistic missile fleet, the missile carrying submarines. Not only would it give a precise location to the submarine, it would allow the submarine to locate itself without transmission on its own part. It would require only a brief exposure of an antenna not transmitting any radio signals or the like nor would any lengthy solar observations or celestial observations be required. It would be a world wide system, in other words, the satellite in an appropriate orbit, a polar orbit going from pole to pole would over a period of time, several times in the course of a day, pass over every spot on earth so that, presumably, a ship or submarine located any place on earth could at some time during the day, even with only one satellite up, locate itself very, very precisely if it knew what the satellite's ephemeris was.

Q: It certainly was a tremendous improvement on the direction finder of WW2 wasn't it?

Adm. W.: Since the whole concept hinged very heavily on the ability of the submarine to locate itself precisely, as well as to know the direction north and the direction to the target and that sort of thing, but it was very unlike a fixed system on earth which could be surveyed in with great precision, a submarine at sea or a ship at sea carrying a missile system is constantly changing its position so being able to locate itself with great precision is tremendously important. Of course one had to locate one's self continuously not just periodically and that is where Dr. Draper's development of the Ship Inertial Navigation System was so important but even SINS (ship inertial navigation system) being a mechanical instrument will, over time, drift and needs to be reset just like a very precise clock and it must be periodically set or it will drift away. In effect, Dr. Draper's SINS became the clock and the TRANSIT navigation system became the precise resetting mechanism and the two together gave the submarines a precision locating system. TRANSIT was very important and its development by the Applied Physics Laboratory was critical to the fleet ballistic missile program.

I can go on if you would be interested in an interesting side issue that developed.

Q: I would indeed.

Adm. W.: TRANSIT was well accepted and well recognized but for some reason or another was not being adequately funded at this particular moment while I was military assistant in the Department of Defense.

Q: And the funding would come through that department?

Adm. W.: Correct. The Department of Defense was not making funds available which were necessary in order to fully support the system.

Q: Lack of appreciation?

Adm. W.: No, that's what I thought and of course I worried about that, but what was actually happening was that in the eyes of a senior official in the office of the Secretary of Defense, whose name was Dr. Eugene Fubini, principle deputy to Dr. Harold Brown who was then Director of Defense Research and Engineering; Dr. Fubini was convinced the navy was trying to use TRANSIT for something more than merely navigating fleet ballistic missile submarines but rather to use it as an entre for itself into the space business. In other words, a decision had been made by the Department of Defense earlier on that the roles and missions of the three services would be divided up and that the role of space activities was to be given to the airforce; yet here was this navy space project which was well justified for its purpose but nevertheless was, at least in Dr. Fubini's mind being exploited or prostituted by the navy to be the genesis or the germ from which a full-blown navy space program would evolve.

Q: Why not talk a subject like that out once you have that question?

Adm. W.: There is some reason to believe that he was right, that the Bureau of Aeronautics where the development of this particular system resided, did have a space office and did have people in there who felt that the navy had a legitimate role in space and they didn't necessarily subscribe to the arbitrary division of roles and missions, giving space development to the airforce.

When I finally perceived that this was what was going on I approached Levering Smith, who at that time was still the technical director in the S.P. office and asked him if he would be willing to take on the responsibility of managing the TRANSIT program if I could get it moved from the Bureau of Aeronautics into the S.P. office. He said he would.

Q: You were undertaking a big job weren't you?

Adm. W.: Yes. Well then I went back and approached Dr. Fubini and asked him about how he would feel about making funds available for completing the activation of the TRANSIT system if that management change were made and he immediately agreed. It was clear that this was the breakthrough that he was looking for.

Q: What insight you demonstrated.

Adm. W.: I don't know whether it was insight or not, I thought it was a lucky stroke because I then promptly wrote a paper that released the funds to the navy and directed that the program be managed from the Special Projects office. In those days the office of the Secretary of Defense under Mr. McNamara had a great deal more authority than they do today. That was that. There were a few noses bent out of shape in the Bureau of Aeronautics but apart from that things went swimmingly and the TRANSIT system which we called the navy navigational satellite system, from that day forward, has been considered a part of the fleet ballistic system navigational sub-system; so the navigation system includes a space program. This is a long answer to an earlier question you asked.

Q: What relation did your outfit have with WESSEG?

Adm. W.: WESSEG--weapons system evaluation group--probably the office of the Secretary of Defense and specifically the director of Defense Research and Engineering assigned as much work to WESSEG as did the office of the Joint Chiefs of Staff. Those two organizations placed tasks on the director of WESSEG who in turn used the Institute for Defense Analyses (IDA) as their contract agency for helping them perform their analyses. Probably the most significant thing that WESSEG did while I was in the office of Secretary of Defense was to settle upon a rationale and logic for sizing up annual missile tests samples. In other words, in order to assess the readiness, the reliability and the accuracy of the operational ballistic missile inventory one must conduct tests. As I have mentioned, these tests are destructive tests, they destroy the articles tested, they are very costly but they are very essential because that is the only way that one really has of testing a complete system. The question arises then as to how many of these tests are necessary in order to establish a good statistical basis for confidence in the planning factors that are to be used by the joint targeting staff in Omaha and how often does one need to re-test having established confidence this year, do we still have it next year and the year after that, if not, how many more tests must we conduct next year, and so on. This rationale and the careful balance between desire to establish a statistical basis for confidence on the one hand and to avoid unnecessary expenditure in conducting very costly missile tests on the other was the problem given to WESSEG which they worked out during my stay there.

Q: In April of 1963 we lost the USS THRESHER. Did that have any impact? There was a deep submergence review group set up with the idea of developing something to attempt to meet a need in case of another disaster.

Adm. W.: There was a major review conducted within the navy on the whole subject of submarine safety and deep submergence. It had a couple of impacts on the program, the fleet ballistic missile program. Here again I was more of an observer than a direct participant. One effect that it had was the institution of the so-called SubSafe--Submarine Safety Program--which was a major upgrading of the level of safety in the critical piping systems, in hull systems of the nuclear submarine force and that affected the ballistic missile submarine program by increasing the workload necessary to complete an overhaul or to complete the new construction of a ship. This had an effect on schedules.

Q: It tightened things up considerably.

Adm. W.: It did indeed. That program is still in place. Another thing that came out of it was the so-called Deep Submergence Program. This program was not directly related in any way to safety, it concerned safety in that part of it was to develop capability of rescuing crews that were trapped at deep depths in the submarine in a future disaster--God forbid!, but development of a rescue vehicle capable of removing the crew safely from a submarine at considerable depths was part of that program, but only part of it.

Q: Did it go way beyond that?

Adm. W.: It went way beyond that. The recovery of objects at much greater depths and other things that are too classified to discuss. That program needed to have a project team to manage it. The Special Projects office was approached to find out if they would be willing to take this on even though it had nothing directly to do with the fleet ballistic missile program, and Admiral Smith agreed to do that. He has explained to me his rationale in accepting that task at the time, as one being that the office was short on work to do at that particular moment in history. The POLARIS A-3 program was essentially behind it, at least as far as research and development aspects were concerned; POSEIDON had not yet been fully conceived and development started so there was a hiatus, a valley, between the levels of activity that had preceded it and were yet to come in research and development. Admiral Smith saw this task as being one which could help fill that valley by involving many of his engineers in the office, keeping them gainfully employed, you might say, and technically engaged until the next weapons system development came along.

Q: Again a very incisive point of view, wasn't it?

Adm. W.: Indeed. He turned over the management of that

particular project to his chief scientist, Dr. John Craven, and it was run that way until the POSEIDON program actually got under way at which point S.P. promptly spun that effort off and it became a separate project and Dr. Craven took with him several of the engineers from S.P. and for a time he was the project manager for the Deep Submergence program in the navy, here in Washington. Ultimately he turned the job over to someone else and went off to Hawaii. The project was removed from S.P. when it had served its purpose as far as S.P. was concerned and it had filled the workload gap.

Q: In September of 1963 the Senate voted to ratify the US, British, Soviet Treaty banning nuclear tests except under ground. This was a confirmation of something that had begun before. What effect did it have on your particular efforts?

Adm. W.: As you said, this was more a ratification.

Q: This made it very legal, from our point of view.

Adm. W.: Since underground testing was still permitted it did permit the continuation of nuclear warhead technology development with testing restricted to underground testing. It did stop the investigation of some of the more exotic phenomena that one could postulate that could only be demonstrated by an atmospheric or an exo-atmospheric nuclear test. So some of the postulated threats to the survivability of missiles and communication systems and the like, some of these things that were postulated by our scientific community couldn't be directly proved or disproved.

Q: Were they shelved?

Adm. W.: They simply became concerns that were not readily dispensed with and we were quite frequently pushed into doing some very conservative things in the designs of our new systems to make certain that we were safe against these phenomena.

Q: Did this lead to a sense of frustration?

Adm. W.: What it really led to was spending more money. There is a popular misconception that by stopping nuclear testing or restricting nuclear testing one is capping the arms race by some means. It has been my observation more often than not the effect of restricting nuclear testing is to force the developers into doing things in a less than optimum manner--if we can't do the obvious thing then we will find some alternative way of doing it which, generally speaking is less optimum and therefore, in general, less efficient and more costly.

Q: Then what is the purpose of the treaty?

Adm. W.: The purpose of the treaty has to be found somewhere else other than in the argument given.

Q: Is it psychological?

Adm. W.: The atmospheric testing was adding radioactivity

and radioactive fallout into the environment and that certainly has stopped. As it turns out it stopped others from testing in the atmosphere from time to time but one cannot argue that the testing of a nuclear weapon by India or by France or by South Africa, which is a very rare event but nevertheless it happened, adds anything like the amount of radioactive material into the atmosphere that the much more vigorous test programs that the Soviet Union and the United States would have had they been going on in the atmosphere. There is one reason for doing it, for banning it, but I think we should look at these things with realistic perspective and not credit these limited arms control measures with more than they deserve.

Q: But that isn't necessarily the kind of information that is made public at the time a treaty is under debate or under consideration, is it?

Adm. W.: You don't see that very often. Generally speaking you see extremists on both sides. You will see an extremist shouting that one must stop all nuclear testing if we are going to achieve our ultimate goal of eliminating all nuclear weapons, which is totally unrealistic, in my view. It is not realistic and not even desirable because it is my belief that the existence of nuclear weapons is the only thing that has prevented a third world war. On the other hand you will find the extreme hawks shouting that any kind of arms control measure is a nefarious scheme aimed at subverting the legitimate national interests of this country in achieving military domination over our enemies. That also is totally unrealistic I don't think that in this world that kind of domination could exist, nor would it necessarily be desirable.

Q: SUBROC came into to being too in 1963--not came into being but tests had been made and apparently it was a successful thing. Was that within your purview?

Adm. W.: No it wasn't really, I was aware of SUBROC because it was referred to by many people as sort of a miniature POLARIS in that it was launched from under water, from a torpedo tube that travelled to the surface and flew some distance before it dropped back into the ocean and became a torpedo, and it was a nuclear weapon, so in many respects it had similarities to POLARIS but our office was not directly concerned with SUBROC.

Q: Were you concerned in any remote way with the A-3 POLARIS test missile from the OBSERVATION ISLAND, the eject launch system? This was in September of 1963 apparently?

Adm. W.: The OBSERVATION ISLAND was a missile test ship that was developed along with COMPASS ISLAND--these are surface ships--so-called EAGs. They were developed, designed and built for our fleet ballistic program early on, COMPASS ISLAND for navigation testing and OBSERVATION ISLAND for weapons system testing, including the launching of missiles at sea from a surface ship. Several generations of weapons systems were tested, not just POLARIS A-3 but also earlier versions of POLARIS as well, from OBSERVATION ISLAND. I am not sure I am familiar with the specific test to which you refer but we had POLARIS A-1, A-2 and A-3 tested from OBSERVATION ISLAND.

Q: It was labelled the eject launch system of steam instead of compressed air.

Adm. W.: Oh, I see, yes, what that is referring to is the development of an improved launching system. The original POLARIS launcher was one which literally used compressed air, or compressed nitrogen, carried in bottles in the submarine and they literally blew the missile out. Later on a much more compact and efficient design was developed which combined what amounted to a solid propellant, a small solid propellant rocket used to eject the missile. The rocket motor exhausted into a chamber where it was mixed with water in a controlled manner so that the result was a mixture of gas and steam and this gaseous mixture was what actually ejected the missile and it was called a steam eject system. I think the question you refer to was the first test of that system which was done on that ship.

Q: Then there was another mention of a missile, work on which was discontinued--the TYPHON missile?

Adm. W.: That I am not familiar with. I do recall the name and I can't recall whether it was a surface-to-surface or a surface-to-air missile. In any case I wasn't involved.

Q: No you weren't involved in it, I just wondered why it was discontinued.

Adm. W.: So often these things are discontinued when we find that we simply can't afford to do everything we could imagine doing.

Q: One other thing, what was the prevailing thought in the Department of Defense on the round-the-world trip of the ENTERPRISE, the SAVANNAH and the BAINBRIDGE--atomic powered ships?

Adm. W.: I really am not your best witness for that.

Q: The skipper, Smoke Strean, took it around and Smoke felt he was left out on a limb because Admiral Ricketts was the one who really backed this project and then he died and everybody turned against it. Strean was enroute and he had to deal with the problems as a result.

Adm. W.: I think there is one thing I could say and that is these events you refer to all have to do with the application of nuclear propulsion to surface ships which was, and remains, somewhat controversial. With few notable exceptions, and rather rare exceptions, you don't hear much controversy about the appropriateness of the application of nuclear propulsion of submarines. There just isn't anything that competes with that in a sensible way. It gives a submarine a capability that simply doesn't exist otherwise. There is no simple cost-effective measure for arguing that it would be better to have a diesel powered submarine except in certain very limited applications--coastal work or the like.

Q: It is firmly implanted in the doctrine of the country isn't it?

Adm. W.: For world-wide ocean operations nuclear power makes a submarine in fact a true submersible, a submersible that needs only to surface when necessary to change crews or to re-provision for logistic purposes. Without nuclear power, and this has been observed before by others, a submarine is really a surface ship that is capable of submerging for short periods of time, rather than the other way around. So it makes a major difference for a submarine to have nuclear propulsion where with a surface ship it is more of an economic argument.

Q: I added some of these items.

Adm. W.: Many of which I couldn't really respond to.

Q: In my mind at least they round out the picture of your years in the Department of Defense. There were probably others that haven't come to the surface.

Adm. W.: In many of these areas I was just an observer, I was there when a lot of these things happened but I was not a principle actor.

Q: So now, do we go back to S.P.?

Adm. W.: All right.

Q: This was in August of 1965.

Adm. W.: As I have said, I accepted Admiral Smith's invitation to rejoin Special Projects Office and to manage, as the head of the Missile Branch, the ongoing POLARIS improvement program that was aimed at adding ballistic missile penetration capabilities to the POLARIS A-3.

Q: As a footnote we might say that it preserved your talents for the navy for the time being.

Adm. W.: It also kept me very happily engaged in work that I would rather do than almost anything else. It also gave me the job of carrying out the development of POSEIDON. The POSEIDON, as I also said earlier, had a front end payload on it that was given the name MIRV because it consisted of multiple warheads each of which was capable of being separately targeted by a guidance system. At that time there was a great deal of concern about such capabilities--MIRVs--by the Arms Control Community because, in theory at least, it gave a single missile the ability to threaten the survivability of several other missiles, at least missiles that were land based and capable of being targeted. So, in theory it might tempt one nuclear nation to pre-empt and attack another nation and therefore become somewhat destabilizing; the implication was that he who hit first would have a huge advantage in catching the other side with his missiles and bombers on the ground. This was, at least in theory, true for land based missiles because land based missiles were themselves vulnerable to other land based missiles and he who launched first had the advantage, at least in theory.

Q: That's an argument that continues anyway.

Adm. W.: It continues to this day, witness the arguments for MX to this very moment.

Q: It is applied in different areas; I read something about the weakness of the economic situation in Russia, that it would be a temptation to launch first.

Adm. W.: Certainly the whole name of the game in the arms control business is to make the nuclear confrontation, if you will, between the great powers stable rather than unstable--to discourage initiating nuclear attack rather than to provide incentives to do it.

MIRVs on land based missiles were seen to be destabilizing and still are. It wasn't at all clear that MIRV missile systems in ballistic missile carrying submarines was destabilizing nevertheless it tended to be swept in under the same acronym and locked in with the land based systems.

Q: Has this ever been discussed within the treaty discussions?

Adm. W.: Of course I haven't been part of the treaty discussions.

Q: No, but you have obviously followed the points made.

Adm. W.: I think both the Soviets and ourselves and negotiators fully appreciate the very significant differences between the land based systems and the sea based systems, as far as their survivability is concerned and their inherent stability, so I think the answer has to be yes. As is so often the case, sometimes our worst enemy is not the Soviet Union but ourselves. Pogo said it very well when he said, "We have met the enemy and they are us." I am referring to the criticism that was coming largely from our own people here in the United States who are very concerned about MIRVs, at least these concerns weren't being espressed publicly by the Soviets particularly. They, I am sure, complained about them so long as it appeared we had a lead but once they had achieved that capability for themselves they ceased complaining. The reason I mention it in conjunction with POSEIDON is because POSEIDON had such a design but the warheads on POSEIDON were very small in yield, in explosive power, and the accuracy of the system was not great so the combination of a relatively small warhead and relatively poor accuracy meant that these systems did not really threaten the survival of land based missiles buried in hardened shelters. In order to make such a system really threatening one would have to go away from the many small warheads and go to a few large warheads to get much more explosive power in each one, or, alternatively greatly increase the accuracy.

The approach that was being followed under the direction

of the office of the Secretary of Defense at that time, in the early days of the POSEIDON development, was to have an alternate payload configuration which consisted of three very large warheads that would replace the fourteen very small warheads that was the principle configuration for that front end. These three very much larger warheads would give the system the capability of attacking with some probability of success against three separate, hardened military targets. About this time, early in the POSEIDON development program, it was brought to our attention in the Special Projects office that there was a new scheme for ballistic missile guidance which combined the pure inertial system that we had been using on POLARIS in its several generations and on POSEIDON, planned for POSEIDON, combining that inertial system with a stellar feature, in other words giving the system the capability of taking a star sight once it was out of the atmosphere and that this single stellar system would greatly increase the accuracy of the system. It compensated in large measure for the uncertainty in the launch location of the submarine itself and some of the other pre-launch, pre-flight errors; so we started a program of development of such a guidance system that could have been used to go into POSEIDON as an improvement to its guidance system. At least in theory it appeared that with the improvement in accuracy that would be possible by this means, one could achieve the same capability against hardened targets with the small warheads that the large warhead payload was intended to provide, and in fact it gave us the excuse for terminating the development of the large warheads for POSEIDON which was a very desirable thing because that was going to be quite costly and it was going to be a great complication to our logistics. What I am saying is, we saw a way of having a single front end for POSEIDON, a single development for the front end which could do all things for all people. The trouble with this was it appeared that our submarine based ballistic missile systems were going to be afflicted with the same disease, at least from the view of the 'doves'--those who concerned themselves with arms control matters--that already affected the land based systems and so there was a great outcry from certain people in the Congress and elsewhere about this development. Not too much longer after this point where we had terminated the development of the large warhead and shifted to the development of a highly accurate guidance system, in response to some pressure from the then Senator Brook from Massachusetts, Secretary Laird agreed to cancel the development of the improved guidance system.

Q: A casual observation is that this was rather slow in coming, was it not--the star guidance system for a navy set-up?

Adm. W.: It might have seemed a natural thing for the navy to want to do and we pushed on with it as quickly as it was technologically feasible. It was a very sophisticated thing you know, having a missile take a sight on a star and then use the information to update the data that had been provided it before it was launched.

Q: I was thinking of the star sighting as an age-old technique of the navy.

Adm. W.: And it is a perfectly natural thing for the navy to be interested in doing once technology permitted it. I have gone into this lengthy discussion to make two points, one, that the technique of stellar sighting which we pioneered for missile guidance systems on POSEIDON and was dropped for POSEIDON, it was dropped because it would have made POSEIDON too accurate for the time--the political environment of the time.

Q: This is a commentary too--that it had to depend on political approval.

Adm. W.: That's right and this was a technology that was politically unacceptable at that moment. On the other hand we had done enough work on it to demonstrate to ourselves that it was indeed feasible and could be done and it was ready for exploitation when a different need arose later on and that later need was the TRIDENT system. Some years later when propulsion technology allowed us to extend the range of these missiles from intermediate ranges to ICBM ranges, from submarine missiles instead of being 1000 miles or 2000 miles in range it became possible to have 4000 or 5000 mile range missiles. Now a small error at the launch site becomes a large error at the impact point and the stellar system was available then because we had worked on the technology earlier to help us solve the problem of maintaining the accuracy at very much greater missile ranges.

Q: So all was not lost?

Adm. W.: All was not lost, indeed, all was saved. It was the only solution that was really practical and fortunately it had been proven feasible in the POSEIDON program.

By about 1968 the POSEIDON program had proceeded to the point that it was ready for flight testing. We commenced flight testing of the system at that time and it was clear with the start of flight testing that the, until then, undemonstrated MIRV concept for providing assured penetration of ballistic missile defenses the idea of having separate warheads that could be spaced to avoid interceptors so that each would have to be successively intercepted, was a viable technique. The improvement program for POLARIS A-3 that I described earlier (the one that added penetration aids and the like) that we had code-named Project ANTELOPE became unnecessary and the program, having completed its development, was never put into production. Not because it failed but simply because it was overtaken by a superior system.

Q: Tell me, when you have the testing of these developments do you have problems with unofficial observers, Russian observers, trawlers--that kind of thing?

Adm. W.: I think the answer in general is yes, but perhaps not what you are thinking. We have trouble because they tend to get in the way sometimes. They are intensely interested and they follow too closely.

Q: You don't care?

Adm. W.: Well we don't want them to get in the way and be a nuisance, we certainly don't want them to interfere with the conduct of the tests.

Q: Are you concerned about them learning too much through the tests?

Adm. W.: Some people are but I'm not. The reason for that is the business we are involved with is deterrence and deterrence has to be based upon absolute confidence on the part, not only of the national leadership, but also the leadership of your opponent--that you are capable of doing what you are threatening to do. Unless he believes it then deterrence is not on solid ground.

Q: You are almost willing that he should know.

Adm. W.: The only things we wouldn't want him to know obviously, would be a key piece of information that he might be able to exploit to somehow or other defeat the system, or cause it to be ineffective, to cause it to fail.

Q: You can always be certain his efforts will be bent in that direction.

Adm. W.: Surely, but it is in the nature of the strategic missile system that they don't have many features that are subject to external interference. They are not guided missiles that are being steered by radar so that jamming the radar frequency could cause the missile to go out of control; they don't depend upon external signals that can be interferred with. They are self-contained ballistic missiles and in this sense are very much like bullets that are fired out of a gun. Once they leave the gun barrel there is not a whole heck of a lot one can do about it except to shoot the bullet down in its flight, or to so configure the target that it can't be found--you hide it or armor it so heavily that it couldn't be penetrated. This is a poor analogy but to some extent all of these techniques are involved in ballistic missile defense business. Anti-ballistic missiles attempt to shoot other bullets down with bullets. Some of the techniques for moving missiles about and hiding them--that you have heard about in the MX debate--are aimed at doing just these things. As far as learning something about your offensive system which would permit the other side to defeat it by observing flight tests, there is very little of that kind of information that one can get. What one can learn is that the system works and that it works well and reliably and we are very happy to have the other side know that.

Q: They are not so happy to have you know what they do.

Adm. W.: I don't know what makes them happy.

Q: Does this mean then that you felt for the moment your labors had ceased and you could go off to business school?

Adm. W.: That indeed is what I did do in 1968. I did take advantage of an opportunity to go for a few weeks to the Harvard Business School.

Q: How did this happen; what was the motivation? Was this career planning on the part of Levering Smith or what?

Adm. W.: No, Levering didn't particularly push this. In the Special Projects office we had a career planning board aimed not just at naval officers but at all of the people. As a matter of fact since 20% or less of the people in that office were military we spent more time doing the career planning for the civilian engineers and managers than for the military. But at that time we were sending one person a year to this Harvard Business School course and I don't know who it was but somebody suggested that maybe I would like to go. At that point I had moved up from being the head of the Missile Branch to being the deputy technical director to Captain Bob Gooding, who had relieved Levering Smith when he moved on up to be the director. Captain Gooding was technical director and I moved up to take over as his deputy and that was a position which, like any deputy, would allow you to make a little time available with the cooperation of your boss so he agreed and I agreed and off I went. It was a delightful interlude.

Q: For how long a period was this?

Adm. W.: It was a total of some thirteen weeks in two successive summer sessions of about six or seven weeks each.

Q: So you weren't absent for all that time?

Adm. W.: For about a month and a half in the summer of '68 and again in '69.

Q: What did it add to your fund of knowledge?

Adm. W.: Not a great deal. It was an interesting experience because it exposed me to things that are of great concern to our industrial community, to our business community, that were only of secondary concern to me as a naval officer.

Q: But useful.

Adm. W.: Useful because it gave me a perspective that otherwise I would not have had. Probably the most valuable thing I got out of it were the associations with other managers, business people and the like, who were about my same age and about the same level in their organizations but were from the business world or the industrial world. Generally these were not defense contractors, the people with whom I was familiar; these people were from businesses that had nothing to do with the military in large part. The courses dealt with marketing and economic issues and business strategy and the like which was quite new to me and quite interesting but not necessarily apropos the kind of world I was in. So I considered it more a sabbatical than anything of direct concern in my job.

Q: Wasn't it a working sabbatical, I suppose in the realm of economics you had to catch up a bit?

Adm. W.: Oh yes, I had to run like crazy just to get on board much less catch up. I enjoyed it and it looks good on the Personal History form and it sounds impressive but I don't really feel that it was terribly important.

Q: Did you take your family with you on these successive summers?

Adm. W.: No, that was not encouraged at all.

Q: It had to be a summer of concentration.

Adm. W.: Indeed. I would like to mention one thing and that is the British program. I did mention earlier that we had...

Q: You did mention it and I had a latent question on that. You also told me and showed me a framed certificate which indicated that you had a very close relationship with the British and that you had done something about developing their purchase plan originally.

Adm. W.: Let me encapsulate the history of that British program. I believe I mentioned how the cancellation of SKYBOLT led to their being offered POLARIS, that they accepted POLARIS which led to the signing of the sales agreement between the US and the UK designating the director of Special Projects office as the US project officer acting on behalf of the Department of Defense as the US agency directly concerned and their counterpart in the UK being a British Rear-admiral and he in turn would be project officer on behalf of the Ministry of Defense. That relationship went along very, very successfully from 1962-63 on until the British had deployed four submarines and had established a continuous patrol. In due course the British were faced with a dilemma and it was this, do we continue to modernize our POLARIS force to stay in step with the Americans, or not. When we were undertaking the development of the POSEIDON this became a very critical question for the British, should they convert their POLARIS submarines to a POSEIDON capability so that they could stay in step with the US, or should they not. This led to a lengthy debate within the British military circles, essentially between the Royal Navy and the center scientists of the United Kingdom, the center scientists being opposed to the notion of buying POSEIDON and being more inclined to modify POLARIS with a design of their own.

Q: Did they not feel that they should keep pace or did they think that was adequate for their own defense?

Adm. W.: I can't reconstruct all the arguments they used internally. Some were concerned with finding useful work for the laboratories in the United Kingdom to perform. It would be more interesting to find a new development that would be done in those laboratories than it would be to simply make a Chinese copy of something that had already been done in the United States. So the center scientists that were responsible for laboratories like the Atomic Weapons Research Establishment (corresponding for example to Los Alamos in the United States) and the Royal Aircraft Establishment (corresponding to our other government laboratories these center scientists and not just the people at these laboratories but also their political masters in the hierarchy of the British bureaucracy were very much more inclined to develop something that could be done in Britain as opposed to copying or buying something developed in the United States.

Q: I suppose there was a monetary consideration there too?

Adm. W.: Yes, they maintained it would have been more costly to buy POSEIDON. That, as it turns out, is debatable because their cost estimates for modifying POLARIS turned out to be grossly understated and by the time they finish that program (and they are not through with it yet) it is rather clear that they will spend a great deal more than originally represented.

Q: And the product, the end result?

Adm. W.: Will be of limited value.

Q: And not equal to POSEIDON?

Adm. W.: In no way. That certificate you mentioned refers to the support that our office provided while I was there, in the development of their improvement program for their POLARIS. It also refers to our assistance in helping them get the approval for TRIDENT. What I am saying is that they chose to improve POLARIS rather than buy POSEIDON but for the longer haul they have decided to get back with the United States and to buy the TRIDENT system which we are now just deploying and they will, some years from now, also deploy in their submarines--a new class of submarines.

Q: That was a new realization that came to them then?

Adm. W.: Yes. It was a new realization of recognition of the immense cost to a nation that can only afford a limited number of submarines--the immense cost of going it alone as opposed to staying in step with the United States and buying whatever it is we develop for ourselves. This was a matter that pitted the Royal Navy against their civilian scientists; the Royal Navy was at somewhat of a disadvantage in this debate because they did not have (in my opinion) a body of naval officers that were conversant with the nuclear program and were capable of speaking on an equal basis with the civilian scientists on nuclear technology.

Q: They had not raised up a group.

Adm. W.: Correct. They were dependent upon these civilian scientists to a degree that we in the United States were not.

Q: Is that a British custom?

Adm. W.: I don't think it is going to be a custom forever because I think they have learned something from it but whereas in my own case, I was able to take charge of a group of government and non-government activities and acted as sort of chairman of a joint undertaking to develop a nuclear payload; there were others in the navy who were able to do the same thing in Dr. Draper's organization for a missile guidance system, others like Levering Smith who were able to work in the field of solid propellant rocket motors, the Royal Navy had no one, wearing a uniform, who had such technical preparation, which is as far as I am concerned a visible demonstration of the value to the US Navy of having a few people who are specialized in the advancing technological fields looking to the future when these things might turn out to be important.

Q: The British also have to be concerned about political attitudes; if Anthony Wedgwood Benn ever gets in as Prime Minister there won't be any nuclear submarine program.

Adm. W.: I take that with a grain of salt. There was a time when the British POLARIS program was similarly threatened early on, after the program was undertaken under Prime Minister McMillan, it was to have been a five submarine program.

The Labor Government, the Labor party, had loudly opposed this and promised to cancel the program if it got into power. Well, when it did get into power they reviewed the bidding and chose not to cancel it but rather to symbolically reduce it one submarine, so it became a four submarine program rather than a five. I take, somewhat with a grain of salt, the statements that are being made by the opposition party, the Labor party, today. I feel that if they came into power they would review the arguments and quite likely be persuaded that it would be in the national interest to continue the submarine ballistic missile program.

Q: I think you are right.

Adm. W.: I hope for their sakes that I am right. To the extent that they are having such capabilities in the US interest as well, for our sakes also.

That's the background for the nice plaque that I showed you that was given me by the First Sea Lord. He I believe appreciated the help that our office provided in winning the approval of Prime Minister Thatcher and her government for the long-range improvement of their system by the addition of TRIDENT. That was accomplished before I left.

Q: Did this entail trips to Britain on your part?

Adm. W.: Oh yes. As the US project officer for the administration of the POLARIS sales agreement, the director SSPO meets with his counterpart formally three times a year and we alternate between London and Washington so any given year we will meet twice in London and once in Washington or, twice in Washington and once in London--we alternate back and forth.

Q: On those occasions do you have conversations with the political powers too?

Adm. W.: Yes, usually I will pay courtesy calls on others. During my most recent trip, before I retired, I visited with other senior officers in the navy and I visited with the Minister of Defense and with other senior officials. I must say, on a personal note, that the Royal Navy's program, the program of the United Kingdom and the responsibilities that I carried out toward that program have to be one of the more pleasant aspects of that career in S.P. Certainly the British are delightful people to work with.

Q: A cultured group with whom you are working?

Adm. W.: Indeed yes. It is just pure pleasure and it is nice to know that it is something that is in the interest of the US Navy and the US government because anything that is that enjoyable usually doesn't also turn out to have all these other attributes to it.

Q: That is a very kind and a very nice thing to be able to say.

Adm. W.: Well, so much for the POSEIDON and so much for the Royal Navy's failure to adopt POSEIDON.

Interview No. 5 with Rear-admiral Robert H. Wertheim

Place: At his residence in Annandale, Virginia

Date: Monday, 9 February, 1981

Subject: Biography

By: John T. Mason, Jr.

Q: I am looking forward to this with great pleasure but I am also looking forward with not too much pleasure because you tell me it is the last of the series.

Today we are going to talk about the TRIDENT program, the genesis of the program, the evolution of it as it evolved out of STRAT-X, I expect?

Adm. W.: Yes. I would like to now pick up the thread, in 1966. At that particular time my old associate, Dr. Lloyd Wilson who, in the early days of the POLARIS program, had been working with me on the front end of POLARIS, had by 1966 become a deputy director of Defense Research and Engineering under the director who was by then Dr. Johnny Foster, former director of the Livermore Laboratory. Dr. Wilson found himself faced with a dilemma which was that the United States Airforce wanted very badly to go ahead with a project for a new strategic missile, a much larger missile to replace MINUTEMAN in the ICBM silos. It was a huge missile and it troubled Dr. Wilson because he foresaw no alternatives being offered by the other services, specifically the navy; there was only this airforce proposal. He felt rather strongly that the Secretary of Defense should have other options offered before he made a selection of a new strategic weapons system. So, Dr. Wilson discussed this subject with me late one night over a bottle of gin and by the time the evening was over the notion had come out that what we really needed, what he really needed, was an organized competition, highly structured competition of concepts and this scheme was dubbed STRAT-X, (STRAT of course standing for strategic and X standing for nothing) in which the Institute for Defense Analyses acting as sort of the central organization for pulling it all together with organized teams, each team to advocate a different concept. The teams would be competing against a set of ground rules which would be drawn up by the director of the study; the ground rules basically were the least cost for achieving a specified weight of offensive payload arriving on target system, specifically the Soviet Union, in the face of a hypothetical defense system which would be invented and tailored to respond to that specific threat. The idea of course was to come up with measures of effectiveness which would compare on a cost effectiveness basis, these alternate schemes.

All kinds of approaches were considered--air launch missile systems, land launched global systems, fixed systems, sea based systems both on surface ships and submarines. One of the schemes was called ULMS (Underwater Long-range Missile system). This was conceptually a very large submarine carrying large, relatively low technology missiles and a large number of such missiles; the whole system designed to be the least possible cost--after all that was one of the criteria used as a measure of effectiveness. Another sea based scheme was the so-called BMS (a surface based ballistic missile system).

Q: These were contributed by the navy contingent?

Adm. W.: Correct. These were advocated by teams which reflected navy influence.

Q: Were you on STRAT-X?

Adm. W.: No. At that time I was in the Special Projects office having returned there after my tour of duty in the Office of the Secretary of Defense, but I was working closely with Dr. Wilson, under the table you might say, because we were old friends and in this case we were co-conspirators. We were conspiring to try to get the right thing to be done. The navy was not actively advocating a new strategic system but this was Dr. Wilson'a way of getting proposals on the table.

Q: What role did McNamara play in setting up this conference or, did he have any role in it?

Adm. W.: I think he had virtually no role, this was an activity that was set up by Dr. Wilson, at his initiative, with the approval of his boss who was the director of Defense Research and Engineering.

Q: Somewhere I read that he had said, "Does the US need a new generation of ballistic missiles," a question he raised that the conference should consider and so, how should it be based?

Adm. W.: The issue of "Is it needed?" wasn't really addressed by STRAT-X, the only issue that STRAT-X addressed was, assuming that it is needed what is the most effective and least costly approach. It was an extremely efficient way to carry out this kind of undertaking because it was a very competitive environment, it took alternate concepts and weighed them against a set of criteria which were quite realistic, it allowed the countermeasures--it allowed innovative people to try to imagine responses that the Soviets could come up with, technological feasible responses and then modified the proposals again in counter-reaction to the counter measures. That cycle could be repeated several times in a relatively few months in a process which, through the normal budget process would take a year or more. So, in a matter of a few months STRAT-X was capable of advancing these proposals.

Q: How was this assembled? How were these men named to serve on STRAT-X?

Adm. W.: As I said, the Institute for Defense Analyses, which is a not-for-profit organization that serves the Defense Department, can call upon universities and government laboratories in the various services for people to assist them. They were given the task to perform, they organized the teams.

Q: It was quite a large number?

Adm. W.: Yes, it was quite a large number. I did not participate directly in the study but of course I was a very interested observer and made information available when requested. Suffice it to say the ULMS that emerged from this study was one of the most attractive alternatives that came out of the study. Now ULMS bears only a faint resemblance to TRIDENT, which was ultimately the system that the navy proposed and was ultimately accepted by the Department of Defense and the Congress. The genesis of the idea was STRAT-X and I have to give Dr. Wilson credit for prodding this out of the navy. In my opinion, it would not have evolved anything like as soon as it did, maybe never, without that kind of impetus from on high.

Q: What was Dr. Fred Payne's role?

Adm. W.: Fred Payne was the study director. He had had the position that Dr. Wilson occupied in the office of the Secretary of Defense at an earlier time. He had that position when I was working there as a military assistant. He was extremely good at a readiness kind of study, a fine analyst himself and a well organized individual.

In any event, in 1967, when the STRAT-X study was winding up, it was also the time that I moved up from my position as head of the Missile Branch to Deputy Technical Director, so that was a period of transition for me as well. That's where I was when the Chief of Naval Operations established formally an advanced development objective for the ULMS system which gave it a formal status within the navy. There was very little money available for pursuing it, it was just a study effort but nevertheless it had a formal position within the navy for its long-range plans.

Q: Was the CNO at that time Tom Moorer?

Adm. W.: I think it was. It was a few months after that in the middle of 1968, that the Op-98 headed by Admiral Miller who was deputy Chief of Naval Operations for Strategic Offensive and Defensive Systems (I believe that is what that office was then called) that at his initiative the Special Projects Office was re-named the Strategic Systems Project Office (SSPO) which is the title it retains to this day. That was to reflect a broader charter that went beyond the POLARIS and POSEIDON and was to encompass all new strategic offensive and defensive systems that the navy might choose to undertake and it reflected the broad charter that Op-98 had. In fact, looking back, we see that the functions and the responsibilities of the office really changed very little only the name.

Q: He had a special interest in what is called the SLMS, the surface aspect--that proposal.

Adm. W.: Yes that was a scheme that was also a survivor of the STRAT-X study, it was a finalist, it also looked very cost-effective compared to other schemes for basing strategic weapons systems, certainly compared to many of the land-based and air-based schemes. However, it was fundamentally less survivable because it was on surface ships which are at least conceptually capable of being tracked and followed either by Soviet surface ships or by satellites or whatever. It would be much harder to assure one's self that that system was not capable of being knocked out by a preemptive attack from the other side. It might have been more attractive than other land-based systems but certainly it was less attractive than the submarine-based system.

Q: It is interesting that the idea is surfacing again; currently it was thrown out, I suppose, as an expedient proposal on the part of the Secretary of Defense--the possibility of missiles on surface vessels.

Adm. W.: Yes, again I suspect it looks attractive in comparison to the horrendously difficult environmental issues associated with the mobile land-based system—MX. It is not as good as a submarine-based system but it is certainly a lot better, in many respects, than a land-based system, or perhaps I should say better in that it avoids some of the difficulties.

Q: One got the impression, when he tossed this out, that it was kind of a trial balloon and it was an expedient way of hurrying the re-arming of the nation.

Adm. W.: The basic issue here is the so-called Triad, the strategic Triad which is the name we have given to the land-based, the air-based, and the sea-based legs of our strategic offensive forces—having three fundamentally different basic schemes giving us a basis for confidence that we are not likely to find ourselves threatened by some technological breakthrough that would affect all three of them. You can imagine a scheme that would reduce the confidence in the land-based system; we see it now and that is the threat of increasingly accurate Soviet missiles—huge missiles with large numbers of warheads that could dig out the silos—the land-based systems. We should also worry about air defenses that could threaten our bomber force; and we could also, many people do, worry about the possibility of Soviet anti-submarine warfare breakthrough that could threaten our submarine systems. But it is hard to imagine all of these things happening simultaneously so a Triad of forces seems to be worthwhile.

Q: A communications aspect is threatened currently, is it not, with the news we get on their testing out something to destroy satellites?

Adm. W.: Yes, that is of great concern, not just to communications but also lots of other capabilities for guidance for which we depend upon our satellites--surveillance, communications, navigation--lots of our capabilities today have a space element in orbit around the earth.

Q: That would encompass all three elements.

Adm. W.: It could, although that is not by any means the only way we have of communicating, fortunately. We still have the old-fashioned radio and the like and if you have a system, such as the submarine-based system which is survivable, capable of lasting for weeks and months if necessary until it gets the message, we can afford to resort to other means of communication. What you worry about is a system such as our current land-based schemes, or our bomber systems which must be used or lost--they are going to be destroyed if they are not used. The leg of the Triad that is currently at risk, serious risk, are the fixed land-based systems--MX is the title that has been given to the next generation of large, land-based ICBMs, to replace MINUTEMAN, that will hopefully be based in a way that will make them again survivable. The difficulty with this is that while most people will agree that a new ICBM missile—the missile, the weapons system itself is a very desirable thing—we can't get a general consensus on a way of basing it. So, getting back to your original question, the attractiveness of a fleet of surface ships is that it gives us a way of taking these new ICBMs and putting them on a platform that is away from the environmental issues. In the end it comes back to the same scheme that you referred to earlier that came out of STRAT-X—it is a surface based system, it may be a superior way of basing a missile but its still another sea-based system and a less capable one, less secure, less survivable than the submarine system.

Q: Just as vulnerable as any surface ship.

Adm. W.: Of course. But it still can be much more desirable than the best of the land-based schemes. The ultimate limitation on all of these schemes is, in my opinion, people. The navy is faced with a crisis of major proportions in skilled personnel necessary to maintain and operate these and all the other systems that the navy has to maintain. This could easily become the limiting factor, not necessarily the shipbuilding capacity, and not necessarily our ability to get funds from the Congress to buy these new systems, but rather our ability to attract and retain the skilled manpower necessary to operate and maintain. These are things which the Chief of Naval Operations is acutely aware of and speaks at length on given the opportunity. So we have to (when I say we I am speaking of those within the navy who would advocate one system or another) be acutely aware of our need not to oversell, not to let our enthusiasm for a particular scheme or other cause us to rush out and advocate it without making certain that the human resources, as well as fiscal, are available to make this all happen.

In this period following STRAT-X, after I had moved up to SP-200, to be deputy technical director in our office, getting back to a personal note, I was, much sooner than I had expected, asked by Admiral Smith who was then the director, to step up and relieve Captain Bob Gooding who was the technical director and who was moving on to command the Naval Shipyard in Boston. I was to take over as technical director which was the top technical job in SP. This occurred as I have said, somewhat sooner than I would have expected but I was delighted to have that opportunity.

Q: Obviously you were prepared for it weren't you, with all your experience?

Adm. W.: Well, you always wonder whether you are really prepared when the time comes. This happened in 1969 and in the meantime we were continuing at that time, as technical director I found myself managing the continuing operational support of the POLARIS, which was then the only system that was operating, the continuing development, the preparation for the production and deployment of POSEIDON, and the very early conceptual study work for ULMS.

Q: You had a three-fold problem too?

Adm. W.: That's right. All these things tended to overlap.

For a moment, I'll hark back to POSEIDON because in this time period, the late 60's, we were getting ready for the version of POLARIS submarines to the POSEIDON configuration and preparing for the production of the weapons system. The development of the system of course was still very much in progress and we ran into an unexpected difficulty with the Congress. That was that in order to carry the POSEIDON system it was necessary that a POLARIS submarine be converted. In other words the mount tubes--the launcher--had to be completely ripped out and much larger system installed to carry the much larger POSEIDON missile. This was a major shipyard undertaking.

Q: Of what duration?

Adm. W.: It was on the order of a year and a half to two years. It was planned to be done, and was carried out in conjunction with a regular shipyard overhaul. Nevertheless the commitment to do it had to be made well in advance of the ship's arrival at the shipyard in order to buy the fire control equipment, the navigation equipment, the launching equipment--all the rest that was going to be needed by the shipyard in order to perform the conversion.

Q: Roughly what amount of dollars were involved in a conversion at that time?

Adm. W.: It is hard to separate out the cost of a conversion from the cost of the rest of the overhaul because they were done concurrently and I am sure it could be extracted with a careful audit but we are talking about tens of millions of dollars--50 to 60 millions of dollars is not an unreasonable estimate for this cost.

Q: How many were you intending to convert?

Adm. W.: The numbers started at about 22 of the original 41 and then grew to 31 total. All but the oldest ten submarines ultimately were converted to POSEIDON from POLARIS.

Q: And simultaneously, did you begin a program of building new submarines that met all the specifications of the POSEIDON?

Adm. W.: No, we didn't, we were not building new submarines. These were all conversions of submarines that had already carried POLARIS. None of the POSEIDON submarines had initially been deployed with POSEIDON; they had all been deployed with an earlier missile. The reason I am bringing this up is that it was necessary for us to go to the Congress and ask for the funds to convert POLARIS submarines to POSEIDON some years before the POSEIDON development was complete, and even before the first POSEIDON missile had been flown. There were some Senators, and presumably others, with long memories who could recall that the navy had come in with schemes for installing new weapons systems and committing ship platforms to them before the development of the weapons systems had been completed, then later finding that the weapons system development was delayed or didn't meet its specifications or for some other reason the two weren't ready for one another at the appropriate time. Senator Russell who was the powerful chairman of the Senate Arms Services Committee believed (or maybe it was the Appropriations Committee in any event he was in a very, very influential position) and he simply said no he would not endorse the tearing out (in his view) POLARIS capabilities, that POLARIS was a fine weapons system that worked very well indeed, and accepting on faith that this new POSEIDON thing with its mysterious MIRV capabilities and the like (which he didn't fully understand), he had heard grandiose promises before out of the navy about how well things were going to work and he was not going to buy a pig in a poke, he wasn't going to allow a good system to be taken out of the force in favor of a new system which was untried.

Q: Does this say that the navy hadn't properly mended its fences?

Adm. W.: I think what it said was that we had to do a job of educating Senator Russell, that the Special Projects office and the Strategic Systems Project office as a project, that the management both in its technical disciplines as well as its business practices was competent and capable of dealing with this particular problem--the problem of concurrency.

Concurrent commitment to production while development is still in progress; so we were forced to delay by a full year, the commitment of long-lead monies to the conversion process and we spent that year working very hard to do just what you suggested: mustering the facts, the data, and the evidence necessary to convince a skeptical Congress that we were indeed capable of anticipating and coping with the problem associated with concurrency.

Q: Did you have others among the Senators who were protagonists, who were convinced that it could be done and should be done?

Adm. W.: It is hard for me to say. I was the technical director and the political fight was being led by my boss Admiral Levering Smith who was the director. I was given the job really of making these things happen rather than fighting the issues in Congress. Admiral Smith did a very effective job in his low key but highly professional way of mustering the facts and the evidence necessary to ultimately convince Congress. We were delayed a year in getting the initial funding we needed for the conversion. Fortunately we had allowed enough time so that that year's compression really didn't impact the program in any significant degree and we were able to proceed on schedule.

Q: Was Russell convinced or did he suffer ill health at that time?

Adm. W.: He was convinced. He had grave doubts but he allowed himself to be convinced and the funds were approved. It is an interesting contrast with a situation that later faced us in TRIDENT, and I will talk of that further on. In the case of POSEIDON, in order to prepare for the new system we had to commit to removing an existing system, in other words, the submarine platforms on which the new system was going to be installed, had to be modified to a degree that forced a shipyard overhaul conversion and that has a very long-lead process and means that commitments must be made way, way in advance while development is still in progress. In the case of the TRIDENT system later on, we found a very different situation. Here we are installing in POSEIDON submarines, submarines that have already been converted to POSEIDON, a new weapons system by a process we call a back-fit which is not the same as conversion at all. In this we deliberately sized the TRIDENT missile so that it would fit in place of a POSEIDON without having to change the launch tube in any significant degree. We designed the entire weapon system with the idea in mind that we could bring in any POSEIDON submarine alongside the dock, anywhere there is a modest industrial facility available, and change it out in the course of a couple of months--from POSEIDON to TRIDENT.

Q: Thank you for giving me that definition. You used it in a previous session and I didn't quite know what it was.

Adm. W.: As we use the terms a conversion is literally the use of SCN or Ship Construction Navy funding--it is paid for differently and used from a different appropriation--in other words it is a major undertaking. A back-fit--we have used that term to refer to just simply switching from one weapons system configuration to another that doesn't require the services of a shipyard and is not paid for with SCN money but rather with other procurement money in the navy.

Q: I'm going to see that that word gets into the Naval Terms dictionary. It isn't there.

Adm. W.: Obviously you have looked it up, or tried to. Jargon is an important thing that distinguishes experts from amateurs.

Q: One other comment, that is that what you were asking Congress at that time doesn't exactly fit into their scheme of things--their pattern of doing things through the generations.

Adm. W.: As a matter of fact, this attitude of the Congress was heavily reinforced by the Secretary of Defense. There had been a major study of defense procurement undertaken during this time period under under Secretary of Defense Packard and Packard, who was a very successful businessman and engineer came in and undertook to revamp defense procurement procedures particularly program and project management. One of the conclusions reached by the Packard sponsored study on procurement was that many of the difficulties that had been given a great deal of publicity through the years on defense procurement stemmed from commitment to production before development was complete. In other words, this term concurrency again, so, he came up with a scheme to assure that a new system would not be committed to production until concrete evidence had been demonstrated, had been provided through demonstration, that the system was satisfactory and the term for this became 'fly before buy'--we will fly the system before we buy it. Concurrency which had been the key to our accelerated and successful development of all the POLARIS systems and all the early ICBM systems and the like, concurrency of development and production was the only way we could possibly have done these things in such short order. Suddenly this became instead of a good word, it became a bad word; it implied poor management practice. In our world, in order to continue meeting the commitments that we had set for ourselves and had accepted for ourselves we had to find ways of convincing people to allow us to continue the practices that had been demonstrably successful in our program in the past. It is rather a strange thing to have to justify doing what you had already demonstrated was the key to your previous success. But that is what we had to do.

Q: Was Packard himself involved in this?

Adm. W.: Yes, Packard personally endorsed these policies.

Q: I mean the exceptions that you were presenting.

Adm. W.: Packard unfortunately left the Pentagon before he

had really had time to follow the results of his own policies through to the end. He was consulted later on as an adviser and moderated his views when handed facts, but by that time he was no longer in a position of influence. Suffice it to say the facts had been mustered successfully both for POSEIDON, as I have indicated with some difficulty, and later on we had the same problem with TRIDENT, nevertheless in both cases we were successful in convincing the decision makers that we should be allowed to continue following the practices that we had in the past. We modified them to some extent, usually in a way to further improve on our past performance where we had found some procedure or other was less than satisfactory, so we attempted to improve on them. If there is any key at all to the success of the navy's fleet ballistic system, through the years is the fact that the management organization and its style of operating and its team of prime contractors have all remained intact through these years and have therefore been capable of learning from their experience and applying lessons learned to successive generations. This is a feature that is missing from most of the navy's procurement systems. Generally speaking we tend to start new systems as if they were from the ground up, starting all over again, and the lessons we tend to apply often don't really apply.

Q: David Packard was applying good business practices to government methods and your exception was a rare exception which didn't really fit into a business pattern.

Adm. W.: Perhaps that is right. There are certain things about a ballistic missile system in particular that are unlike anything else. Our acquisition procedures that we had developed in our office through the years reflected those unique features in our practices. It wasn't easily understood by someone just coming in cold from the outside world. If you are deciding whether or not to build a radio set and put it on the market and sell it and you would like it to sell for such and such a price because you feel there is a place in the market for such a set with these capabilities and in this price range, it is entirely reasonable in building such a set to make certain that you know what it is going to cost to build and that you test it out so as to be satisfied that it performs as you expect it to before you order it into production. You cannot afford to do that with a large ballistic missile system which you are incapable of testing without destroying the article you test. You may very well test it and find it works fine and you decide you want to put it into production but you have no assurance whatever that the thing you want to produce will in fact end up being the same as the thing you tested earlier. You have to invoke very, very special procedures to make certain that the article in production has not changed from the article that you tested in your development program. That is why you have to maintain continuity--production continuity--from the experimental article right into serial production and that calls for very special processes and procedure which we evolved and matured in the history of our program.

Q: At this point I would like you to comment on something George Miller said because it has bearing on this positive asset that you emphasize in the S.P. program; he seemed to disagree. He said, "Technicians like to build things they know now to build, they like to build things they are accustomed to building. If you have been there long enough, as certain people have, you hate to go out and lay your reputation on the line again after you have made such a brilliant reputation. So the questions are, 'what range missile does the US need, etc., and what range do the technicians want to build'?" He makes that point that he obviously didn't think it was such a good thing that there was this continuity in the personnel and the methods in S.P.

Adm. W.: It is hard for me to comment unemotionally on that. Suffice it to say that Admiral Miller was having some difficulties with our office and with Admiral Smith in particular in getting the response out of him that he thought he wanted. Admiral Miller had some very grandiose ideas about what the navy ought to be doing in the strategic areas; not only should we be pursuing, in addition to our submarine launch ballistic missile systems which S.P. was advocating adequately, but we should also be pursuing, at least in his view, surface ship ballistic missile systems and sea-based anti-ballistic systems, among other things. He saw his role as in the vanguard of leading a complete movement of US strategic capabilities to sea. He foresaw all strategic systems in the future being sea-based. To the extent that he felt he was not getting adequate support out of S.P. for pursuing all of these schemes at once, he was disappointed, he was looking for more support. It is hard for me to do a motivational analysis on anyone; he saw perhaps the answer should lie in conservatism of S.P. and its technical people.

Q: I suppose that is what he is underlining in this book.

Adm. W.: In fact, other people will criticize technicians for attempting to do too much, for being too enthralled with technology, with eagerness to commit to doing things that are on the fringes of feasibility. It is perhaps refreshing to be a technical type being accused of being too conservative. I think that any realistic individual looking at the TRIDENT system and what it accomplished--literally doubling the range while maintaining the accuracy of a submarine based strategic weapons system and doing it in a system that was capable of being installed in existing submarines without taking them the line for more than a couple of months--that was a major undertaking and to do this all in a system that demonstrated itself and has demonstrated itself to be the most dependable of any system that we have ever deployed, I think I can state categorically that TRIDENT's initial reliability is higher than any system that we have deployed before. This major step in technical capabilities as well as integration into an operational system was not accomplished by being ultra conservative, it was done by applying very advanced technology but in a way that allowed us to capitalize on past experience. I really don't think that Admiral Miller's charge is entirely fair in this case. When were these words written?

Q: He didn't have the advantage of a retrospective view of what was accomplished when he said this. It must have been around 1975-'76.

Adm. W.: Again let me say, knowing that you were going to be held accountable for the results is a very sobering influence. Admiral Miller of course was not around to be held accountable for promises and commitments he was prepared to make. S.P. and its director and its successive generations of directors typically had been held accountable and that is a very moderating influence. There is nothing quite as sobering as knowing that you are being held accountable.

Q: It does make you cautious.

Adm. W.: That's true, but not necessarily unwilling to apply the vast technology, knowing in fact that that is necessary to achieve an objective.

Through that period, from the end of STRAT-X right through 1970, these ULMS trade-off studies were continuing. In our office we were studying various combinations of missile sizes and submarine sizes. Now, instead of it just being a study group put together by a defense organization, these were navy studies being carried out with the assistance of our contractors, the naval sea-systems command, Admiral Rickover was very much involved because these were nuclear submarines and he had interests of his own to pursue, but the basic issue of what should the size of the vessel be, how many missiles should there be on the submarine, how large should the submarine be, should it really look like that configuration that won the game in the STRAT-X competition or should it be more nearly like an extrapolation of the POLARIS configuration--all of these issues were being strongly, not just debated, there were engineering trade-off studies, cost studies and the like were being conducted on them.

Q: Is there something comparable to the STRAT-X assembly of technicians and scientists continued so that the navy's development of this program, the airforce development and so forth, is there some over-all perspective of them?

Adm. W.: Unfortunately the answer is no. I say unfortunately because in the strategic area, unlike other warfare areas, strategic weapons systems tend to cross service lines. You find airforce and the navy both involved in strategic weaponry but they don't tend to compete directly against one another. They tend to compete within the service against other service requirements and needs so we tend to see funding for the navy's strategic program competing against navy General Purpose Force funding and it is not easy to trade off a new strategic missile that meets a national objective perhaps against a new frigate or some element in the rapid deployment force or something of that sort. It is very difficult to get an analytical handle on that. I have maintained for a long time that the strategic forces should in fact be fenced and competed against one another across service lines. STRAT-X allowed that to happen, it has not continued and this is an area of considerable frustration to me. I have strongly advocated it, so far without any great success.

Q: What is the deterrent to doing it? It seems to make common sense; it is a common sense point of view.

Adm. W.: It was easier to do under McNamara. When McNamara and Hitch came in and set up their very strong centralized management in the Defense Department, they had a strong staff, it was a natural thing for them to package these programs out then and trade them off against one another at the OSD level because that really is the lowest common denominator, the lowest administrative level where all of these things can be considered together. As you know, when McNamara departed the baby was thrown out with the bath water, Secretary Laird returned to the practice of setting budget limits for each of the three services and then allowing the services to optimize within those budgets. As long as they could solve their problems within the funding that they had then generally the Office of the Secretary of Defense would approve what they proposed to do.

Q: That was the traditional Congressional point of view wasn't it?

Adm. W.: Exactly, and there were many people in the Congress that McNamara irritated greatly because they saw him as intellectually arrogant (including Laird) and he was strongly criticized, with some justification, for his attitude and so when he was evicted, or departed (whatever the right word is) and Laird took his place the pendulum swung hard over in the other direction, and as I say they threw the baby out with the bathwater. I think much of what Laird did was appropriate, correct, certainly for all of the general purpose forces, but I feel to this day that strategic forces, or meeting national objectives as opposed to service needs, should be dealt with as an entity. It is not.

Q: This could be a development in the future.

Adm. W.: Perhaps. I keep hoping. In any event the ultimate configuration of the submarine and its weapons system for this new generation was finally selected and approved by the Department of Defense in 1971 and the configuration, as I think many people now know, the plan was one which would allow the development and construction of a large new nuclear powered submarine which would initially deploy with a missile which was sized to fit not only that submarine but also it would fit into the existing submarines. This missile was ultimately titled TRIDENT I. I refer to it as a missile but in fact I should be calling it a weapon system the missile being a part of that system.

Q: TRIDENT I with the thought that it would be the first in a series?

Adm. W.: Yes, first in a series. The submarine itself would be capable of carrying much larger missiles than TRIDENT I. These generically were referred to as TRIDENT II and they were seen as coming along later, at some time in the future.

Q: But not actually undertaken at that point?

Adm. W.: No, other than in cartoon form. They would need to be undertaken, at least conceptually, in order to help the shipbuilders and the ship designers to size the submarine properly to provide adequate stability margins and the like so that the ship would be capable of carrying much heavier weights and sizes, and be capable of accommodating the electrical and optical alignment needs of a much more accurate system that might be called for in the future. These sorts of things needed to be coordinated with the shipbuilder early on, when he was designing the initial ship to carry only TRIDENT I, in order to minimize the conversion necessary later on when ultimately we got around to putting in the larger missile.

Q: There again for the shipbuilders there has to be a sense of continuity too in this program?

Adm. W.: Yes.

Q: What shipbuilders are specifically involved?

Adm. W.: In the case of the TRIDENT system there is only one and that is the Electric Boat Division of General Dynamics. In the case of POSEIDON there were a number of shipyards. I can't recall them all but I believe there were some naval shipyards involved in the conversion program as well, just as they were in the original POLARIS submarine construction. With TRIDENT it was only one--Electric Boat Division. As I indicated, the design of the initial weapon system to be capable of being installed in existing submarines as well as the new TRIDENT submarine, actually permitted these two major elements of the program to proceed more or less independently of one another. The submarine construction program followed its own course, and as you know if has fallen considerably behind schedule (now approximately three years behind), in the meantime the weapon system was allowed to proceed and be deployed when it was ready and it was so deployed without being held up as a consequence of the ship delays.

Q: Ship delays due to lack of appropriations?

Adm. W.: No. The problems at Electric Boat Division--I

am really not the best person to recite all those and I am sure history will show that whatever anyone says at this stage would not really be the best description.

Q: Was there adequate financing from the Congress?

Adm. W.: I don't think lack of funds has been the problem at all. I believe it has been almost entirely due to the difficulties which the contractor and the navy will continue to litigate and argue about for some time in the future. The fact is there is enough blame to go around--lay a little on everyone. We have tried to keep our skirts clean in the Strategic Systems Project office and it turned out that this business of the separation in effect of the weapons system and the submarine construction program, to be a blessing in disguise for S.P. because when that particular organizational relationship--that particular configuration of weapon system and ship was selected it made it possible to organize the program somewhat differently. A project manager was set up, designated PM-2, contrasted with the PM-1--project manager number one which was the title S.P. carried within the Naval Materiel Command; PM-2 was the TRIDENT program manager and he was set up as being sort of the over all czar of the entire TRIDENT program. The two elements of the program--one the weapons system was managed by SSPO and the ship system was managed by the Naval Sea Systems Command. This meant it was no longer necessary for the director SSPO to go to the Congress and seek funds for the shipbuilding program or to explain to the Congress why difficulties, short falls and the like in that program were occurring since in fact he had no control over it anyway-- that that part of the program was being managed by the Naval Sea Systems Command and they might just as well be testified to by that organization. So PM-2 and Naval Sea Systems Command have had the fun of going to the Congress and telling them all about that shipbuilding program at the Electric Boat Division while S.P. could stick to its business of developing....

Q: Could focus on the problem at hand.

Adm. W.: That's true.

Q: Were there any outside pressures or developments which propelled S.P. into a more rapid development of the system?

Adm. W.: I think I made reference earlier on to an abortive undertaking in the POSEIDON program of developing a stellar assisted guidance system. That system, while the development was never completed nor was the system put into production for the purpose originally intended, actually it allowed the advance of technology for stellar aided guidance to be carried to the point that we were able to commit to using it in the TRIDENT so that TRIDENT I system in fact carries a successor version of that guidance system in it. That is a very significant element of advanced technology and that is the key to our ability to meet the objective of standing off at twice the greater ranges from our targets and still be able to deliver weapons on them with the same or greater accuracy. The other major technological area was in the propulsion system. Obviously in order to get twice the performance for a weapon system missile without allowing that missile to grow in size means that you are going to have to pack a lot more energy in it somehow so the solid propellant motors have a much higher level of technology in them--in TRIDENT than in POSEIDON. There are other areas of advance as well, micro-electronics, integrated electronics and the like, new materials applications, composite structures replacing older use of aluminum and allowed unnecessary dead weight to be cut back therefore more weight to be available for propelling the missile and delivering payload. All of these were areas.

Q: Was there an element of our potential adversary making advances in his own field? Was this a help in propelling us forward?

Adm. W.: It became clear I think to nearly everyone that the Soviets were doing a great deal more in this area than they had in the past. Originally they had been concentrating almost exclusively on their ICBMs, they developed in their YANKEE submarines you might say an analogue of our POLARIS but they didn't stop there, they continued to develop a new system, later generations of submarine based missiles and the like so they were continuing to work in this area as well.

Q: That acted as something of a spur didn't it?

Adm. W.: Something of a spur; its not a direct spur, it is more an endorsement than a threat because you see submarine ballistic missile systems don't threaten other submarine ballistic missile systems. They can't be used to target each other the way our land-based systems can. I say it is more an endorsement because what it really says is, to those who would argue that you shouldn't be putting new systems to sea in submarines because perhaps the other side knows some secret way of detecting submarines and destroying them all before they could be used, to see the other side investing billions and billions of rubles in new submarine ballistic missile systems of their own, sort of refutes that argument because they think it is a pretty good idea too. In many respects, I think the world is better off, it is a safer place to live in when both the Soviet Union and the United States chooses to put a major element of our strategic forces to sea in submarines where it is not necessary to put a hair trigger on their release; where they are secure, where they are dependable and where the leaders of both sides know they do not have to make quick decisions, that their systems will still be there if they want to delay a day, a week, or a month in making a decision as to their use.

Q: You have already talked about Mr. Packard's directives, do you wish to elaborate on the new dogmas on management?

Adm. W.: I would make a general comment that S.P. has over a period of years, tended to tailor its acquisition practices, procedures by which it draws up its weapon system interfaces, controls them, and contracts for their current development and the transition of these systems from development to production. All of these areas have tended to become tailored to the specific needs and the unique requirements of the submarine ballistic missile program to reflect lessons learned, less than satisfactory things, in other cases things that went very well in earlier programs, so that each successive program is to some extent better than its predecessors. Too often, it seems to me, we find people coming in with preconceptions about how defense acquisition, or project management should proceed and this certainly was the case with Mr. Packard and it has been very much the case with many of his successors. They come in with theories on how things should proceed--untested theories in general or theories which, if they have been tested have been tested and conclusions have been drawn on unsuccessful programs, programs that had fallen flat in one way or another, and they tend to apply these new rules and regulations across the board. In order for an organization like S.P. to continue practices which it has evolved and matured over the years and optimized for its own purposes, inevitably requires exceptions to the new wisdom--the new rules and regulations; so we constantly find ourselves having to justify doing things which have been demonstrably successful in the past as opposed to being used, perhaps as a model, for other programs to follow in a more positive sense in hopefully trying to replicate a successful program like ours.

Q: You are dealing with a bureaucracy which is somewhat different I suppose from what exists in private business.

Adm. W.: I don't know whether it is because it is just a bureaucracy or whether it is just naturally a part of human nature to want to look for simple solutions. It was so easy for the Blue Ribbon Committee that was set up by Mr. Packard to look at the problems associated with weapons system acquisition to conclude that most of the problems lay in premature commitment to production of systems that had not yet completed their development, or to conclude that having an independent organization evaluate the readiness of a system for production was superior to putting that responsibility on the project manager with the unstated presumption that the project manager is so self-serving that he would always attempt to put the best possible face on his product rather than searching out deficiencies and fixing them. These are simple solutions based upon simple concepts of what went wrong in previous programs. In fact it is my strong belief that every project and program is, to a considerable extent, unique. The key to a successful undertaking is of course applying fundamental good business practices but adapting them in every case to the unique requirements of a specific program. Very rarely do we start a new project completely from ground zero, we are always dealing with some extrapolation of something in the past-- even in the case of the original POLARIS which was as close to starting from a dead stop as anything can be. We were putting it into a submarine which was already on the building ways.

Q: Your theory that every project is unique--why isn't this discernable--every human being is unique, differing from every other.

Adm. W.: Again, I feel if we follow that logic train to its ultimate conclusion, we would reach the conclusion that the best approach to follow is to get very good people to head up these projects, give them a great deal of authority and then hold them there from the beginning to the end of the project--entrepreneurs if you will--you have all the tools necessary to do the job. A bureaucracy is very reluctant to give that kind of authority and it does it rarely.

Q: And sometimes only under duress.

Adm. W.: And under great pressure, great strain. Admiral Raborn had it in the early days of the POLARIS program, his airforce counterpart, General Bernard A. Schreiver who was running the airforce ballistic missile programs, had it. General John Bruce Medaris of the army who was running the early JUPITER program down at Huntsville, had that kind of authority but it is rare. And it certainly is rare today. The directors of S.P. who succeeded Raborn I think have successively had a little bit less.

Q: Did you feel that you did have a little bit less?

Adm. W.: Oh yes, definitely but in all fairness, I don't believe that has kept me from doing what needed to be done. And I believe it is because I have had enlightened leadership. I had a boss in the case of Admiral Alfred J. Whittle, Jr. in particular, who is the Chief of Naval Materiel. He had a great deal of regard for me and knew that I wasn't going to come to him with a request for an exception for special treatment unless it was really important, that if a rule or regulation or a requirement was imposed on us, even if it was kind of dumb and it really didn't make an awful lot of sense for us, if I felt I could live with it I would and he knew that. Also I think he knew I wasn't going to come and ask him for relief unless it was something which was really going to hurt the program otherwise. I had very, very good support from him but that level of supervision, if you will, didn't even exist in Raborn's day.

Q: He was at the top of the heap.

Adm. W.: Well it just wasn't the Chief of Naval Materiel that he had to worry about. In many respects he reported directly to the Chief of Naval Operations and all the intervening staffs and organizations simply were by-passed. I would like to comment that after taking over as Technical

Director I was very much surprised in 1971 to be the recipient of the Navy League's Parsons Award. This was an award set up in honor of Admiral Parsons who I believe we mentioned had such an important influence on my career. To ultimately receive an award from the Navy League named after this great man honoring me for advances in science within the navy gave me more pleasure than I can possibly describe. It was all out of proportion I think, to even the rather considerable satisfaction it would have given in any case.

Q: I suppose in an intangible way it was a sort of blessing from him.

Adm. W.: Perhaps so, but I felt it was sort of in effect a closing of the circle, although there was another decade of navy service before I retired. That was certainly one of the most gratifying moments of my service. The following year I was selected rear-admiral as an ordnance weapons engineer, which was another closing of the circle following an earlier admonition by a detailer about sticking to the technical field and specializing to the extent I had was the kiss of death for ever amounting to anything in the navy.

Q: Later on it sort of became a foregone conclusion didn't it? When you got to be Technical Director.

Adm. W.: Not really, not at all. Remember the first such officer in my particular field of specialization ever to become flag officer was Levering Smith and Levering was not selected by the navy, he was given his stars by presidential over-ride.

Q: I hadn't realized that!

Adm. W.: His name was added to the list before it went to the Senate for confirmation, by the President.

Q: That's a rare way of doing things isn't it?

Adm. W.: Extremely rare, the only thing that even approaches it is the way Admiral Rickover got his. Following Levering's promotion there had only been one other officer who was an ordnance specialist in the navy, to have been selected flag and it was Admiral Jack Chrisman who had preceeded me as deputy Technical Director and had moved on to Ordnance Systems Command. It was extremely rare and the opportunity for selection was very little greater than zero--it wasn't by any means automatic. Nevertheless it happened and it has happened since and I think that now the navy would maintain there is some opportunity for an officer who has chosen to specialize in weapons management, weapons engineering within the engineering duty community.

Q: That is a great step forward isn't it, in terms of getting men of talent to pursue that avenue?

Adm. W.: I think it is and as a matter of fact I think it is a great step forward for the navy because it assures the navy that they are going to have a way of retaining the services of people who don't insist that they be made flag officers; all they insist on is at least having some opportunity however small; some opportunity for being selected flag at some time in the future.

Q: They don't have the ceiling over their heads.

Adm. W.: There is an immense difference between an opportunity that is identically zero--absolutly no chance--and an opportunity that is greater than zero no matter how small.

So, the TRIDENT program proceeded under the new organizational arrangement. In S.P., in setting up the program, we chose to model it from a business management point of view very much on the successful POSEIDON--we used the same contract forms, we tried to tie our development to production transition process into the same schemes that we had followed in POSEIDON but again applying lessons learned in POSEIDON; attempting to improve on the POSEIDON experience where in particular, the POSEIDON as originally deployed was not as reliable as we had expected it to be. We found that we had gotten into difficulties when we moved from experimental manufacture into full scale engineering production--full scale production--subtle changes had crept in and these later on resulted in flight failures and we had to go back and re-institute more severe quality control measures and the like in controlling production, inspection and processing. In TRIDENT we took all of that into account and made changes which gave us greater assurance that there would be no unintended change creeping in during that transition process—a very critical process going from low rate manufacture into larger volume production.

Q: Just a moment ago you said you pursued the same type of contracts and so forth for the TRIDENT program that you had for the POSEIDON keeping in mind the fact that you had developed this contractural arrangement through a marriage of the McNamara idea and the previous one. Did this create added difficulties in terms of TRIDENT? Was it a much bigger job in the advance preparation for a contract figuring out what was involved?

Adm. W.: The effort of attempting to apply our own lessons learned, to the TRIDENT, made it a bigger job. One of the things we had learned was how important it was to carefully define at the outset of the program—the front end of the contract—precisely what our objectives were, precisely what our priority was among competing objectives so that we could best align the contractors efforts with the navy's needs and objectives. This is easily said, much more easily said that it is to actually spell it out in hard contractual language. We spent much more time at the start of the TRIDENT program doing that kind of project definition before we awarded fully structured formal contracts.

Q: You knew what you were stepping into.

Adm. W.: Exactly. One of the conclusions I have reached is that the time spent at the front end of the program, getting agreement on those very things, attempting to spell out in contractual language exactly what the government's objectives are and how the contractor should trade them off when he finds them in competition and finds he has to give on one objective in order to meet another--he needs to know which is the more important, and quantitatively, and to spell that out in a way that will result in communicating the message to him best. This is a challenge that simply cannot be underestimated, it takes a great deal of effort, a lot of understanding and knowledge, it takes a great deal of mutual appreciation on the part of the contractor and the government representatives. Here again S.P. profited by the long association that we have enjoyed with our contractor team--prime contractors who have been with our program since the beginning. Individuals in those organizations who are, if anything, dedicated to the objectives of the program as much as any of the government participants are.

Q: Am I right in thinking it was doubly difficult with the TRIDENT program because it was in a state of evolving and so there were perimeters that weren't actually known definitely?

Adm. W.: I think to a considerable extent that has been true of all of them, of all of the programs. We have yet to start a program where we have awarded contracts and have been able to leave them alone and say we are satisfied with the definition as it existed at the outset. We always run into surprises during the course of development, things unintended, unexpected changes, some of them come out of the development process itself, others are imposed by changing external conditions. For instance, in the case of the TRIDENT development we found that we had probably set our technical objectives too high in the missile propulsion area. We had put too great an emphasis on missile range performance and that tended to force the contractors into trying to squeeze too much energy into the missile motors and as a result we were surprised by finding it was possible, under certain abnormal conditions, to cause the motor to detonate instead of burn. That was clearly unexpected and so we had to back off on that performance objective during the course of the program; we had to go back and re-emphasize the safety to a degree that we hadn't before simply because we hadn't appreciated this particular hazard. So, that was an internal problem, or a development-revealed problem with our original definition. As an example of an external problem, the 1973 mid-East war leading to an oil embargo and a tremendous boost in the inflation rates; that impacted us in 1974 when all of a sudden we found that we had a need for funds, an unexpected need for funds because the cost of everything had gone sky-high for us, just as for everyone else. As an external environment we had to modify the program to accommodate that; we just chose not to ask for more money but restructured the program to stay within the available funds during that year.

Q: What caused you not to ask for additional funds?

Adm. W.: Two things really. One, the submarine program, by that time, was clearly slipping (the schedule for the TRIDENT submarine) and it was not at all obvious why we needed to hold to the original schedule. The needs for having the new TRIDENT system on the original schedule were not so great that we couldn't afford to slip the program in order to stay within available funds. Secondly, these technical difficulties that I referred to were giving us fits and we felt we could make good use of additional development time without going to heroic measures to hold to a tight schedule. Finally, we knew if we asked for the money it would probably come out of the navy's hide and hurt the navy more than it would hurt anything else; and, Congress would probably not give us more money, they would simply say, "Fine, we approve of your taking it out of some other program," and we didn't feel that the need justified that kind of solution.

Q: Going back to your original illustration, what was the compelling emphasis on increased range at that point?

Adm. W.: Security of the submarines. If one increases the range of the missile one greatly increases the amount of ocean that we can deploy submarines in. This meant that by giving our ballistic missiles in these submarines ranges in excess of 4000 miles, once the ship cleared port in the United States, it was capable of covering targets in the Soviet Union. It made it possible for instance, to remove the submarine squadron that had been based in Rota and return it to continental United States without ever changing the coverage, so that dependence upon overseas or foreign tender sites was eliminated, at the same time the entire ocean became available for deploying submarines instead of a narrow arc of ocean close to the European land mass.

Q: Does it follow then that the need for these overseas bases is eliminated?

Adm. W.: As far as the TRIDENT equipped submarine is concerned, yes. The only one that now remains, as I am sure you are aware, is the base at Holy Loch in Scotland, which supports POSEIDON submarines.

Q: And that was always much more secure than Rota.

Adm. W.: And they were much more comfortable there anyway where we know we are welcome.

In November of 1977 I relieved Admiral Smith as the Director of Strategic Systems Projects (SSPO) and that, as far as I am concerned, is another one of those peaks.

Q: That was really getting to the top of the mountain.

Adm. W.: As far as I am concerned it was. There isn't any other job in the navy that I aspired to at all.

Q: That is precisely why you stayed in the navy, because this was something that you really wanted to do.

Adm. W.: I really had never expected to become director, I really felt that the top job for me was Technical Director and being asked to relieve Admiral Smith when he chose to depart the navy was icing on the cake. I must admit that there is nothing quite comparable to having the full responsibility. One can develop a taste for that sort of thing.

Q: And this underscores your sense of modesty as I discern it.

Adm. W.: I'll not comment on that.

It was my great pleasure, in the ensuing three years, to complete the TRIDENT weapon system initial development and production and deployment and see the system actually tested in its operational submarines, and see the weapon system prove out as reliable--even more reliable--and its performance even better than we had committed to back in 1971.

Q: In the process, were you enabled to spent a prolonged period on a TRIDENT equipped submarine?

Adm. W.: I tried to go to sea with the weapons trials,

what is called a demonstration/shake-down operation, of each of the submarines as they came out of the back-fit process. I tried to ride every submarine when it went through its DASO process, the DASO being what you might say is the graduation exercise for the submarine completing either shipyard initial construction or the conversion. In the case of the TRIDENT back-fits they are being equipped with the TRIDENT capability. Every ship I possibly could I would ride during that period, the DASO period, and it culminated for about half the time in the launching of the missile in the ocean areas around Cape Canaverel. These are also wonderful opportunities to take people to sea for a day to show them what the fleet ballistic missile system is and what it is capable of doing.

Q: That's a VIP program? For highly selected guests?

Adm. W.: That's right, they were highly selected, we would take those selected people on board the submarine and the nice thing about it is that unclassified trips at sea can be had by many other people on the surface ship that accompanies the submarine and they can actually see the missile launched. Other participants in the program who aren't necessarily VIPs, even members of the family of people in the program can ride that ship on occasion. I have done that on only one or two occasions in all the years I have been in the program. My wife has had the opportunity to do it a couple of times and she says it brings tears to her eyes. It is a very impressive sight to see a missile emerging from the ocean and launching itself thousands of miles down range, especially I presume if one is a close member of the family of one who has spent the bulk of his life working on it.

Q: That adds to the emotional impact.

Adm. W.: It is hard for members of the family not to be involved emotionally with something like that.

Q: Did you, as the director, have any involvement in the maintenance of morale problems in the force and that whole area?

Adm. W.: Do you mean the operating submarine force?

Q: Yes.

Adm. W.: Not directly. Indirectly I think that we may have helped a little by making certain that the operators of the systems were given systems that worked well and were given help in maintaining those systems so that they knew they were not being thrown into the abyss with a strange weapon system that they were going to be held accountable for maintaining without any help. We had a very, very tight closed loop system for following up on any deficiency in the weapon system. I would like to think that knowing that kind of help was available, the help and morale of the people who were serving in the program, certainly going to sea and staying submerged for two month patrols, out of contact with families excepting for emergency messages, is a potential morale killer, but for two decades POLARIS submariners have been doing just that and their esprit and elan is as high as any in the navy. A lot of credit goes to a lot of other people, not necessarily S.P. but S.P. I think has done a lot to make certain that the equipment these people have been given to use and the maintenance support to help them with their maintenance problems, have reflected the importance the program has to the nation, and that is bound to help morale. I think the key to anyone's morale in this business is the knowledge that the sacrifice that he or she is making is in a good cause, it is a job that is worth doing, it is important to the country, that it is appreciated by one's countrymen, working with first-class people--all of these elements have been present in the fleet ballistic missile program both on the supply side in the part of the world that I have been living in, as well as the user's side--the operators. I think that is a very important team.

Q: Your path and that of Admiral Rickover must have converged much more frequently as director?

Adm. W.: Because of the organizational relationship, the set-up back in 1971 by the Chief of Naval Operations, namely the establishment of a separate project office--a TRIDENT Program Manager which allowed the separation of S.P., SSPO from the submarine community directly, this meant that Admiral Rickover interfaced much less with the director of S.P. than he had in the earlier days of POLARIS. So the answer to your surmise is, not really; I had very little interaction with Admiral Rickover.

One thing that did occur late in 1980 I would like to mention as an event of some significance--this was the decision on the part of the United Kingdom to follow the US example and to proceed with TRIDENT as a successor system. You will recall I mentioned they had chosen not to do that in the case of POSEIDON and as a consequence they did not have the POSEIDON conversion--they hadn't converted their POLARIS submarines to POSEIDON therefore they were not in a position to back-fit those boats to TRIDENT as we were doing. Their decision in effect was to replace their POLARIS submarines out in the more distant future with a new weapons system.

Q: Maintaining them currently in operation?

Adm. W.: Maintaining an improved version of the POLARIS in operation in the interim. This decision was ratified for a couple of reasons the most important of which was that they had done a complete review of all the alternatives available to them if they were to maintain an independent nuclear deterrent and in reviewing all of these alternatives land based, sea based, air launched, cruise missiles--the whole gamut of possibilities, they concluded that what they really wanted was to continue with the submarine based ballistic missile system. In other words, our staunchest ally and a very, very astute group of scientists and politicians on the other side of the Atlantic Ocean for whom we should have the highest affection as well as respect. Their economic condition permits them not a TRIAD but only a single capability. Faced with that decision it chose a version of our submarine ballistic missile system.

Q: Can you enumerate the major factors that induced them to make this decision?

Adm. W.: All I can really say, since I wasn't a participant in their internal debate and discussions, is that they produced a white paper which they presented to the Parliament explaining their decision, and they concluded for a given capability they felt this was the most certain and least costly way to achieve it. Their other capabilities, the other systems they can procure cost them less but would not have given them equal effectiveness; given the effect they wanted to maintain--assured capability of delivering a certain amount of payload to the Soviet heartland under the most pessimistic assumptions--the least costly way of doing that was with the TRIDENT system on nuclear powered submarines.

Q: They see this as essential to maintain their status as a major nation?

Adm. W.: I presume so. It was a vote of confidence, or an

endorsement if anything, not only of the system we had developed by also the relationship that we had established with them and maintained through the years. They were, in effect, buying a continuation of that relationship as well as the system.

Q: Did you consult with the committee drawing up the White Paper? Did they ask for your advice?

Adm. W.: Not directly. Of course I worked very closely with my Royal Navy counterparts in providing them with that information which classification permitted me to give them. I was also called upon to brief senior members of the British Government and their technical bureaucracy when they came over to this country and were given the various alternatives that the US was prepared to offer them in the way of assistance. These were meetings which were sponsored at the White House level and, in our case, were authorized and supported by the Office of the Secretary of Defense. There were members of the State Department present and International Security Affairs and the like. At these sessions we were authorized to be quite open in spelling out alternatives and I, and my technical director presented our characteristics of the various sea-based alternatives, TRIDENT being one but not the only one. Others gave them information about land-based options and cruise missile alternatives and the like. This was all information which they used in preparing their own analysis.

Q: By virtue of your office and your activities, were you thrown in with the National Security Council?

Adm. W.: Oh yes, not on this particular issue but actually it was the NSC staff that was sponsoring these meetings with the British. On other occasions the President's science advisor has set up committees to look into one or another aspect of the strategic programs and have been called upon to brief them and present options and alternatives to them. This was particularly true in the formative days of the ULMS and TRIDENT. There was a lot of healthy skepticism as to whether or not it would be possible to build a SLBM that would have the range that we were projecting for TRIDENT and if we did that it would be capable of coming anywhere within the ball park of the target. So accuracy and range objectives were brought into technical question and we reviewed this with our scientific peers and that forum.

Q: So the educational process was in operation?

Adm. W.: The bureaucracy has checks and balances galore.

Q: Were you thrown in with Zbigniew Brzezinski?

Adm. W.: I have never met Dr. Brzezinski although on one occasion he was supposed to have ridden a DASO submarine with me and he cancelled out of it. That would have been the only occasion for our meeting. He was more concerned

I think with policy than with engineering decisions.

Q: But policy has to be based upon the engineering decisions and what they result in?

Adm. W.: Indeed. Perhaps he trusted people that were giving him the information, I hope.

That I believe brings us pretty close to the present day.

Q: You were director for three years.

Adm. W.: Yes, for three years, and then came the decision to retire.

I have been asked about the timing of that decision.

Q: When did you make it?

Adm. W.: About a year before I departed.

Q: It is not a job you can leave at the last minute.

Adm. W.: No, and certainly not one that I would leave without the complete support of my superiors, and certainly not a position that I would leave at all happily having spent so long in that program. In many respects it is tempting to stay on forever--as long as one could--because after all it is the best job in the navy for a person such as myself. However, thinking about it realistically I have lectured people, in the past, about the importance of tying the personnel changes at the top, in a project, to key events in that project; in particular the key to successful program mangement is to insist that the individual who makes the commitments be required to see those commitments through and be held accountable for the results at the end.

Q: And actually you are talking about TRIDENT I?

Adm. W.: That was right, but now we are facing into a new generation and TRIDENT II is now the next program that will be undertaken by the Strategic Systems Project Office; the large, new TRIDENT submarine will be going to sea, the first one will be completed this year and there will be successors coming out every year thereafter but anticipating the lead time for developing and producing a new system, it turns out that the TRIDENT II is the larger, new missile that will make full use of that TRIDENT submarine and will start its development during this coming year. I felt that however much I might enjoy that job it wouldn't be fair for me to stay and be the one responsible for going to the Congress and making commitments about what we were going to do, what we were going to be capable of delivering, for how much money, and on what schedule, for a new weapons system and not be the one that stays there to deliver it.

Q: And you anticipated the length of time would be what?

Adm. W.: It would be six or seven years and that would be unrealistic, to expect to be able to stay that much longer.

It would be well past the statutory retirement age. So, I had a technical director, Admiral Glenwood Clark, Jr. who had a history in the program not unlike my own. He came in as a lieutenant commander, had progressed through various increasing positions of responsibility within the office, he had succeeded me as technical director, and at that point had been in the program for some fifteen years. He is an outstanding engineer, an outstanding program manager, he demonstrated that he had fully learned and understood the principles on which S.P. had based its successful development, production and support, and had proven that he was capable of managing this program by demonstrating it in various positions of responsibility; he had been selected flag officer while he was technical director; he was available to relieve me and he was acceptable to my bosses as a successor. There was no assurance at all that an equally qualified individual would be available some years hence. I am certain that he would have left the navy before I was ready to leave had I committed to staying another six or seven years. The timing was such that both from the program point of view as well as the readiness and availability of a suitable successor to continue what I hope is going to be a long history in the future, as well as in the past, of successful program management.

Q: In the S.P. organization, how can you provide and don't

you provide for understudys--people like Clark who is qualified in every sense--considering the frailties of the human body?

Adm. W.: S.P. is marginally large enough to permit a few selected individuals to make a career in it. I say marginally large enough because obviously a systems command like the Naval Sea Systems Command or the Naval Air Systems Command is plenty large enough, the navy has corps of officers who specialize in their activities and they have full careers as aeronautical engineers and naval engineers. The same thing is true of other groups in the navy such as the Naval Constructors and the Naval Facilities Engineering Command; but a typical project is not, it is too small to have career rotation in it and career broadening, and most projects do not last that long anyway. S.P. is different. In many respects it is more like a small systems command than it is a large project in the sense that it has this continuity, it has this open-ended responsibility and it has field activities as well as headquarters activities that allow a broadening of individuals so that we can afford to have a few people coming into the program that are technical officers who can stay and be promoted and raised aloft. But, it is a fragile thing, a tenuous thing because you are running a risk when you are dealing with such a small number of people that you are not going to have the right person when you need him. Fortunately so far we have.

Q: You see what I was concerned about.

Adm. W.: Yes, and I am comfortable, very comfortable with the qualifications of Admiral Clark and he has some excellent younger officers following along behind him and, hopefully, we will be able to keep a few of them and entice them to stay. Most of them seem to be well motivated to stay and are challenged by what I believe will be the next very exciting new development in the program and that is the exploitation of the TRIDENT as a base for the next generation of strategic missiles at sea and the increasing importance of the sea-based leg of our national strategic TRIAD. I think with the difficulties of a land-based system becoming more and more apparent to everyone it is inevitable that people are going to appreciate and want to exploit the sea-based option. I think it is in good hands with Admiral Clark.

Q: Would you say something about what compels a new generation to develop on the horizon--say a new generation of TRIDENT? What are the factors that converge to make this so?

Adm. W.: I believe those factors are the same as those which characterize almost every new weapon system and that is a convergence of need and opportunity. There has to be a need obviously, nobody is going to spend money on something that doesn't provide a capability that is required even if the appreciation for the need wasn't there until the opportunity presented itself. On the other hand it has to be technologically feasible, it has to be possible, and that often becomes apparent only when certain scientific or engineering break-throughs occur. The original POLARIS was, I believe I have described in our earlier conversations, a beautiful example of the convergence of need and opportunity. Each of the successor systems has reflected that to a greater or lesser degree. I don't believe that either one in isolation will result in convincing the totality of our bureaucracy that a program should proceed.

Q: When you were talking about the British a short time ago and their limited funds for the development of new programs and the amount of agonizing they evidently engaged in before they made this most recent decision, I wondered why when they had POLARIS and it was adequate some years ago, why it wouldn't be adequate today for them in their circumstances? Certainly it still had fire power.

Adm. W.: Yes; and of course it is adequate today and it will continue to be adequate, it will have to be adequate for them for a long time in the future. What we were talking about when we discussed TRIDENT for the British is a follow-on system to POLARIS which will not become available to them for many, many years. What they had to think ahead to was the time when their existing submarines would have to be replaced because they would approach an age where it would become more costly to maintain them than they were worth to them and they would want to have a successor generation of submarines. Then the question is, "Do we want to do that, do we want to continue with submarines or should we proceed with something else and if it is to be a submarine system, what system?" It will be well into the '90s before the British begin to replace the POLARIS. Another factor that affected the British of course was the availability of US support. Our POLARIS systems will be completely out of US inventory long before the British are, and they with a few submarines cannot afford the testing that is necessary to maintain confidence in the dependability of an aging system. They have depended very heavily upon the US testing of a much larger inventory of identical systems in order to maintain their own competence.

Q: In a sense they are a kind of satellite and they are attached to us.

Adm. W.: That's right. When they become unique, as they will, when the US POLARIS systems are completely out of the inventory, they will be unique, they will have a configuration unique to them alone. It is going to be very lonely for them and we will continue to support them by providing them contractual assistance, some engineering advice and logistic support and all that. But, since the data upon which they base their competence is going to be limited without any US inputs to it, it is going to become increasingly tenuous and that is why they want to move into a system that will share the US configuration and that is TRIDENT. I think they learned a very harsh lesson when they chose not to move with us when we modernized with POSEIDON.

Q: I suppose that was tending to move into a philosophical realm. I was about to ask, if ever we can envision the time when there will be a cut-off to the development of new generations of such weapons, or is this an impossibility?

Adm. W.: No, certainly it is not an impossibility, I think that we can hypothesize a certain stance that would cause us to lose interest in modernizing a fleet ballistic missile system and that would be the time when the nuclear submarine no longer represented a secure and survivable base for such operations.

Q: Something else taking its place?

Adm. W.: Well, let us assume that science provides a break-through that literally turns the oceans transparent so that one could keep track of submarines the same way we now, or presumably will some day soon be able, to keep track of surface ships. The ocean is a remarkably benign medium for submarines and a terrible medium for submarine hunters. It is an electrolyte, it conducts electricity therefore it is not penetrated easily by electro-magnetic radiation, it is inhomogeneous--it has layers of warm and cooler water which tend to distort the sound beams--it has currents, it has fish, it has other ocean traffic both surface and sub-surface both generating noise, it has all kinds of miserable things which make it hard to find a submarine particularly if you are looking for a special kind of submarine as opposed to all other things that might sound like it. So, its a great place to hide, a marvelous place to hide today. But we can imagine a situation where that changes, a hypothetical scientific break-through; when that happens then we will no longer be willing to make these multi-billion dollar investments in putting missiles in submarines.

Q: Of course you can't hold back the imagination of man which is involved in the development of new generations of weaponry.

Adm. W.: That's true and we will continue (when I say we I mean my successors now) I think to have a responsibility to suggest alternative ways of further modernizing and improving and advancing the capabilities in a system like this in which we have invested so much so that our political leadership can decide what they want to do. No one else can realistically make such proposals. We also have the responsibility of postponing that day of reckoning, the day when that scientific break-through could occur as much as we possibly can. That's another responsibility that the S.P. has--it is managing a continuing advanced development program aimed at pursuing all the technologies, all the relevant technologies necessary to assure the continuing survivability of the SSBM force, trying to anticipate any possible break-through and develop alternative procedures, counter measures, techniques, tactics to postpone this as far into the future as possible the day when anyone could, with any justification, say "I know how to threaten the continued survivability of the SSBM force." I don't perceive that happening myself, but part of that confidence in that not happening is based on that scientific program. We have to run scared.

Q: This calls always for a constant re-examination of all these factors in the ocean that you mentioned earlier which serve as a deterrent. It must be fascinating.

Adm. W.: Yes; it is and it was fascinating.

Q: So, it must have caused you certain pangs to leave the job at that point, even though you gave very cogent reasons for doing so, but it must have caused you some pangs to step down and, momentarily at least, think in terms of retirement?

Adm. W.: I had severe pangs, I still suffer them occasionally. To walk away from a position like that for which one has prepared during his entire career, is not easy. Certainly I had severe withdrawal pains. Nevertheless it was the right thing to do I believe.

Q: And you are a man of conviction so you have maintained, at least externally, a very pleasant countenance in the light of that. But now it has ameliorated somewhat, has it not, by going into a new realm which has some connection-- it has to do with national defense at least? Would you say a little about what you are stepping into?

Adm. W.: First of all let me say that I don't have any illusions at all about ever (of what's left to me of my professional life) finding a position which would combine all of the elements of satisfaction that I have enjoyed in my navy career. The only thing that could possibly have kept me in that long had to have been that sense of satisfaction with what I was doing.

Q: You have said that from time to time when the temptation came to leave or were on the verge of leaving, you stayed because of all these satisfactions.

Adm. W.: Almost to the point of convincing myself that I never really would leave. I determined, when I did leave, that whatever I did with myself I wanted to continue somehow or other to apply what limited talent I had and the experience I had to national security matters. I wanted to continue to somehow or another, in one role or another, contribute to the nation's security. Why? Because I was equipped to do it and certainly that, more than anything else, would rationalize whatever I had done with my life up until then. Perhaps that is self-justification as much as anything. I have chosen to make myself available, at no cost, to the Office of the Secretary of Defense to consult when and as they desire, and the same is true as I have made a similar arrangement with the Los Alamos Scientific Laboratory at Los Alamos, New Mexico who have asked me to serve them in a similar capacity. I am working on an Arms Control Study with the Carnegie Institution, and continuing to advise the Joint Strategic Target Planning Staff in Omaha as a member of their Scientific Advisory Group; so these activities have continued and will continue. In the meantime I have been considering a number of options for full-time employment which would allow me to continue with these other things on the side. I have recently been invited by the Lockheed Corporation to take a position as their senior Vice-president for Science and Engineering, which would give me a position on the corporate staff of assisting the company president in deciding the allocation of research and development investments across the entire corporation. Recognizing that in our free enterprise system, unlike the Soviets, the government depends very heavily on its defense industry to carry out projects and programs in support of the country. We do not have national production facilities and the like comparable to the Soviets. We depend on private, competitive enterprise to carry out our major projects. Lockheed Corporation is one of the largest defense contractors in the nation, it is active in military aircraft, space, missiles, shipbuilding, electronics--all of these areas and others that are too classified to discuss. It performs functions for the government, for the Department of Defense, and other defense agencies that cannot be done as well by others. The opportunity to influence the course of events within decision making at the top in such a corporation appeared to me to be one of being able to apply my background and experience constructively, expecially when they indicated that they would be willing to allow me to continue these other consulting activities for the government. So, being a far cry from being a director of a Strategic Systems Projects it certainly was an opportunity to be useful and that's why I have chosen to go along with that.

Q: Well I think it is a great opportunity for the employment of all your manifold talents and I am delighted. Thank you for giving me this record which I am sure will be one of the stellar ones in our collection.

Appendix

to

Reminiscences

of

Rear Admiral Robert Halley Wertheim
U. S. Navy (Retired)

Remarks by RADM R. H. Wertheim, USN
           Director, Strategic Systems Projects
For the   National Security Industrial Association Luncheon
           11 April 1980

It is good to be here with so many friends. I accept the consequent risk of preaching to the choir.

I. Evidence of Success

While all the returns are not yet in, the data available today supports a conclusion that the TRIDENT weapon system development has met or exceeded all of its objectives.

The principal development objective of the TRIDENT Strategic Weapon System was to make vastly greater patrol areas available to our SSBN Force through increased missile range -- and to do this without compromise to reliability or accuracy. Our range goals have been exceeded by a substantial margin.

With regard to reliability, 21 of the 24 valid flight tests in the development program were fully successful. What is of even more significance, this reliability record is holding up in the rapidly growing number of tests of production missiles from operational submarines.

With regard to costs -- neglecting inflation, the development came in within 6% of the figure we had committed at the start of engineering development and missile production unit costs are below our design-to-cost goal.

While I can't give you accuracy figures in an unclassified forum, suffice it to say that our data base indicates that we are well inside our performance objectives.

Two SSBN's that were until recently deployed with POSEIDON are today operationally deployed with the TRIDENT Weapon System, a third is in its final pre-deployment phase and additional POSEIDON ships are being backfitted. I am confident they will be deployed on schedule. At the same time, weapon system equipments are being delivered, installed and checked out in support of the new TRIDENT submarine construction schedules, and missiles will be ready for them when they arrive at their new base at Bangor, Washington.

All concerned in our government-industry team (many of whom are here today) can take justifiable pride in these statistics.

II. Factors in Success Story

It is often hard to pin down the reasons for successes or shortfalls of a project in such a way that either successes can be repeated or failures avoided in subsequent similar undertakings. It is my impression that those who write military procurement directives put a disproportionate emphasis in the latter. It is somehow easier to proscribe than to prescribe.

I would like to address some of my remarks today to the other side of that coin as well -- that is, the positive elements that I believe have contributed to the TRIDENT I success story. First of all, it must be emphasized that TRIDENT I is the product of the same organization - including most of the same prime contractors - that were first assembled by Admirals Red Raborn and Levering Smith to develop and produce the POLARIS Program. This team has provided life-cycle support and when necessary the evolutionary modernizations of our Fleet Ballistic Missile System over the past quarter century.

Also important to note that the Strategic Systems Project Office organization is tailored to its task - it reflects the architecture of the weapon system that is its principal product. The project is managed by logical FBM weapon subsystems which are capable of being separately specified and separately tested. Thus we have branches and contractor teams with cradle-to-grave responsibility for launcher fire control and guidance, navigation, test instrumentation, ship installation and missile. Within well-defined interfaces, each of these teams have all necessary authority to develop, produce, and support a workable subsystem within budgetary and schedule constraints.

This vertical organization and many of the management discipline put into effect at the outset of the program have demonstrably stood the test of time and are as valid today as they were 25 years ago.

Continuity of people, program and style of operation pays off in many ways. Not the least of those is the important discipline of knowing where the buck stops. The people who are responsible for the design of the equipment are also responsible for the consequences of that design, whether they show up in terms of produceability, maintainability or reliability.

Having to live with one's mistakes is a marvelous way to learn from them and this learning process is readily apparent in the evolution of the Fleet Ballistic Missile System from POLARIS to TRIDENT.

Changes have taken place -- some of them significant ones -- in the way we do our business. For example, all of the three generations of POLARIS were developed under CPFF contracts. Starting with POSEIDON, and with further refinements in TRIDENT, we shifted to completion type, multi-year, fully structured incentive contracts. We found that the extensive time and effort put in at the outset in negotiating the incentive structure served the program well. The process forced us to sort out and quantify program objectives and priorities so that our contractors could make the trade-offs we wanted during their conduct of the program. Out contracts have as an objective the alignment of the government's and the constractors' interests such that if the project succeeds, we all prosper and if it falls short, we suffer together.

This is one of the factors that accounts for the teamwork that has characterized our programs over the years. An even more important one is the knowledge shared by each of us, military and civilian -- in government and industry alike -- that we are participating in an undertaking of supreme importance to our country and that each individual matters to the success of the program. This sense of personal responsibility and involvement extends from the top to the bottom of our organization and is probably the single most important factor in our success. When the principle of "<u>MANAGEMENT BY OBJECTIVES</u>" was first articulated, we found that that was what we had been doing all along.

III. Contrasts -- Then and Now

Much of the change that has taken place over the years, however, is in our external environment. Admiral Raborn used to tell us "We don't have problems in the POLARIS Program - only Challenges." I have tried to sustain that attitude, but recently one of my engineers replied: "But, Admiral, some of these 'challenges' are insuperable."

It is hard to explain to anyone who was not a part of the POLARIS Program in the early days, the exhilaration and sense of purpose we all shared. The Chief of Naval Operations, Admiral Arleigh Burke, had written a letter delegating full authority to Admiral Raborn to get the job done, and Red made the most of it. He carried the letter around in his pocket, but since everyone knew about it, he rarely had to invoke it.

At first, I suspect that the normal bureaucracy was only too happy to step aside and let him have his way, because it did not want to be even remotely accountable for what could well have turned out to have been the greatest procurement disaster in the history of the Navy. By the time it was generally appreciated that the idea of launching long range ballistic missiles with nuclear warheads from a submerged submarine really wasn't all that nutty, it was too late to "help" in the many areas of special interest to functional staff members who do not share in the P.M.'s responsibilities. The sense of personal commitment in SP was pervasive. Let me tell you a little story on myself.

One day in 1960, after the first POLARIS was safely deployed, I was meeting in my office with the Technical Director of Sandia Laboratories, Jack Howard. Jack and I had worked closely together in the design, development and initial production of the integrated POLARIS re-entry body/warhead. I suggested it was time he met our Technical Director, Captain Levering Smith, and he agreed. I took him to Levering's office and introduced them. After the normal pleasantries, Jack volunteered his views on why the highly accelerated joint AEC-DOD efforts on this nuclear weapon had been so successful. The principal reason, he said, was because for the first time the Navy had had the good sense to delegate to its

MEMBER THE FULL AUTHORITY TO MAKE DECISIONS AT JOINT COORDINATING COMMITTEE MEETINGS AND TO COMMIT THE NAVY ON THE SPOT. AFTER A LONG SILENCE, LEVERING POINTED TO ME AND SAID, "YOU MEAN HIM? HE NEVER HAD THAT AUTHORITY!" SORRY ABOUT THAT, JACK.

AS ADMIRAL RABORN'S SUCCESSOR SEVERAL TIMES REMOVED, IT IS HARD NOT TO BE A BIT WISTFUL ABOUT THE SUPPORT THE DIRECTOR OF SP ENJOYED IN THOSE DAYS.

FOR EXAMPLE, THE ORIGINAL SP STAFF MEMBERS WERE SELECTED AND LITERALLY PUT TO WORK THE VERY NEXT DAY. TWENTY-FIVE YEARS LATER AS MANY OF THESE VETERANS RETIRE, I FIND THAT ADMINISTRATIVE PROCEDURES FOR BRINGING THEIR SUCCESSORS ON BOARD CAN TAKE THE BETTER PART OF A YEAR. WITH A HIRING FREEZE, OF COURSE THE TIME BECOMES INDEFINITE.

WHEN OUR FIRST DIRECTOR TESTIFIED BEFORE THE CONGRESS ON HIS ANNUAL BUDGET REQUESTS, HE PRESENTED A SINGLE INTEGRATED PROGRAM TO FOUR COMMITTEES. IN CONTRAST, LAST YEAR NAVY WITNESSES MADE TWENTY-THREE APPEARANCES BEFORE CONGRESSIONAL COMMITTEES AND SUBCOMMITTEES TESTIFYING ON ELEMENTS OF THE FBM PROGRAM WHICH WERE IDENTIFIED AS PORTIONS OF THE NAVY'S "PROGRAMS" FOR R&D, WEAPONS PROCUREMENT, OTHER PROCUREMENT, SHIP CONSTRUCTION, MILITARY CONSTRUCTION, OR OPERATIONS AND MAINTENANCE. BALANCING THE NAVY BOOKS ON ALL THESE ACCOUNTS IS A LABOR-INTENSIVE PROCESS OF SUB-OPTIMIZATION WHICH ADDS NO VALUE TO THE PROGRAM OR ILLUMINATION FOR THOSE WHO NEED TO UNDERSTAND MY FUNDING REQUIREMENTS. OBVIOUSLY, NONE OF THESE CHANGES HAVE PREVENTED US FROM GETTING OUR JOB DONE, BUT THEY HAVE MADE IT HARDER.

IV. THE NEW DOGMA ON MANAGEMENT

I EARLIER STATED MY IMPRESSION THAT THE AUTHORS OF OUR PROCUREMENT DIRECTIVES TEND TO PLACE THEIR EMPHASIS ON THE NEGATIVE -- THAT IS, THEY WRITE RULES WHICH ARE INTENDED TO MAKE SURE THAT BAD THINGS THAT HAPPENED BEFORE CAN NEVER HAPPEN AGAIN. SINCE THERE ARE LOTS OF BAD THINGS IN OUR WORLD, AND THERE ARE LOTS OF VERSIONS OF WHY they happened, there are lots of rules to guard against them. There appears to be less interest in understanding why some projects work out well, and in writing rules which would attempt to make repetitions of such success more likely.

About 10 years ago, David Packard as DEPUTYSECDEF called for a new emphasis on project management and wrote a landmark memorandum on the subject. In it Mr. Packard said:

> "In order to be effective, program managers must be given adequate authority to make decisions on major questions relating to the program."

No disagreement on that.

Amongst other things, his memorandum established as DOD Policy that <u>unnecessary</u> concurrency between development and production should be avoided. The general policies in the Packard memo were later promulated, with somewhat less flexibility to the military departments by DOD Directive 5000.1. With regard to T&E it stated in part:

> "...A determination of operational suitability will be made prior to large scale production commitments..."

Within the Navy, the screws were tightened further. OPNAV Instruction 4720.9 and NAVMATINST 4720.1 were promulgated which require "approval for service use" before production will be approved. This requires a determination by the CNO or other delegated authority that there has been:

> "(1) Demonstrated reliable performance, in accordance with design specifications, in the intended or existing operational environment.
>
>   (2) Demonstrated ability to be operated and maintained by Navy personnel with the level of skill anticipated to be available under fleet service conditions.

(3) Sufficient evidence that the equipment can be supported logistically in a deployed status."

All of which may have sounded eminently reasonable as a way of avoiding repetition of acquisition shortfalls which - rightly or wrongly - had been ascribed to premature commitment to production -- but it put us in SP between a rock and a hard place if we were to apply POLARIS and POSEIDON experience to the TRIDENT missile program.

To understand this, it must be appreciated that the nature of the major end item of the FBM system is a complex, costly item of expendable ordnance which cannot be fully tested without destroying the missile tested. Much of what we think we know about the ballistic missiles that are operationally deployed is based upon extrapolations from those we have destructively tested, and the validity of that extrapolation depends upon our ability to assure that no change has taken place in the materials, tools, processes or personnel used in their manufacture.

In every generation of the FBM system, from POLARIS A-1 onward, we had taken extraordinary care, through application of rigid engineering and production management disciplines, to avoid unintended change as we moved from experimental missile manufacture into rate production. In order to avoid line breaks between development and production hardware required production expenditures beginning about the time of the start of full-scale development flight testing, which was some 2-3 years before IOC. Such concurrency was accepted and even applauded for POLARIS A-1, A-2, A-3 and POSEIDON as a way of minimizing acquisition time.

For TRIDENT however, we were faced with a dilemma between the new rules and the old reasons. In the end, it was necessary to seek an exception from the Deputy Secretary of Defense in order

TO USE IN TRIDENT THE CONCURRENCY PROCEDURES WHICH HAD BEEN DEMONSTRABLY SUCCESSFUL IN ALL OUR PREDECESSOR FBM GENERATIONS AND WHICH WE HAD GOOD REASON TO BELIEVE WERE ESSENTIAL TO THAT SUCCESS. DEPSECDEF ULTIMATELY FOUND IT APPROPRIATE IN THE TRIDENT PROGRAM TO: "WAIVE TO DEGREE NECESSITATED BY THE PROGRAM, THE REQUIREMENTS OF DOD DIRECTIVES 5000.1 AND 5000.3 CONCERNING FULL AND COMPLETE T&E PRIOR TO COMMITMENT TO PRODUCTION."

IN A SIMILAR VEIN, THE CNM WAS PERSUADED TO AUTHORIZE THE DIRECTOR, SSP TO DEVIATE FROM THE CNM'S NEW AND SPECIFIC REQUIREMENTS REGARDING THE TREATMENT OF RELIABILITY AND MAINTAIN-ABILITY," ...WHEN, IN THE DIRECTOR'S JUDGMENT, ALTERNATE METHODS/PROCEDURES WILL PROVIDE THE DESIRED RELIABILITY AND MAINTAINABILITY OF THE TRIDENT MISSILE SWS DEVELOPMENT AND INITIAL PRODUCTION."

I MUST CONCLUDE FROM THIS THAT IT IS SOMEHOW EASIER TO TREAT SP AND ITS PROGRAMS AS <u>EXCEPTIONS</u> TO A GENERAL SET OF RULES THAN TO USE THEM AS A FAVORABLE <u>EXAMPLE</u>.

V. While the Tears are Wet

IF THERE IS ANY MESSAGE I MUST HAVE DRAWN FROM MY EXPERIENCE, IT IS THAT THE RULES CAN AND MUST BE SET ASIDE WHEN JUSTIFIED BY OVER-RIDING PROGRAM NEEDS. AS ALWAYS, THE BURDEN OF PROOF IS ON THE PROJECT MANAGER WHEN HE WISHES TO TAKE ISSUE WITH THE CONVENTIONAL WISDOM. THAT IS OF COURSE EASIER FOR AN OUTFIT WITH A TRACK RECORD LIKE SP THAN FOR A TYPICAL NEW P.M. WITH HIS MATRIX MANAGEMENT ORGANIZATION. EVEN FOR US HOWEVER, IT ISN'T EASY TO PLAY THE ROLE OF THE SMALL BOY WHO COULDN'T BRING HIMSELF TO ADMIRE THE EMPEROR'S NEW CLOTHES. TIMING IS ALL-IMPORTANT. AS THE WISE OLD LAWYER ADVISED HIS YOUNG COLLEAGUE: "ABOVE ALL REMEMBER THIS -- PRESENT YOUR BILL WHILE THE TEARS ARE WET."

IT IS ALSO TRUE IN THE BUSINESS OF PROGRAM MANAGEMENT, THAT

THE TIME TO GET THE RESOURCES COMMITTED AND ANY ESSENTIAL WAIVERS AUTHORIZED IS RIGHT UP FRONT BEFORE THE COMMITMENTS ARE MADE. UNFORTUNATELY, THIS IS THE VERY TIME WHEN MANY WOULD BE TRYING TO PUT THE BEST POSSIBLE FACE ON A NEW PROGRAM IN ORDER TO GET IT PAST ALL THE HURDLES IN THE PATH TO APPROVAL. I SUSPECT THAT PROGRAMMATIC POST-MORTEMS WOULD SHOW INITIAL OVERCOMMITMENT HAS BEEN THE GENESIS OF COST OVERRUNS AND PERFORMANCE SHORTFALLS AT LEAST AS OFTEN AS PREMATURE PRODUCTION COMMITMENTS.

VI. CONCLUSION

I WOULD LIKE TO CONCLUDE THESE GENERAL PHILOSOPHICAL OBSERVATIONS WITH A FINAL COMMENT ON THE MANAGEMENT OF THE FLEET BALLISTIC MISSILE PROGRAM. IN CARRYING OUT THE NAVY'S RESPONSIBILITY FOR WHAT HAS BECOME THE NATION'S MOST DEPENDABLE DETERRENT TO NUCLEAR WAR, I AM CONVINCED THAT THE KEY TO FUTURE SUCCESS WILL CONTINUE TO BE THE HARD WORK OF DEDICATED PEOPLE IN AN ORGANIZATION AND CONTRACTUAL STRUCTURE THAT ALLOWS APPLICATION OF RELEVANT EXPERIENCE AND OF THE POLICIES AND PROCEDURES THAT EXPERIENCE TEACHES US WORK WELL AND ARE RIGHT FOR THE PROGRAM. I AM ENOUGH OF AN OPTIMIST TO BELIEVE THAT THE SYSTEM WILL CONTINUE TO ALLOW THAT TO HAPPEN.

CHANGE OF PROJECT MANAGER AND RETIREMENT CEREMONY

30 October 1980

STRATEGIC SYSTEMS PROJECT OFFICE MANAGEMENT INFORMATION CENTER

CAPT Bunting: Please remain standing during the invocation given by Chaplain Chambliss.

Chaplain Chambliss: Lord of longevity, be our special guest and the guardian of our ceremony on this memorable occasion. The greatness of our nation is heavily dependent upon those individuals who, like Admiral Wertheim, volunteer their professional services, for freedom's sake. In due course, each careerist contemplates and must face this day with its torn loyalties and unavoidable ambiguities. In the months and the years of new leadership before us, help us to gain strength of character, so that we will be courageous in spirit, and maintain the high example set by this superb career, as he now leaves the Navy. Be with us today and always, I pray. Amen.

CAPT Bunting: Please be seated. Admiral A. J. Whittle, Chief of Naval Material.

ADM Whittle: First I'd like to apologize to everyone for having held up the ceremonies. It's now 1530. But I'm sure that most of you will recognize that it was in a good cause when I tell you that I was attending a CNO executive board meeting for a missile project. And since the issue was in doubt, I stayed until it was over. I can express myself quite briefly and succinctly on the subject of Robert Wertheim, not only briefly and succinctly but sincerely. I know of no one in the United States Navy more professional. I know of no one more dedicated, and I know of no one whom I trust more. On the subject of his retirement, I have mixed emotions -- regret at losing his services, and envy, because as you may or may not know, Bob and I are classmates, and long-time friends. I will miss him as much, if not more, than will those of you here in PM-1.

As I've told you before, when I talk to students at the Defense Systems Management Course, I use PM-1 as an example of the best managed programs in the United States Navy, and we have had four superlative program managers, shortly to have a fifth. If I said anything else, I'd be repeating myself, except for one facet of this program that is unique, and that is that it is not only one of the best programs in the United States Navy, it is also the best example of handling a foreign military sales program that I know of. I think that our Royal Navy friends will agree with me. Thank you.

CAPT Bunting: Rear Admiral Robert H. Wertheim, Director, Strategic Systems Projects

RADM Wertheim: Admiral Whittle, distinguished guests, family and friends. Let me say that I am not at all surprised that Admiral Whittle was inconvenienced by staying to help fight for one of his projects. It's quite typical of him, and let me say that it's been an honor and a pleasure to serve with you, sir. He mentioned that we graduated together from the Naval Academy. That was a little over 35 years ago. Only two or three short months later, after my class graduated, the Japanese surrendered. We modestly accept that that was a coincidence.

It's also not so obvious to those of us who have been aging slowly, to realize that most Americans have been born since then, and therefore cannot remember first-hand an unlimited war. The impact of World War II should be remembered. There were six years of conflict involving most of the civilized world. There were some 40 million lives lost, countless millions more that were disrupted, injured, displaced. The costs to the nations involved were countless trillions of dollars, including irreplaceable resources. It ended finally with the dropping of the first, and prayerfully the last, nuclear weapons ever detonated in anything other than tests. Now, in the 35 years since Nagasaki and Hiroshima, it's been the existence of those nuclear weapons and the means for their certain and inescapable delivery on enemy targets that has deterred unlimited warfare, either conventional or nuclear. Deterrence, I believe, has worked since World War II, in spite of tensions and provocations between great nations which have historically resulted in world wars.

Now, I don't think it is necessarily any basis for complacency on our part, because things change. During most of that post-war period, the United States of America had either a monopoly on nuclear weapons or unquestioned superiority. That condition no longer exists. The gap between us has closed, and some would say that it may have even become a little more than closed. At the same time, the threats that we can perceive to the other legs of our strategic Triad have been growing as well, and that has the effect of increasing the relative dependence of our national leadership on the system for which we are responsible, the Fleet Ballistic Missile System, for deterring nuclear war. It's the only leg of the Triad that is unquestionably survivable. The decade of the 80's that lies just ahead of us I believe will be a very dangerous time for our country. There's no doubt in my mind that the credibility of our deterrent will be tested, maybe more than once during this period, in this time that we call the window of vulnerability.

I'm also quite certain that during this period, this Office is going to be called upon for another critically important challenge, and that will be the modernization of TRIDENT to meet what will inevitably be an expanding responsibility for the Navy, for our strategic deterrence. And of course we will be called upon to do it promptly, on schedule, and at the least necessary cost, as we have in the past. This of course, will be in addition to the continuing missions that we have of supporting our operational forces, of providing an authoritative scientific basis for projecting the continued survivability of our missile submarines through our security technology program, and meeting our continued commitment to the United Kingdom, which has now been extended with the new TRIDENT Agreement well into the twenty-first century. And I might also add that I, too, am honored by the presence of my UK counterpart, Rear Admiral Grove, here to mark that responsibility.

I am confident that SP is in good shape to meet all these challenges, under a new leader, not only because Glen Clark has unique technical and managerial qualifications for the tasks that lie ahead, but also because of his personal integrity, and his uncompromising dedication to quality, upon which the confidence in our system has always and must continue always to be based. Most important, in my opinion, is that he is backed by the finest team of men and women, in uniform and out, in the government, and in our industrial support contractors, that has ever been assembled to manage a project. SP is armed with another asset, in my opinion, and that's 25 years of experience in conceiving, designing and developing, producing and supporting the Fleet Ballistic Missiles Systems through their life cycle--five generations. Oscar Wilde wrote that "Experience is the name that everyone gives their mistakes." And I think that we have made our share. We've also done a few things right. And hopefully, we've learned from both of them. For as another writer, George Santayana, put it, "Those who cannot remember the past are condemned to repeat it." On my own behalf, I have no better prescription for job satisfaction than to serve with a team of professionals armed with unambiguous responsibility for authority for a well-defined task whose importance is universally accepted. I'll be forever grateful to the Navy for having given me the opportunity here in this program.

Best of all, has been the opportunity to share it, share it all, with my wife, Barbara, and two fine sons. For the past 34 years, Barbara has been the one who has kept the bad times in perspective, and multiplied the pleasure from the good ones, which were much larger in number. I leave the Navy and this program with sadness, but with the great satisfaction of knowing that it is in good shape and in good hands. I will now read my orders.

"BUPERS order number 164817 dated 23 September 1980. When directed on 31 October 1980, detach from duty as Director, Strategic Systems Projects and proceed to your home of selection. You will regard yourself relieved from all active duty effective at 2400 on the date of detachment. Your request to be transferred to the retired list is approved by the Secretary of the Navy effective 1 November 1980. On 1 November 1980, you will be transferred to the retired list with the grade of Rear Admiral, pursuant to the provisions of 10, US Code 6322."

CAPT Bunting: Rear Admiral G. Clark, Jr.

RADM Clark: I will now read my orders: "BUPERS order 168450, dated 10 October 1980. When relieved, detach in October 1980 from duty as Technical Director, Strategic Systems Project Office, report to Chief of Naval Material for duty as Director, Strategic Systems Projects" Admiral Wertheim I relieve you as Director, Strategic Systems Projects.

In a very few days we will celebrate the 25th anniversary of SSPO, or as it used to be called, and I think is in some cases still preferred, SP or Special Projects. It will certainly not be a very exciting time, and it will certainly not be filled with horns and whistles. And I dare say that it will go completely unnoticed, by the world external to SP, and I suspect hardly more than a modest acknowledgement within our own headquarters. But for anyone who cares to analyze it, the first quarter of a century will find a very impressive record: five generations of Fleet Ballistic Missiles, with each successive generation being more capable, more survivable and more reliable. From what appeared to many outsiders to be a pretty screwy idea--the thought of launching a nuclear warhead from a submerged submarine, and expecting it to hit a target thousands of miles away--the FBM system has become this country's major deterrent to nuclear war, and I expect, to a major conventional war as well.

Admiral Wertheim spent the bulk of his professional career making all of this happen, having played a key role in this program for most of these 25 years. While his contributions to this feat are indeed remarkable, and certainly too numerous to mention, I believe his most lasting contribution is the role that he played in developing what I'd call, SSPO's way of doing business, or by some others perhaps, SSPO's Management Disciplines or Philosophy. He quite clearly recognized their importance to continued success of the program, instilling this basic philosophy, and rather fundamental philosophy, throughout all levels of our government and industry team, particularly as we approached the point in the life of our project when many of our senior people would be retiring, and as it has turned out almost all at the same time.

In this connection, Admiral Wertheim, I believe you have prepared us very well. You've been more than a Director, providing sound management and technical direction and guidance. You've been our coach, and our teacher, with the patience and wisdom to help us grow, to do our thing, to let us make our own mistakes, but always, very patiently, put us back on track when we veered off course. With this very capable team of government and industry people, which you and Admiral Smith have so successfully created, I proudly accept this responsibility which you pass to me today. Be assured that we will always do what needs to be done in the very highest traditions of SP and the very high standards of quality that you have set for this program.

As you well know, we have a custom in SP, one that involves

the providing of a plaque, which symbolizes participation in the FBM program. You are certainly not going to escape without receiving one. You'll note that it is a bit larger than some of the others that we give, but it's not nearly big enough to mark all the contributions that you've made to the FBM program. You'll also note that it's signed not by the Director, but by the previous three Directors, the ones that have preceded you: Vice Admiral Raborn, Admiral Galantin and Vice Admiral Levering Smith. We are going to miss you, and I hope you come back to see us at the lunch bunch.

RADM Wertheim: Thank you very, very much.

ADM Whittle: Before we proceed, I would like to point out that for the last two years plus, as a neophyte in the Naval Material Command, I've been coming to Admiral Wertheim for guidance and counsel, and he has given it to me freely, and I'm telling you this because I know a lot of you complain about NAVMAT a lot.

I have a certificate here that says that: "This flag of the United States of America was flown over the Capitol of the United States at the request of Senator Harrison H. Schmitt in honor of a distinguished son of New Mexico, Rear Admiral Robert H. Wertheim, United States Navy, upon the occasion of his retirement from active duty, effective 1 November 1980. George M. White, Architect of the Capitol." And here are the colors.

ADM Wertheim: Guess I'll have to get a flag pole.

ADM Whittle: Right!

I have here a letter from the Secretary of th Navy, which I would like to read:

"Dear Admiral Wertheim, You approach retirement from a long and distinguished military career. Please accept the gratitude of the Department of the Navy, with my personal appreciation for your more than 35 years of dedicated service to our Navy and our Nation. Early in your career you showed marked qualities of leadership and a potential for increasingly valuable service. Your recognized judgment and extensive experience concerning engineering matters have been of value in many situations. The citations and medals that you have received clearly reflect outstanding service during your military career. Especially noteworthy are the awards of the Distinguished Service Medal, the Legion of Merit, the Joint Service Commendation Medal, and the Navy Commendation Medal. In all situations, your total efforts have greatly benefited our Navy and Nation. Of special value have been your many contributions in your most recent position as Director, Strategic Systems Projects. In an extremely challenging environment, you have successfully managed the most multi-faceted program of the highest national importance. You will leave behind a brilliant record of achievement, one which will long serve as an example for those who follow. I join your many friends to wish that your retirement years will provide you with good health and warm memories and the deep satisfaction that comes from the knowledge that you have done your best for your country. Sincerely, Edward Hidalgo."

And now we get the bottom line: "Certificate of Retirement from the Armed Forces of the United States of America. To all who shall see these presents, greetings. This is to certify that Rear Admiral Robert H. Wertheim, having served faithfully and honorably, was retired from the United States Navy on the first day of November, 1980."

Barbara, will you join us? We have a tradition of presenting a certificate of appreciation from the Navy to the wives of officers who retire. I think in this case it is not enough, because Barbara is one of those who has made lasting contributions throughout Bob's career. And we will miss her as well.

I think that takes care of everything.

CAPT Bunting: Please rise for the Benediction.

Chaplain Chambliss: The Lord bless you and keep you. The Lord make His face to shine upon you and be gracious unto you. The Lord lift up the light of His countenance upon you. And give you peace, now and forever. Amen.

Op-36D/dn
(SC) P16-1/00
Serial: 00108P36

NAVY DEPARTMENT
OFFICE OF THE CHIEF OF NAVAL OPERATIONS
WASHINGTON 25, D. C.

~~SECRET~~ Unclassified

2 December 1947

From: Chief of Naval Operations

To: Ensign Robert H. Wertheim, USN, 448603
USS MALOY (DE-791)
c/o Fleet Post Office
New York, N. Y.

Via: Commanding Officer

Subject: Special Assignment

Enclosure: (A) Instructions for completing enclosures (B), (C), and (D).
(B) Six copies of Personnel Security Questionnaire.
(C) Two fingerprint cards.
(D) One copy of AEC Security Acknowledgment Form.

1. After a careful review of your military background, experience, and qualifications, you have been selected as one of a group of Naval personnel to participate in one phase of the U. S. Navy's activity in the field of atomic energy.

2. In connection with this special assignment, it is necessary that enclosures (B), (C), and (D) be completed at once and returned to "Chief of Naval Operations (Op-36), Room 3834, Navy Department, Washington 25, D. C."

3. Your attention is directed to the classification of this correspondence. The enclosures hereto do not in themselves have a military security classification. Information concerning them, however, must be limited to those who need to know. They may be returned via non-registered mail. Air mail is preferred.

Op-36D/dn
(SC) P16-1/00
Serial: 00108P36

NAVY DEPARTMENT
OFFICE OF THE CHIEF OF NAVAL OPERATIONS
WASHINGTON 25, D. C.

~~SECRET~~ Unclassified

Subject: Special Assignment

- -

4.   This assignment will involve a permanent change of station on orders to be issued by the Bureau of Naval Personnel. The date of your reporting for new duty in the immediate vicinity of Albuquerque, New Mexico, will be 2 February 1948.

5.   Except for limited BOQ accommodations for bachelor officers, no Government quarters will be available. As in other congested areas, non-Government housing for families is not always readily available.

6.   Transmission by registered guard mail or United States registered mail is authorized in accordance with Article 76 (15) (e) and (f), United States Navy Regulations.

D. C. RAMSEY
VICE CHIEF OF NAVAL OPERATIONS

- -

FIRST ENDORSEMENT

U.S.S. MALOY EDE 791
C/o Fleet Post Office
New York, N. Y.

EDE 791/P16-4/448063
Serial 001-47

8 December 1947

From: Commanding Officer
To: Ensign Robert H. Wertheim

1.   Delivered.

J. H. GEYER

- 2 -

Unclassified

Index

to

Series of taped interviews

with

Rear Admiral Robert Halley Wertheim, USN (Ret.)

AEC (Atomic Energy Commission): objection to the use of
        beryllium for re-entry body of POLARIS, p. 128-30:
        p. 134; p. 186-7;

ANTELOPE SYSTEM: developed for the front of the POLARIS A-3,
        p. 218; p. 267;

BACK-FIT: term given the installation of a new weapons system
        (TRIDENT) in POSEIDON without changing the launch tube
        in any significant degree - term also had wider use and
        application, p. 294-; p. 324;

BALLISTIC MISSILE SYSTEMS: Wertheim's discussion of the system
        and procurement concurrency, p. 295 ff;

BERYLLIUM: Wertheim's decision to use a raw metal in building
        the re-entry body, p. 127-30;

BMS (Surface based ballistic missile system) proposed to
        STRAT-X, p. 281; p. 301-2;

USS BORDELON - DD: Wertheim detailed to her - joins the ship in
        Okinawa, p. 40-41; starts as Asst. Engineering officer -
        suddenly with reduced personnel on board - Wertheim becomes
        communications officer, p. 43; after electronics school in
        San Francisco, Wertheim sent to rejoin the BORDELON - but
        she has departed for U.K....he is consigned to the USS
        MALLOY, p. 51;

BROWN, Dr. Harold: sent from Livermore Laboratory by Dr. Teller
        to become a member of Wertheim;s Re-entry Committee on
        POLARIS, p. 114; as Director of Research and Engineering
        (DOD) he calls Wertheim to a job in the Pentagon, p. 209-11;

BURKE, Adm. Arleigh A.: his strong backing of POLARIS, p. 94;
        p. 198; he hears the news of Dr. Teller's remarks at
        Woods Hole (Project NOBSKA) about the future of nuclear
        technology in the 60s - the break through for POLARIS,
        p. 102-3; p. 109-110; p. 126-7;

BU SHIPS: p. 126;

CARLSBAD, New Mexico: p. 4-6

CHAPARRAL: (Spanish name for a Road Runner) name given by
        Wertheim to the ground launched SIDEWINDER, p. 198-9;
        navy objection to the CHAPARRAL, p. 199; army and marines
        use it, p. 200;

CHINA LAKE: Wertheim goes to experimental station in July, 1961, p. 185; p. 195 ff; works on a development of SIDEWINDER to be launched from the ground or ship, p. 197ff; the CHAPARRAL, p. 198 ff; the TARANTULA, p. 202, the value of an assignment there for Wertheim, p. 204-5; the value of naval laboratories in general, p. 205-7;

CLARK, RADM Glenwood, Jr.: Wertheim's Technical Director becomes Director of SSPO upon Wertheim's retirement, p. 333; p. 335

CLAW (Clustered Atomic Warheads): a special air force study, p. 139;

CRAVEN, Dr. John: Chief scientist with S.P. - takes over the Deep Submergence Program and it becomes detached from S.P. p. 254;

CUBAN MISSILE CRISIS: its impact on us and on the Russians, p. 242-3;

DEEP SUBMERGENCE PROGRAM: This developed as a result of the loss of the SS THRESHER: Admiral Smith takes it on in S.P., p. 252-4;

DOD: Wertheim called be Harold Brown (1962) for a position in the Department as military assistant to the Director for Strategic Systems (Dr. Richard Montgomery), p. 209 ff; Wertheim's remarks about the many projects undertaken in DOD while he was on the staff, p. 237-8;

DRAPER, Dr. Charles Stark: joins the S.P. to develop the guidance system of POLARIS, p. 105 ff;

EISENHOWER, General Dwight W.: p. 41-2; p.65;

ELECTRIC BOAT (division of General Dynamics) - under contract to BuShips, p. 124-5; experiences delays in building the new submarines for the TRIDENT Weapons System, p. 306-7

ELF (extra low frequency) submarine communications project, p. 204

ENTHOVEN, Alain, p. 229;

FLEET BALLISTIC MISSILE PROGRAM: the great value in the development of the Navy's TRANSIT System p. 245 ff, and Dr. Draper's SINS (ship inertial navigation system), p. 247-8; p. 259-60
see also: POLARIS; POSEIDON; TRIDENT.

FLY BEFORE BUY: term given the concept of defense procurement as sponsored by Under Secretary David Packard, p. 296;

FUBINI, Dr. Eugene: principal deputy of Harold Brown - (Director of Defense Research and Engineering) - holds up funds for the navy's TRANSIT program, p. 248-50;

USS GEORGE WASHINGTON: first of the POLARIS subs - used successfully in testing of the first POLARIS missiles, p. 186;

GOODING, VADM Robert C.: Technical Director of S.P. after Levering Smith, p. 270;

HARVARD BUSINESS SCHOOL: Wertheim attends sessions in 1968, p. 270 ff;

HITCH, Charles J.: Assistant Secretary of Defense (1961-65), p. 229;

HOLY LOCH: the only overseas base still existing for subs (POSEIDON) - TRIDENT does not require use, p. 322;

USS HYMAN - DD: Wertheim joins her after graduation (Aug. 1945), p. 25; p. 28-29; scheduled for participation in invasion of the mainland of Japan - finally given task of taking surrender of certain Jap held islands - Kusai, p. 30-31; Ponope, p. 32 ff; joins TF 77 of the 7th fleet, p. 37 ff;

JOHNSON, President Lyndon Banes: announces the advent of POSEIDON (1965), p. 222;

JULIAN, Comdr. Alexander Jr.: succeeds Wertheim in SP (Aug. 1961), p. 194-5; Wertheim comes back to SP in 1965 and relieves him as head of missile branch, p. 227;

JUPITER: name given Army's ballistic missile, p. 101-3; p. 118;

KENNEDY, The Hon. John F.: meets with Prime Minister Harold MacMillan - SKYBOLT and POLARIS are topics of discussion, p. 212-3;

KUSAI: a Japanese held island - by-passed by U. S. forces - surrenders to DD HYMAN on Sept. 8, 1945, p. 31-2;

LAIRD, The Hon. Melvin: Secretary of Defense, p. 303-4;

LOCKHEED Corp; p. 118-119; p. 231; p. 233; Wertheim becomes Senior VP for Science and Engineering (March 1981), p. 342-3;

USS LOS ANGELES: Wertheim detailed to her (1954) as main battery officer, p. 85 ff; the REGULUS is assigned, p. 85; p. 92;

USS MALOY: Wertheim transferred to her (1947) - her task to develop electricity for use in Maine - a winter-long tour at the pier in Portland, p. 52; the communications officer sees a secret despatch at the right moment, p. 53-4;

McLEAN, Dr. William: Technical director at China Lake, p. 195;

McNAMARA, Robert Strange: Secretary of Defense, p. 208; p. 221; the powerful position of SecDef in his time, p. 228; p. 229; his total package concept for government contracts, p. 230; his proclivity for prejudgements of issues to be followed by a study to support the decision, p. 236-8; p. 282; p. 303-4;

MERRILL, Capt. Greyson: the first Technical Director of SP, p. 100; Wertheim serves as his assistant, p. 101-2;

MILLER, RADM George: head of Op. 98 (1968) - deputy CNO for strategic offensive and defensive systems, p. 284; his special interest in SLMS - a proposal before STRAT-X, p. 285; conservatism - Wertheim's response, p. 299-300.

MIRV: p. 136; p. 141 (Multiple, Independently Guided Re-entry Vehicle System); the concept of MIRV emerges, p. 219; p. 223-4; p. 261-3; p. 267;

MISSILE TESTING: and Russian observance, p. 267-8;

M.I.T. (Mass Institute of Technology); p. 75 ff; Wertheim's professors ask him to stay on for a doctorate - Navy declines for him, p. 78; the nature of Wertheim's thesis, p. 79-80; the next detailers' reactions to the Wertheim records, p. 83;

MONTGOMERY, Dr. Richard: Assistant director for Strategic Systems in the office of Defense Research and Engineering (DOD), p. 209; Wertheim works as his military assistant, p. 209-10;

MX: title for land based ICBMs to replace the MINUTEMAN, p. 287-8

NAGASAKI: Wertheim's visit there - lasting impressions, p. 37-8; his views on the use of the bomb to end the war, p. 38-9; p. 56;

U. S. NAVAL ACADEMY: Wertheim's appointment, p. 12-14; the accelerated class, p. 14 ff; summer cruises, p. 19-20; the honor system, p. 21-22; aviation indoctrination, p. 22; Wertheim's interest in submarines, p. 24-25; graduates with distinction (1945), p. 26; social life at the academy, p. 26-7;

NEW MEXICO MILITARY INSTITUTE: p. 15; Wertheim attends in 1940, p. 10-11;

NIKI ZEUS: Army's anti-ballistic missile system, p. 138;

USS NORTON SOUND: Wertheim wanted to go ultimately to study nuclear physics - but due for sea assignment first - so he elected for the NORTON SOUND, p. 58 ff; she was engaged in testing guided missiles, p. 60 ff; (LARK, LOON, VIKING); Wertheim learns something about the psychology of gathering data after a test, p. 66-7; a survey of the scientific and technical people whom they dealt with on NORTON SOUND, p. 67; storage problems on the NORTON SOUND, p. 68 ff;

USS OBSERVATION ISLAND: (EAG) - a missile test ship, p. 257-8;

PACKARD, The Hon. David: Under Secretary of Defense - his study of defense procurement and its impact on the SP program, p. 295-6; p. 310-12;

PARSONS, RADM Wm. S. (Deke): decided to add some junior officers to the team assigned to the atomic program in Alberquerque, p. 49;

PAYNE, Fred: the study director for STRAT-X, p. 284;

PEHRSON, Gordon: p. 175-6;

PERT (Program Evaluation Review Technique), p. 171; p. 173-6;

PG (post Graduate) School: p. 71; first in Annapolis and then in Monterey (1951), p. 71-2;

POLARIS: p. 69-70; advent of POLARIS caused the phase out of REGULUS I, p. 93-4;
POLARIS A-1 and subsequent A-2 and A-3, p. 133 ff; the birth of the multiple re-entry vehicle, p. 135-7; p. 176-9; the formal approval for POLARIS A-3 comes in 1960, p. 185; 1960-61 Wertheim busy gaining acceptance and approval for front end of the A-3 - Pentagon, AEC, JCS technical concerns and economic concerns about the A-3 system, p. 188-9; development of the ANTELOPE system for front end of A-3, p. 218; navy advocates a bigger bang to compete with airforce and hard military targets, p. 219-20; also p. 267; POLARIS B-3 (multiple war heads) the proposal of Levering Smith, p. 221-2; B-3 suddenly announced in the press by President Johnson as POSEIDON, p. 222; p. 272; the conversion program to the POSEIDON configuration, p. 290 ff; p. 313;

PONAPE: surrenders in Sep. 1945 to the US HYMAN...HYMAN
stays on for three months as a station ship, p. 32-3;
U. S. use during the war was live training for U.S.
pilots without too great opposition, p. 34-5; HYMAN's
task to keep the Japanese military busy until repatriated, p. 35;

POSEIDON: background to the President's announcement about
POSEIDON, p. 221-2; Levering Smith proposes that Wertheim
become head of missile branch and manage development of
POSEIDON (1965), p. 226; Wertheim takes on the project
and faces the necessity of working with the total Package
Procurement Rules as established by the SecDef, p. 231 ff;
the compromise system as worked out by Wertheim and S.P.,
p. 232-3; p. 234; p. 236; difficulty and delay with the
congress over conversion of the POLARIS subs to POSEIDON,
p. 290 ff; p. 317-18; Wertheim has a chance (after 1965)
to carry out the development of POSEIDON, p. 261 ff; the
new idea for ballistic missile guidance that combined
the inertial system with a stellar feature, p. 264 ff;
dropped momentarily because of political pressure, p. 265-6
later resumption and feasibility for TRIDENT, p. 266 ff;
ready for flight testing of POSEIDON in 1968, p. 267;
p. 273; the conversion of POLARIS subs to the POSEIDON
configuration runs into difficulties with the CONGRESS -
ESPECIALLY Senator Russell, p. 290-1; p. 308;

RABORN, VADM Wm F. Jr.: now his - the S.P., p. 98; p. 102;
his inspirational leadership, p. 105 ff; p. 107; how
he deals with potential opposition of aviation to the
development of POLARIS, p. 108; p. 110-111; p. 125;
the team's quarterback, p. 125-7; p. 130; his use of
PERT, p. 173-; p. 187; his freedom from control in the
development of POLARIS - successors had less freedom,
p. 313-14;

RAMAGE, VADM Lawson P. (Red): brings news from NOBSKA conference
to Burke - transformation of the POLARIS project, p. 102-3;

RAMO-WOOLRIDGE CORP: hired the finest scientists for the Air
Force ballistic missiles program of ATLAS, THOR, TITAN,
p. 172;

RE-ENTRY COMMITTEE of S.P.: see entries under S.P.; POLARIS:

REGULUS I: p. 85 ff; security provision on board, p. 88;
launching procedures, p. 88-90; launching from a sub,
P. 91-4;

RICKOVER, Admiral Hyman G.: p. 26; p. 302; p. 316; Wertheim, as
Director of SP, had very little interaction with Rickover
because of the system of a Project Manager for TRIDENT,
p. 326-7;

RUSSELL, The Hon. Richard: Senator from Georgia - he raises objections to the plans of SP for the conversion of POLARIS subs to the POSEIDON configuration, p. 292-3;

SANDIA BASE: Alberqueque, N.M. Wertheim gets orders for the base at precise moment when he was preparing his resignation from the Navy, p. 53; the mission - the navy's first atomic bomb assembly team, p. 55 ff; a brief summary on the state of things at Sandia and Los Alamos, p. 58; the situation changed with the revelations about Klaus Fuchs, the Rosenbergs, p. 60; p. 67-8;

SIDEWINDER: p. 197; Wertheim works on a variant to launch from the ground or a ship, p. 197.

SINS (Ship Inertial Navigation System) a development of Dr. Draper at MIT, p. 247-8;

SKYBOLT: the ballistic missile mounted in an airplane - to be used by the British in modernizing their nuclear capability-project cancelled by DOD, p. 211 ff; British given the option of continuing research or going for POLARIS, p. 213-5; p. 236; p. 273;

SLMS: scheme to base strategic weapon's systems on surface ships, p. 285-8;

SMITH, VADM Levering: at China Lake - the Navy's expert in solid propellant rocketry, p. 103; assigned to SP in 1956, p. 103; p. 111; p. 121; p. 130; p. 172-3; p. 179; p. 182; p. 195; he proposes the B-3 - re-named POSEIDON, p. 221-2; Wertheim consults him and Smith proposes him as future head of missile branch, p. 225-6; he takes over TRANSIT program once Wertheim gets it sprung from BuAir to the S.P. office, p. 249-50; p. 261; p. 270; he leads the battle with Congress over conversion of POLARIS to POSEIDON, p. 293-4; the first in that special field of navy work to become a flag officer, p. 316; succeeded by Wertheim as Director of SSPO in Nov. 1977, p. 322.

SP (Special Project): p. 98 ff; Dr. Teller's remarks change the picture, p. 102 ff; Levering Smith joins the team as expert in solid propellant rocketry, p. 103; Wertheim given job of tracking down significance of changes envisioned by Teller's criticism, p. 104-5; the Saturday sessions held by Raborn on progress being made, p. 111-112; internal organization of project, p. 112 ff; Wertheim heads the Re-entry Committee, p. 113; complexion of his committee, p. 114-115; the orginal time table for POLARIS as contrasted with JUPITER, p. 119; the launching of SPUTNIK accelerated POLARIS schedule, p. 120-121; the work of the steering committee p. 122; choice of 16 missiles on the POLARIS, p. 123-4; the quarterback of the team, p. 125-6; "going for broke" with beryllium, p. 127-8; p. 131-2; the PERT system, p. ff; strength in continuity - retraining of key people in program, p. 180-1; SP eventually becomes the Strategic Systems Project Office (SSPO) because it is unique and doesn't fit into the navy's way of doing things, p. 181; Wertheim comes back to SP in August 1965 as head of miss branch - to add ballistic missile penetration capabiliti to POLARIS A-3, p. 261 ff; name change (SSPO) in 1968, p. 284; for TRIDENT a project manager is set up (PM-2) - Naval Sea Systems command has control of the ship building end of things, p. 307-8; Wertheim comments on SP practices and procedures - they reflect lessons learned, p. 310-314; maintaining morale in operational units, p. 325 ff; imperative for S.P. to maintain an advanced development program, p. 339-40;

SOVIET TECHNOLOGY: p. 309; the YANKEE Submarine - an analogue of the POLARIS, p. 309;

STRATEGIC SYSTEMS - DEFENSE RESEARCH AND ENGINEERING - (DOD) - while Wertheim was on the staff he worked on the SKYBOLT project and its cancellation, p. 211 ff; POLARIS project for the British, p. 213 ff; development of projects to assure penetration of Soviet ballistic missile defenses by, p. 216-7; advent of POSEIDON (B-3), p. 221 ff.

STRAT-X: the birth of the STRAT-X concept and the reasons, p. 279 ff; the parameters to the proposal, p. 282; conference organized by the Institute for Defense Analysis, p. 283; p. 301-3;

STRAUSS, RADM Lewis: p. 65;

SUBROC: p. 257;

TELLER, Dr. Edward: his remarks at Woods Hole on nuclear technology, p. 102; p. 104; p. 116;

TEST BAN TREATY: The Treaty banning nuclear tests except underground - Wertheim comments on the ban and the results, p. 254-5;

TFX: p. 236;

TOTAL PACKAGE PROCUREMENT RULES of Secretary McNamara, p. 230-4;

TRANSIT PROGRAM: the navy's navigational satellite program, p. 245; the immediate value to the submarine ballistic missile fleet, p. 246-7; Dr. Eugene Fabini holds up funds for its development, p. 248-9;

TREASURE ISLAND - ELECTRONICS SCHOOL: Wertheim sent there from the BORDELON for a crash course in electronics, p. 46-7; a significant happening for Wertheim, p. 49;

TRIAD concept of defense: p. 286-7;

TRIDENT BALLISTIC MISSILE SYSTEM: p. 266; Britian decides to buy the TRIDENT system for the future, p. 275; p. 277; concept for TRIDENT comes ultimately from the STRAT-X conference, p. 283; p. 294; p. 300; p. 304-6; SSPO sets up a project manager PM-2 for the TRIDENT weapons system - while the ship system and its building problems were under the Naval Sea Systems Command, p. 307-8; a successor version of the stellar assisted guidance system carried in TRIDENT I, p. 308; p. 317-19; p. 321-2; increased range of TRIDENT eliminates the need for overseas bases, p. 321-3; Wertheim rides the TRIDENT backfits on their shakedown and DASO trips, p. 323-4; Wertheim decides to retire and turn the helm over to a man who could stay for six or more years and see TRIDENT II to development and operation, p. 332-3;

ULMS (Underwater Long-Range Missile System) - a scheme proposed to STRAT-X, p. 281; p. 283; CNO (1967) establishes an advanced development objective for ULMS, p. 284; p. 290;

UNITED KINGDOM's POLARIS PROGRAM: p. 191-2; p. 213-16; p. 272-278; their decision to improve POLARIS and not go to POSEIDON, p. 274-5; British decision on TRIDENT in 1980 p. 327-330; p. 336-8;

WALKER, VADM Thomas J.: how he pulled Wertheim into the POLARIS program, p. 70; his task under Raborn was to organize a test organization for missiles - asks Wertheim to take charge of progress charts, p. 99; Wertheim demurs - given job on staff of the Technical Director, p. 100 ff;

WERTHEIM, RADM Robert Halley: background, p. 1-14; graduated by the Naval Academy (1945) with distinction, p. 26; his meeting with his future wife, p. 27 ff; his marriage, p. 45-6; the death of his father, p. 61-63; decides (1956) to become an EDO against the advice of his peers, p. 95-7; given orders for duty in NOL but that is changed suddenly - to SP with Raborn, p. 97 ff; the family at China Lake, p. 195-6; his cultural shock when he arrives at the Pentagon (1962), p. 209-10; thought of retirement after twenty years in service (1965) - Levering Smith makes a proposal, p. 226; becomes deputy to the Technical Director of SP (1968), p. 270; becomes Technical Director to succeed Capt. Gooding in 1969, p. 289; gets the Navy League's Parsons Award in 1971, p. 315; selected as Rear

Admiral (1972) - an ordnance weapons engineer, p. 315; relieves Admiral Levering Smith as Director of SSPO in Nov. 1977, p. 322; retires at the end of three years, p. 332 ff; contemplates the future, p. 340 ff; a consultant to various defence agencies - senior VP for Science and Engineering at Lockheed Corp, p. 342.

WESEG: the task of sizing up samples from annual missile tests, p. 250-1;

WHITTLE, Adm. Alfred J. Jr.: Chief of Naval Material - his relations with Wertheim, p. 314;

WILSON, Dr. Lloyd: deputy director of Defense Research and Engineering - concerned about the single proposal of the Air Force for a huge missile to replace the MINUTEMAN - he wanted competitive ideas from Navy, p. 280-3;

www.ingramcontent.com/pod-product-compliance
Lightning Source LLC
Chambersburg PA
CBHW080619170426
43209CB00007B/1466